THE INCREDIBLE ADVENTURES OF

BUFFALO BILL
from BOCHNIA
(68715)

To my beloved husband,
JOSHUA JAY SCHWARTZ,
with all my heart
For having given me a future with his love and for
having given me back my past with this book

THE INCREDIBLE ADVENTURES OF

BUFFALO BILL
from BOCHNIA
(68715)

The Story of a Galician Jew
Persecution, Liberation,
Transformation

JUDITH TYDOR BAUMEL-SCHWARTZ

sussex
ACADEMIC
PRESS
Brighton • Portland • Vancouver

2 4 6 8 10 9 7 5 3 1

First published in 2009 by
SUSSEX ACADEMIC PRESS
PO Box 139
Eastbourne BN24 9BP

and in the United States of America by
SUSSEX ACADEMIC PRESS
920 NE 58th Ave   Suite 300
Portland, Oregon 97213-3786

British Library Cataloguing in Publication Data
A CIP catalogue record for this book is available from the British Library.

Library of Congress Cataloging-in-Publication Data
Baumel-Schwartz, Judith Tydor, 1959–
The incredible adventures of Buffalo Bill from Bochnia : the story of a
  Galician Jew, persecution, liberation, transformation / Judith Tydor
  Baumel-Schwartz.
p. cm.
Includes bibliographical references and index.
ISBN 978-1-84519-380-5 (p/b : alk. paper)
1. Tydor, Chaskel, d. 1993. 2. Jews—Poland—Bochnia—Biography.
3. Holocaust, Jewish (1939–1945)—Poland—Biography. 4. Holocaust
survivors—Israel—Biography. 5. Holocaust survivors—United States—
Biography. I. Title.
DS134.72.T93B38 2009
940.53′18092—dc22
[B]
                                                                    2009031750

Mixed Sources
Product group from well-managed
forests and other controlled sources
www.fsc.org Cert no. SGS-COC-2482
© 1996 Forest Stewardship Council

Typeset and designed by SAP, Brighton & Eastbourne.
Printed by TJ International, Padstow, Cornwall.
This book is printed on acid-free paper.

Contents

List of Illustrations

Foreword by Walter Laqueur

This is the story of Chaskel Tydor, one of a very small group of Jewish survivors of the Nazi death camps of the Second World War. How many survivors were there? There are no precise figures, only estimates; we do know that between 5.1 and 6 million were killed and that in the extermination camps such as Maidanek or Sobibor virtually no one survived. But Buchenwald and Auschwitz (the two main stations in Chaskel's six years of hell) were in a category apart. Buchenwald was a concentration camp for political prisoners from many countries, and for common criminals as well various enemies of the Third Reich. Buchenwald and Dachau, where many thousands perished or were murdered, did not belong to the category of camps in which industrial mass killing was practiced. Auschwitz was both: An extermination camp in which more than a million people were murdered by gassing, frequently immediately after their arrival; but it was also home to some factories, notably Buna Monowitz belonging to I.G. Farben, the giant chemical enterprise. And while the survival rate of the Buna workers as a result of starvation and disease was extremely low, thousands did survive until January 1945 when the Soviet army approached Silesia and these remnants were evacuated in forced marches in which perhaps half again lost their life.

The fact that precise figures are not available is by no means surprising, or suspect as some Holocaust deniers have intimated. Germany was probably the most thoroughly recorded and reliable European country as far as population statistics were concerned. And yet there are no precise figures with regard to German losses in World War Two and the reasons are obvious. During the last year of war following Allied bombardments and other acts of war much of the state machinery broke down, offices were destroyed, files burned, and in the end no one could say with any certainty whether certain individuals had perished or moved on to another place, whether a soldier was missing because he had been killed, or because he had defected, or joined another unit.

If there was so much uncertainty with regard to such an orderly country like Germany in which everything and everyone was accounted for, there was much less certainty concerning such a marginal group like

Jews from Poland. The overwhelming majority was killed, but a few were hiding in the forests, a few survived outside the ghettoes having assumed non-Jewish identities and in possession of forged papers, a few had escaped to the east or south.

And then there were a few like Chaskel Tydor who miraculously survived six years of the camps which had been built to exterminate European Jewry.

I have tried to study the fate of young and relatively young survivors and one of the questions which always obtruded itself was – why did they survive in circumstances in which the odds against survival were so heavily against them?

Chaskel provided an answer.

Chaskel was a religious Jew, a firm believer following all the orders and bans of Judaism even in the most difficult conditions of camp life. And it is also true that his firm religious belief provided a psychological support which non-believers often did not have and which helped him to overcome enormous difficulties, face constant mortal danger, and survive the most difficult conditions. When asked what saved him Chaskel said about 90% help from heaven and 10% good luck. But reference to the intervention of Divine providence leads by necessity to another other question – why should Divine providence protect him and not so many other equally God-fearing and deserving people? Why should he have been singled out from among so many others?

It is my impression, having studied so many cases and talked to so many survivors (including some who appear in this book), that good luck was the most important single factor – to have been in the right place at the right time, and conversely not to have been at a certain place at a certain time and thus having evaded death. This certainly was true in my own case and it must have been true for many others.

But there were certain other factors which I shall try to describe, albeit briefly. Those who were sent to the camps early on, and those who were deported late during the war, stood a better chance to survive. Those like Chaskel, who was arrested and deported even before the war had broken out, learned the fundamental lessons of camp life, namely to take the lowest possible profile, to be seen and to be heard as little as possible, not to attract any attention. Many years after the end of the war I met in the United States a schoolmate who had risen to an important position in the air and space industry. He too had been for years in one of the worst camps. How had he survived? He was quite small of stature and this (he told me) had been the reason for being frequently overlooked during the morning roll-call when the selection was carried out – who was to be kept on for employment and who was to be sent to the gas chambers.

There was another very important factor which Chaskel mentions more than once and which was frequently mentioned to me by others. Those who belonged to an organized group stood a far better chance to survive than those who did not. The SS, which was responsible for the maintenance of the camps, had neither sufficient manpower nor the experience to cope with this task and was quite willing to delegate many of the organizational functions to groups of inmates. Each such group tried, of course, to save as many of its own members; they could make people who were candidates for the gas chambers "disappear within the camps", they could send sick comrades to the hospital and help them in many other ways. The most important group of inmates were the Communists (also fervent followers of a religion albeit a secular one), and Chaskel also succeeded in the course of time to establish a group of young Orthodox Jews. But the Communists for unknown reasons believed that Chaskel really was one of them which, on various occasions, was of great help to him and his friends. The fact that Chaskel's German was perfect also helped; he had attended a German school and worked in Frankfurt in the years of the Weimar Republic.

Chaskel was a modest man with no ambitions of leadership but in the camp when leadership was needed and was thrust on him he emerged in a position of authority; he maintained such a position in the years after the liberation when he was instrumental in establishing Kibbutz Buchenwald.

Chaskel's life can be divided broadly speaking into three periods. He was in his thirties when war broke out. He had grown up in a small town in Western Galicia, but also lived and worked for years in Germany, like many Polish Jews who had escaped to the West at the time of the Russian offensive in 1914 and did not return after the end of the war. He was fully aware of the danger looming – to him, his young family and to European Jewry. But like so many others he could not escape in time for the few doors that existed in the beginning were quickly closed. No one wanted to accept Jewish refugees, even Nobel Prize winners and million-aires had difficulty in escaping.

The second period in Chaskel's life was the time in the camps. How did the survivors fare after the war had ended? How could they face life after this horrible trauma? "Trauma" is the term most frequently used in this context but it is a gross understatement. For it was not only the personal suffering, starvation, disease, the fact that most of one's family and friends perished and that often one had to witness it. It was also the total uncertainty whether one would live one more day, one more hour.

The term "holocaust" has been used in subsequent years far too widely for all kinds of disasters and situations; only a few of them were remotely similar to what went on in the death camps of Eastern Europe during World War Two. Sometimes this usage has been instigated out of ignorance, sometimes deliberately or even frivolously.

The abuse of the term holocaust is a painful issue which will no doubt be discussed for many years to come. But this painstaking biography, a true labor of love by the hands of an experienced historian, deals primarily with the life of one man who had lost his wife and most of his other relations and friends in these Holocaust years and had to face life after the liberation which must have seemed a miracle. How could he have found the way to a new life? Only the strongest mentally (perhaps even more than physically) had survived the camps. Like the Biblical Job, having escaped with the skin of his teeth from the land of darkness and the shadow of death, Chaskel found a way back to a reasonably normal and even happy life. He had a new family, found new work in Palestine/Israel and later in America – including some unlikely places such as South Dakota. The graduates of Auschwitz had survived and it was likely therefore that they would even flourish in almost any circumstance. Chaskel Tydor lived for many more years to play with the grandchildren of his new family and this must have been a great comfort to him. To quote from the book of Job, "The Lord blessed the latter end of Job more than his beginning."

WALTER LAQUEUR
Washington/London 2009

Preface

Every book embodies the hopes and expectations of those who created it, and like a child, is the result of a long period of dreaming, planning, and hard effort. Every book has a parent, or set of parents who nurtured it during its creation, eventually sending it into the world to touch the lives of those with whom it comes in contact. This book is the result of all of the above, and was written with love and honor for my father, Chaskel Tydor, Yechezkel Shraga ben Yehuda Leib Halevi, and in the hope that the steadfast faith which exemplified his life will touch the hearts of its readers.

In the autumn of 2008, fifteen years after my father's death, I found myself at a crossroad resulting from personal and professional upheavals which I had recently undergone. Trying to better understand the path my life had taken I often, and somewhat even morbidly, found myself pondering the statement of Mishnaic sage Akabia ben Mahalalel "Remember whence thou hast come and whither thou goest" (*Avoth,* 3:1), with which Jewish funeral services begin.

And yet, there was also a positive and optimistic side to that statement. Discussing the matter with my husband, he echoed what I had been thinking: that in order to truly know where you want your life to go you must better understand where you came from, what formed your historical and cultural makeup and created your *self*. Looking to better understand that *self* and positively mold my future I embarked upon a journey into my personal past, choosing to begin with my father's side of the family.

Being a historian, I soon realized that I was weaving a tapestry which merged the personal and the professional by examining major events of contemporary Jewish history through the eyes of my father and his experiences. The professional crossroads at which I stood enabled me to set aside time to turn the soul searching process into a process of searching for roots, and with my husband's active encouragement, it became the basis for this book.

I had previously written and edited over a dozen books as a professional historian; in all of them I tried to find the correct balance between "story" and "history". Prof. Yehuda Bauer, one of the world's most eminent Holocaust historians, once stated that to be a good historian you first and foremost must be a good storyteller, because that is what people will remember. Instead of annotating history with stories, as I have done in my academic writing, here I have tried to annotate the stories of my father's adventures with more than a sprinkling of Jewish history to provide the framework and backdrop to the experiences that I describe. I hope that the readers will have patience with this historian turned biographer, and enjoy the combination of the personal and the historical that forms the basis of this book.

Although the book is being presented to the reader as "popular history", much of it is based on academic research which I have conducted either for my previous studies or specifically for this book. The joy of popular history is that one can read it "as is", enjoying the story without delving into the source material. But a historian remains a historian and I hope that the narrative will interest some readers enough to kindle a desire to know more about some of the issues or people mentioned in the book.

Not wishing to interrupt the narrative and burden the reader with citations or footnotes I do not refer in the text to specific documents or cite sources. Instead, I refer interested readers to relevant literature that deals with many of the issues mentioned through a Further Reading section in the back matter, divided into chapter sections. I have also provided a research bibliography that includes the archival collections and secondary works consulted and a list of interviews I conducted at various junctures that formed much of the basis for the book. For readers without a research library at their disposal I have also included a list of online sources for many of the subjects covered in the chapters to follow.

The list of those who touched my life and were the impetus towards and support for the writing of this book is almost endless; many of them are mentioned in the stories which appear in its pages. But there are a number of individuals without whom it truly would not have been written and to whom I wish to express special gratitude.

The idea for the book was first given to me by my beloved husband, Prof. Joshua Jay Schwartz, after we visited Bochnia together and spent time in the house in which my father had been born 104 years earlier. He gently encouraged me to combine my love of Jewish history with my love of family and write my father's story, not only as a testimonial to the father-in-law who he had never met, but as a work which would bring together the various threads which weave the fabric of my life. I am forever indebted to him for his patience, foresight and wisdom which allowed me to pursue this goal and make this book a final chapter in the commandment of "Honoring thy father".

Many members of my family were involved in creating this book, some long before it was an idea in anyone's mind. My mother, Shirley K. Tydor, who told me about numerous events in my father's life of which I had been unaware, some which had me doubled over in laughter, others that brought tears to my eyes. My daughters, Rivka (Beki) and Rina Baumel who were the joy of my father's life in his later years and still remember their Zeide telling them stories at the Shabbat table and hiding chocolate for them to find afterwards. My sister and brother, Camilla Maas and Manfred Tidor, who knew our father for almost thirty years longer than I did although they lived with him under one roof for less than a decade. My late aunt, Yaffa Greiver, who told me about his years in pre-State Israel after the Holocaust; my father's various friends and relatives, some of whom are alive, others who are no longer among us, who told me much about his life in Poland, Germany, Israel and America. I thank them all for their contribution to the stories that you will read here.

The bulk of the first half of the book is based on interviews that I conducted with my father between 1982 and his death in 1993, some of which also formed the basis for my academic study of Kibbutz Buchenwald, the first post-war pioneering kibbutz in liberated Germany, which he was instrumental in founding during the spring of 1945. Only when I knew that his days were numbered did I decide to continue these interviews and asked him to tell me about his early years. During the winter before his death I would come over to my parents' home with my tape recorder almost every evening. After sending my mother for a long needed rest, I would sit with my father, he, wrapped up in his quilted robe in the large wooden armchair, I by his side, practically forcing him to recall the long forgotten stories of his childhood in Bochnia, Munich and Frankfurt. "Who in the world will be interested in such a thing", he would ask me over and over, and I would just smile, point to the tape recorder and say "Don't ask questions, just keep talking". It got to the point where he would see me come in the front door with my tape recorded and sigh in jest to my mother, "Oy veh, *Malach hamoves* ("oh no, the angel of death") is here again". When I would turn on the tape he would begin every session with the words "*Al Korchacho*" ("Against your will"), a reminder of the Mishna in *Avoth* 4:29 "Perforce you were formed and perforce you were born; perforce you live, perforce you shall die, and perforce you shall have to give a strict account before the supreme King of kings, the Holy One, Blessed be he". And yet, I know that he looked forward to those hours of closeness that we had together and am grateful that only when he truly no longer had the strength to sit up and talk did they come to an end.

My gratitude towards many people extends far beyond what I have written here and I hope that this book will be a tribute to all the time and effort that they invested in this endeavor. All positive results of its publication should be credited to my late father's merit; any mistakes are mine and I take full responsibility for all of them.

Above all, I give thanks to the *Ribono Shel Olam*, the Master of the Universe, who allowed me the privilege of being born to a father who would tell me stories week after week as a small child, that interwove Torah, faith, and the history of the Jewish people – all embodied in the adventures of the imaginary little fellow featuring in all the tales, whom he had named "Buffalo Bill from Bochnia".

JUDITH TYDOR BAUMEL-SCHWARTZ
Ramat-Gan, July 2009

Introduction
Givatayim, 1993

It had been a long Shabbat.

Although it was late February and night fell early, that particular day seemed to last forever.

During the chilly morning hours the elderly man slept while various family members tiptoed in to check on him, reassured by the rhythmic rise and fall of his chest. At lunchtime, when the winter sun had slightly warmed the room, his wife helped him out of bed and gently fastened the quilted robe around him so that he could sit at the Shabbos table with his family. Leaning on her arm, he had just enough strength to walk the length of the corridor, stopping every few seconds to catch his breath.

At the entrance to the living room he could walk no further and sunk slowly into the large wooden armchair next to the sideboard. The chair had been one of a stately pair originally belonging to his uncle and aunt and had featured in so many important family events. Half a lifetime ago he and his wife had posed in them for their wedding pictures, taken in his aunt's garden. Soon after, he inherited them and they became their family dining chairs. One had ultimately succumbed to the ravages of time and the other became his living room "learning chair" where he would sit for hours on end, pouring over his *sforim* (religious books) at night. Lately it had been his favorite resting place when he didn't have the strength to make it into his study.

Closing his eyes, he smiled faintly as he heard the *zmiroth* (Sabbath melodies) coming from the table a few feet away, a tired smile of someone who was already hovering between two worlds. Listening to the traditional melodies he was transported back to the Shabbat table of his childhood where he would sing those same tunes as a young boy. Over eighty years later he could still picture the great wooden dining table in Bochnia, the Galician town where he had been born. His grandfather Menachem-Mendel with his flowing patriarchal beard holding court at the head of the table. His father Yehuda Leib, Leibeleh to his friends, with his black beard and glowing eyes sitting beside him. At the other

1

end of the table sat the women – his mother Esther, grandmother Mecha, and his baby sister Yehudis – waiting to hear the other three join their voices in harmony during the Shabbat meal. Now they were all gone. A different world. A different life.

But the melodies lived on. These were the melodies which they had taken with them on their flight across Europe during the First World War. These were the melodies which he had sung with his wife and children in Germany after Hitler came to power. These were the melodies which he had hummed in secret with his comrades in Auschwitz and Buchenwald on Shabbat afternoon, doing forced labor for the Nazis. These were the melodies which he had shared with his fellow survivors, kibbutz members in Israel, as they rebuilt their shattered lives. And these were the melodies which his little *sabra* granddaughters were singing now, standing by the great wooden armchair and holding his hands during what would be the last Shabbat of his life.

After most of the family had gone home, he closed his eyes and dozed in the chair. Where did his dreams wander to, if he was dreaming at all? His parents? Grandparents? Children scattered throughout the world? Friends long gone? His first wife, murdered by the Nazis? His second wife, quietly cleaning up the house after their grandchildren had left for home? We will never know.

Hours later, he sat up suddenly and opened his eyes, looking around the darkened room in confusion. "*Bring mir a tallis und tfillin*" ("bring me a prayer shawl and phylacteries"), he rasped to his youngest daughter, one of the only two sentences that he had uttered all day. Moving quickly to his side she answered him in English, the language in which they usually conversed. "It's Shabbos Daddy, it's nighttime, you don't need them today". He nodded and closed his eyes once again.

Those were his last words.

The next day he was gone.

This is a book about my father, Chaskel Tydor, Yechezkel Shraga ben Yehuda Leib Halevi, spanning close to ninety years of life, three continents, two marriages, and one Holocaust. But it is also the story of much of the Jewish people during the twentieth century, or at least those who found themselves wandering between countries, learning to function in new languages and societies, building and joining various Jewish communities, and continuously adopting different outward ways of life while trying to maintain their Jewish beliefs and practices.

Like many Galician Jews, my father began his life at the beginning of the twentieth century as a Chassidic boy in *cheder*, speaking, learning and breathing Yiddish. With the outbreak of the First World War he and his family escaped to the Central Europe, living as refugees who had left almost all possessions behind. As an Eastern European Jew in Germany between the two world wars, he functioned in German, becoming a firm part of the Orthodox Jewish community in Frankfurt which lived by the dictum of "Torah and *Derekh Eretz*". Experiencing the daily struggles of German Jewry during the early years of the Nazi regime as a young husband and father, he lived in hope that it would be a temporary situation and that reason would one again reign in his new homeland. As the 1930s unfolded, he and his family joined the frantic and often unsuccessful attempts to find refuge outside of Germany before the outbreak of war. Separated from his wife and children, he was deported to Poland, incarcerated in Nazi death camps where he was stripped of his name and identity and became 68715, the number the Nazis tatooed on his left arm; he experienced the loss of family, friends and entire communities in which he had lived. By the grace of the Almighty he survived the cataclysm and became part of the miracle of survival and rehabilitation after the war. In his case, this merged with the rebirth of the Jewish people in Israel where he learned to function in Hebrew. A temporary sojourn in America to find his two older children who had survived the war and been rescued to the United States became a twenty-three year stay during which he remarried and rebuilt his family and fortune, this time in English. Finally, he returned with his new family to an Israel which was licking it wounds after the Yom Kippur war and experienced that country's transformation during the next nineteen years.

Looking back, my father's life was indeed guided by the twin beacons of "Torah and *Derekh Eretz*", literally "Torah and the way of the world". The ambiguous phrase *Derekh Eretz*, which first appears in the Mishna in tractate *Avoth* (2:2), has been variously interpreted as "livelihood", "appropriate behavior among others", "worldly involvement", or "civilized behavior". Originally articulated by Rabbi Samson Rafael Hirsch (1808–1888) as a banner for his Frankfurt congregation, many saw it as the basis for modern Orthodox Judaism. Jews belonging to these communities saw no contradiction between embracing the challenges of modernity and living a full life of Torah. Thus my parents could reside for several months during the late 1950s in Deer Lodge Montana, where they were the only Jews and as 0.5% of the white population, while my father managed a uranium mine wearing a large cowboy hat along with his *tztzis*, the ritual fringed undergarment worn by Jewish men. Soon

3

after, town residents in Rapid City, South Dakota, to where they relocated, became used to my mother striding into the local supermarket, a branch of the chain appropriately called "Piggly Wiggly", once a month, brandishing her large meat knife. Everyone in the supermarket knew that on the day a shipment of Kosher Salami arrived from Denver, no one was allowed to touch the meat before "the Jews" as they were known, cut off "their piece" with their "ritual knife".

Although he never thought of himself as an emissary of Jewish belief and practice, my father brought it with him wherever he went, even in places where any form of Jewish ritual carried a death penalty. In December 1939 he organized the clandestine lighting of Chanukah candles in his block in Buchenwald and a "festive meal" which had the communist Kapos looking on in awe. After Pesach 1940 he started a *Pirkei Avoth* study group among his friends who would walk together in the camp on Shabbat afternoons reciting the chapters by heart. On Purim he sent other Jews in Buchenwald and later in Buna-Monowitz (Auschwitz III) part of his bread ration as *Mishloach Manos*, presents of food that Jews send each other on Purim, to remind them that while their bodies were in a daily hell, their spirits would always be those of free Jews. In Rapid City, South Dakota, where there was no synagogue but there were Jews living within a feasible radius, he organized Shabbos services for their children, teaching them the basic prayers. Some of the parents, who would bring their children to those services in two feet of snow, would stay for the *Kiddush* that my mother would provide afterwards, and began learning about the beauty of Judaism. At least one family from that time which my parents befriended ultimately became observant, and today their children and grandchildren lead a full Orthodox Jewish life. When a group of survivors met with American president Dwight D. Eisenhower at the White House to mark the fifteenth anniversary of the liberation of the Auschwitz-Buna concentration camp to present him with a commemorative scroll, my father was the one who, against his comrades' counsel, asked the president's permission to bless him with the ancient Hebrew prayer reserved for leaders. As the presidential photographer snapped away, one could see the diminutive survivor with a large black *yarmulkah* (skullcap) standing next to a president bowing his head in reverence as my father recited the blessing "who has given of Thy glory to mortal man".

This is just a small taste of the saga of his incredible adventures, many more of which appear in the chapters of this book.

But this is also a book about an entire Jewish epoch as seen through the eyes of my father and some of his family. Unlike many books based

on the life story of Holocaust survivors which concentrate on the protag-
onist's experiences in ghettos, camps, in hiding or with the partisans, this
book tells the history of an era, almost a century. In fact, it tells the story
of much of Jewish life during the twentieth century in Europe, in the
United States and finally, in Israel. In addition to my father's experiences
during the years of the Holocaust, the reader will learn about daily life in
Eastern Europe before the First World War, events in Weimar and
Hitler's Germany during the 1920s and 1930, daily life in Palestine up to
and including the War of Independence, Jewish life in the United States
during the 1950s 60s and 70s, including what it was like to live in
Montana and South Dakota when few Jews inhabited the area, and
finally, the events in Israel following the Yom Kippur War and up to and
including the first Intifada beginning in the late 1980s. I hope that this
broader description and analysis of what much of the Jewish world was
like during my father's lifetime will give the readers a picture of an era.

1

Bochnia, 1903–1914

It was still dark when the knock sounded at the door. The early morning chill slipped into the house as the heavy wooden door swung inwards. "Is Chaskeleh ready?" asked the *belfer*, the teenage assistant who gathered the young boys, shepherding them to *cheder*. The child's mother nodded and pinned the small glass case on to the little boy's winter coat, lighting the candle inside. This was the primitive flashlight that allowed both young and old to see their way while walking through the dark streets of Bochnia. Making sure that he was wearing his new velvet *yarmulkeh* under his winter hat the mother kissed her son's forehead and guided him towards the door.

On his way out of the house the child looked longingly towards the kitchen. Maybe Bobbeh Mecha would have a sweet ready for him to take before she left for the marketplace, after all, only yesterday she had told him how proud she was that he was a *cheder yingel* (*cheder* boy). But today she was busy and just blew him a kiss as he left. Hopefully she would make up for it with a special treat when he came back at lunchtime. Now it was time to think about other things, like the *davening* (prayers) that he was learning in *cheder*. It was important to know how to *daven*. This was what Jewish men did every morning, and he wanted to be like his father and grandfather and make them proud.

These were my father's earliest memories, the ones which framed his life in Poland at the start of the twentieth century. Like tens of thousands of *Chassidic* boys at that time, he spent his formative years in a one room *cheder* (literally "room", meaning schoolhouse) under the tutelage of the local *melamed* (teacher) until his education was interrupted by the First World War. Although there was no supervising Jewish educational authority, the *cheder* curriculum was the same throughout most of Eastern Europe. Beginning with the daily prayers, the young boys would progress to the study of *chumash* (Pentatuch) and at a much later stage to learning *Mishna* (oral law) and Talmud. Lessons lasted from dawn to dusk five days a week with an additional half day on Fridays. The *melameds* came in all forms and sizes. Some were young; others were old. For some, this was their main means of earning a livelihood; for others it was a sideline of the rabbinate, particularly when there was more than one rabbi in a town. Some were born teachers, knowledgeable, caring and devoted to their young charges. Others were barely literate and could only teach their students the rudiments of reading, writing, and simple Bible studies. Most fell somewhere in the middle.

There were no secular studies in the *cheder* my father attended and like many Jewish children in Eastern Europe before the First World War he had almost no contact with the non-Jewish children of the town. In religious and traditional circles which made up the bulk of Eastern European Jewry before the First World War, Jewish and Gentile children were kept away from each other as it was thought that no good could come of such contact, particularly at a young age. Only a few scant years had passed since the massive pogroms in the Russian Pale of Settlement in 1881 and anti-Jewish legislation had been passed in Romania as late as the 1890s. While Jews peacefully coexisted with their non-Jewish surroundings in Western Galicia where my father was raised, in other areas the "*goy*" was still the enemy. There the main contact between Jewish and Gentile children was when the latter attacked the former, throwing rocks at them and calling them "Christ-killers". Even in peaceful areas Gentiles were often viewed with suspicion and many Jews still considered them the ultimate "other".

My father and his contemporaries in Bochnia knew only a smattering of Polish and conducted their life in Yiddish, the language of Eastern Europe Jewry. "How could you come from Poland and not know Polish?!" I asked him incredulously, knowing that many of my friends' parents were from Poland and spoke the language. "They are younger", he explained. "Before the First World War it was enough to know Yiddish. Only those who studied in Poland between the wars learned Polish and some younger ones even knew more Polish than Yiddish."

My father and his contemporaries were of a different generation. They studied in *cheder*, not in *gymnasium*, functioned in Yiddish and not in Polish, and rarely traveled out of town during their childhood. Until my father fled Bochnia in 1914, he had not even visited Krakow, half an hour away. But although he and his and his friends in *cheder* studied neither history nor geography, they were well versed in stories about the history of Bochnia and especially about the Bochnia salt mines, the local attraction which were oldest salt mines in Europe.

Bochnia is a small town in western Galicia, located some 40 kilometers south east of Krakow. Nestled between a series of rolling hills which punctuate the Galician countryside, the town is near the Raba river, one of the small tributaries of the Vistula that branches off as it runs through southern Poland. My father loved to play on the riverbanks as a young boy and he later bought a painting of a broad expanse of river with beautiful foliage that he claimed reminded him of what he called the "Bochnia river". When I finally visited the area eighty years after he had played there, I failed to see the resemblance. Industrialization, it seems, had taken its toll on the Bochnia river as well as the town.

The earliest settlers made their home on the riverbanks at the end of the twelfth century and Bochnia received official town rights some fifty years later, soon after salt was discovered in the area. During the following centuries Bochnia, and the nearby town of Wisnicka where my ancestors resided, became the center of Galician salt industry and the local economy expanded to include other types of commerce, cottage industry and cloth-making.

Jews settled in Bochnia very close to the discovery of the salt mines and documents from 1445 already show them as having received some type of censure pertaining to commerce in salt; however it did not prevent them from remaining in Bochnia and seeking their livelihood in the area. Eighty-five years later the Jews of Bochnia had their own synagogue and a cemetery but they were not allowed to live in peace. Half a century after they had been granted a formal privilege to participate in the salt commerce they were expelled from the town and by the early 1600s most had moved to nearby Wisnicka. Only in 1862 did the Austro-Hungarian Emperor Franz Joseph officially permit them to return to Bochnia, but in practice over fifty Jews had always continued to live on the town's outskirts, keeping up a commercial relationship with the local population, mainly in the salt trade.

The Bochnia salt mine was known throughout all of Europe. Expanding in size year by year, it ultimately reached four and a half kilometers in length and close to half a kilometer in depth. As the mine's area increased and its shafts and passages were widened and broadened they formed an underground city in which an uninitiated visitor could easily get lost. Going down into the mine one found oneself in chamber after chamber whose walls were covered from floor to ceiling in salt. A person standing in one of those chambers while holding a candle would see a thousand reflections shining back at him from the glistening walls. But its most unusual feature was found at its western end. Just as one thought that one had reached the end of the narrowest passageways it opened into

8

an open underground area which led to a large subterranean lake reaching towards the direction of Krakow. Although my family was not financially connected to the salt mines, they played a central role in my father's reminisces of Bochnia, as they did in those of many of the young boys of the time.

In 1856, Bochnia, known as Salzburg in German, was connected to the Austro-Hungarian railway system, making it more accessible to the outside. After Emperor Franz Joseph allowed the Jews to return to Bochnia he decided to visit the town and the entire Jewish community came to greet him at the railroad station. To show their respect to "our Kaiser", as he was known, the local rabbis reached the station in a procession bearing the community Torah scrolls. Franz Joseph appears to have been suitably impressed as he gave them permission to enter the mine and use the lake for boating excursions. Years later, my father remembered going down into the mine and seeing the famous underground lake although he never went sailing on its waters; today its preserved chambers are a tourist site and the largest of the chambers has been converted into a sanatorium.

Like many parts of what was originally known as "Poland", Bochnia and its environs came under the control of various rulers, passing from local hands to those of the Swedes, the Russians and finally the Austrians. Although most of Bochnia's Jews were no longer living in the town during this period, they remained in the area, transferring their outward allegiances during these political transitions, but not changing their language or culture. As Galician Jews they spoke Yiddish although many could function in Russian, Polish, or German if need be. Their dress remained that of Jews in southern Poland: long overcoats for men, shirts and pants, sometimes tucked into boots, sometimes not, caps and often, broad Galician-Jewish hats. Women dressed modestly in long skirts or dresses and after marriage would cut their hair short and cover their heads with kerchiefs, hats, or marriage wigs. In some areas, but usually not that of Western Galicia, married women were expected to completely shave their heads. Those who wanted the more "natural look" would add a black lace band to their headdress and the daring ones might even attach fringes to the front of their kerchiefs in order to replicate bangs, a headdress known today among ultra-Orthodox Jewish women as a *shpitzl*. From the few photographs that we have of women in my family dating from the late nineteenth and early twentieth century, they did not appear to be partial to *shpitzls*, preferring to don either full wigs or turbans.

One of the major factors of that time which influenced my family along with many others in Eastern Europe was the Hassidic movement based upon the teachings of Israel Ben Eliezer, known as the *Ba'al Shem Tov*, the Master of the Good Name (1700–1760). Coming on the heels of the Chemielnicki pogroms and the moral débâcle surrounding the false messiah Shabbetai Zvi, the movement began in the Ukraine and spread rapidly among the disillusioned and impoverished Jews of White Russia, Poland and Galicia. Following the death of the *Ba'al Shem Tov*, later generations of the Hassidic movement instituted two innovations that became central to the movement: the concept of the *zaddik* or *Rebbe* surrounded by his Hassidim, and the Hassidic "court" located in a partic- ular geographical location. Within a short time a Hassid was not known generically but as one belonging to a specific *Rebbe*, such as a Gerrer hassid or a Lubavitcher hassid; Hassidic *Rebbes* were known by their name and that of the town of which they held their court. The first such *Rebbe* was the famous Galician leader of the third generation Hassidic movement, Rabbi Elimelech Weissblum of Lizhensk (Lezajsk) (1717–1786).

One of the main weekly events of most Hassidic courts was the *tish* (table). On Friday night, or during the third meal at the close of the Sabbath, the *Rebbe* would hold court at his table, blessing the food, taking a small bite and distributing the rest to his Hassidim who would vie for the honor of receiving the leftovers. Acting as a pivotal event in the life- cycle of the Hassidic court, the *tish* was often one of the major public events strengthening the connection between the hassid and his *Rebbe*. But even those Hassidim who did not regularly attend their *Rebbe's tish*, such as my grandfather and great-grandfather, still considered themselves attached to a *Rebbe* if they assisted in supporting his court and institutions such as yeshivas.

"So you were a *hassid*!" I exclaimed to my father as a teenager. "Well not exactly," he answered. "My grandfather was a *hassid*, and my father still kept Hassidic customs, but after leaving Bochnia, I definitely did not remain a *hassid*." My father's family appears to have been strongly Hassidic, going back a number of generations. The first center of Galician Hassidism was in Lizhensk and although he knew no details, my father told me that an ancestor, probably a great-great-great grandfather, had been a *shamash* (assistant) of *Rebbe* Elimelech of Lizhensk, approximately two hours north-east of Bochnia. The next Hassidic connection that we know of in the family skipped a generation and was also in a different geographical location, this time an hour south of Bochnia in the town of Sanz (Nowy Sacz). In 1830, Rabbi Chaim Halberstam (1793–1876), known as the "Divrei Chaim" after the title of his responsa and commen- taries, founded a Hassidic dynasty in Sanz and my father's great grandfather became one of his Hassidim.

Our family connection with the Halberstam dynasty continued through his descendants, as his seven sons and seven sons-in-law and grandsons became *Rebbes* throughout Galicia. My father's grandfather became a *hassid* of the "Divrei Chaim's" oldest son, Rabbi Yechezkel Shraga of Shiniava (1815–1889), but there was also a strong connection to the "Divrei Chaim's" grandson, the first *Rebbe* of Bobov, Rabbi Shlomo Halberstam (1847–1905). In 1881 Halberstam established a yeshiva in Wisnicka, my great-grandfather's home town, to which my ancestor had contributed heavily; when Halberstam became Rabbi in Bobowa in 1892 the Tydor family continued its allegiance to the Sanzer dynasty through this grandson. He was not the only *hassid* in Bochnia to do so. With growing numbers of Bobover Hassidim living in Bochnia, the Halberstam family dominated the Hassidic leadership of the Bochnia community until the Second World War.

As much as the "text" of my father's early years was important to his future, it can only be understood correctly within the context of the broad changes taking place in the Jewish world at the time. These were the years of the "great migration" when millions of people, including almost two and a half million Eastern European Jews, were moving westward. Some, like my father's aunts, and great aunts, settled in Western Europe. Most continued on to the United States. Poverty, anti–Semitism, widespread political dissatisfaction, a desire to better themselves, a belief that they could make their fortune in the "new world", and the fact that railway and steamship transportation had recently become both accessible and affordable were the main reasons propelling Jews from Eastern Europe to leave their countries of birth. But the political dissatisfaction also lead to different solutions; the rise of socialism, communism and the establishment of the Zionist movement. A small Zionist movement began in Bochnia around the time of my father's birth, but it made little impression on my family. Although they prayed thrice daily for the return to Zion, no members of our family belonged to the Zionist movement nor did any attempt to find their physical way to Zion in practice. That would only come later.

In addition to being years of mass migration, these were also the years of industrial change and scientific discoveries affecting fields from transportation to communication, manufacturing to medicine. Even little Bochnia, nestled in the Galician countryside, was affected by these changes. The introduction of the railroad in the middle previous century had connected Bochnia to the outside world. The technological advances of the late nineteenth and early twentieth century now brought the town into the era of modernity. In 1886 the first public library opened in

11

Bochnia, and in 1909 private homes were connected to a sewage system. In 1913 a cinema opened in the town center. Thus, even those Jews who did not join the "great migration" were no longer as isolated from the surrounding world as they had been a generation earlier. The children of Bochnia continued to swim in the Raba river but they now dreamed about the Mediterranean Sea and the Atlantic Ocean. After all, they had seen them in the cinema.

Between 1862 and 1939 the Jewish population of Bochnia gradually increased from 200 families to around 3,500 persons, becoming some 20 percent of the local population. In 1872 the cemetery was reestablished, although Jews from Bochnia were also buried in the neighboring town of Wisnicka. The Jews of Bochnia fell into three categories depending on the length of time that they lived in the town: the "old-timers" descended from those families which had never left, the "newcomers" who migrated from Wisnicka after Kaiser Franz Joseph allowed official Jewish settlement to be reestablished, and the "sojourners" who lived there temporarily for business reasons.

While certain boys in *cheder* could trace their Bochnia heritage back for several hundred years, my father's family was only there for two generations and were thus considered "returnees". The town archives list his grandfather, Mendel (Menachem-Mendel) Tydor (the name appears in the archives as Tydor, Tidor, and Tieder), as having been born in Wisnicka in 1845. Having lost his parents in his youth he was raised by two older sisters, both of whom married and moved to Antwerp, becoming part of the great migration westward. When Mendel reached the marriageable age of eighteen, he became engaged to a young neighbor, Mecha Scharf, who was thirteen at the time. Family lore states that Mecha was playing on the porch with her dolls when her father came to tell her that she had just gotten engaged. She asked who the young man was and whether he was nice, and when told that he was, she said "Good, now I'm going back to my dolls". Two years later, when Mendel completed his Torah studies, they were married.

During those two years Mecha had metamorphosed from a little girl into a headstrong young woman. A short time before their marriage she had a hunch that she would be lucky if she would buy a lottery ticket and secretly invested her marriage money in the "Polish Lotteria". Jews rarely took part in the Polish lottery and for a Jewish girl of fifteen such a step was unheard of. As a teenager I always wondered whether Mecha faced down her family over the issue or bought the ticket in secret, but the result was the same. Instead of losing her dowry she won the jackpot, and embarked on a very different life than that which her family had planned for her. Young Mecha won a tremendous amount of money and decided to make the most of it. Hearing that a grocery store in the center of the Bochnia marketplace was for sale, she informed her fiancé that they were going to buy it along with a house in Bochnia where they would live. Mecha was clear in her intentions. Mendel would continue to learn Torah and assist her in his spare time and she would operate the grocery and find someone to care for the house. Thus, sometime in the late 1860s the family moved from Wisnicka to Bochnia and became the proud owners of a large wooden house on Biala Street with an even larger back yard filled with fruit trees.

It is hard to know whether Mecha was house-proud, but she certainly had a big house of which to be proud. The large sloped roof one-storey house they purchased was made of brick and wood, and together with the attached garden stretched from Biala Street to the parallel Rozana Street behind it. In addition to a dining room and kitchen the house boasted four bedrooms along with a shed and wooden outhouse in the garden. From the back door one descended a number of wooden steps and reached the garden, Mecha's pride and joy. There she grew fruit and vegetables, along with grass and shade trees. When I visited the house in 2007 I was astonished at its size, only half of which was in use; the other half had been a pharmacy, but now it was closed. However it was the enormous garden which truly caught my eye, a marvel of different shades of green, glinting in the summer rain. It was in this enclosed garden that my father took his first steps, and under whose trees he played in his childhood.

In between running the grocery store Mecha gave birth to three children. From a young age their oldest daughter Yehidis'l (Judith) was drawn to Torah learning, always having her nose in a book. Unlike many Chassidic men, her father encouraged her endeavors, teaching her what he knew, and eventually arranged for her marriage to a young man named Naftali Horowitz who became the rabbi of a nearby town, Limanowa. Yehidis'l and Naftali had several children, none of whom appear to have followed their mother in learning or their father in the rabbinate. Their oldest son David opened a grocery in the Limanowa marketplace, similar to what his grandmother had done in Bochnia. It is not known whether he was as good a businessman as she. Other than my father's stories little remained from this branch of the family; all were murdered in the Holocaust.

Their second daughter, Chaya Bracha (Chatsha), preferred a more domestic existence and her marriage was arranged to Aaron Tennenbaum, a businessman from Germany. Having moved to Munich, Chatsha gave birth to four children – Ida, Mari, Rosl and David. Although geographically separated from her parents she often came to visit, bringing one or more of her children to meet their grandparents. Thus, from his earliest childhood my father was close to his German cousins. During the late 1930s Chatsha, Aaron, Mari, Rosl and their families escaped to England and thus survived the war. Ida and her family moved to Palestine and from there to America and were later joined by her parents. David, his wife and two daughters disappeared without a trace. Although "*onkel* Aaron" died long before my parents married, I was privileged to know my father's "*tante* Chatsha" until her death at age 96.

Mendel and Mecha had only one son, Yehuda Leib, born in 1874, who became the apple of his mother's eye. More than his sisters, the young boy inherited his mother's striking black hair and piercing dark eyes, and, as Mecha hoped, also his father's love of Torah. But as much as young Leibeleh tried to devote himself to learning, his true passions lay in other directions and Mecha soon understood that he was more suited to commerce than full-time Torah study. She then changed direction, looking for a business for him run, and finding him a wife to help him in this endeavor.

The arranged marriage system which Mecha employed to settle her children's future was quite similar to the one used by ultra-Orthodox Jews today. The concept of "like marrying like" guides the first stage of finding a child's future spouse, with Torah learning being one of the few wild-cards that can break the hierarchy of "rich marry rich and poor marry poor". While a well-to-do family is often willing to consider a poor but promising Torah scholar for their daughters, there is no parallel consideration when seeking a suitable match for their sons. Then as today, a young woman is usually judged by three variables: family background, money, and looks. Young men are also examined in three spheres: family background, money, and Torah knowledge. Other variables considered are mental and physical health of both the individual and their family, and for girls, domestic skills.

Although Mendel was a scholar, he and Mecha were also an established business family in Galicia and could therefore make their choice among families of the same economic station. Their fortune enabled them to marry their older daughter into a rabbinical family and their second daughter to a businessman. It followed that their son would need a wife from a similar business background, who would come with money of her own, and hopefully with domestic skills, good looks, and suitable personality traits. Bearing in mind Mecha's dominant personality she probably looked for a somewhat docile daughter-in-law who would accept her authority. But she also wanted her only son to marry a girl from a Hassidic background and who could also be a business asset to him.

The first order of the day was to find a business for Yehuda Leib to run. Although much of the family fortunes had been invested into rebuilding the house on Biala Street and expanding the grocery store, enough money remained from the lottery winnings to enter into an additional family venture. Mecha had her eye on a flour warehouse in Bochnia which was coming up for sale. At the same time she began searching in earnest for the right bride for her son. Several months later she heard about Esther Laufer, the nineteen year old single daughter of a family from the Chrzanow area who owned a chain of shoe stores throughout Maehrisch-Ostrau. As the Chrzanow district was at least two hour northwest of Bochnia, either the Laufer family was quite well known outside their area or Mecha must have previously exhausted all the potential candidates in a closer radius. Traveling to meet the parents, Chaya and Sinai Laufer, she was introduced to the potential bride, a diminutive and quiet dark haired young woman who combined good business sense with respect for elders – an important trait if you were about to live in one house with your in-laws. Esther was also fluent in German, the language spoken in her area of Galicia, which would be helpful to her husband in trade. Weighing her up as a potential daughter in law, Mecha concluded that Esther would be a welcome addition to the family and made plans for the two young people to meet. It appears they were pleased by what each of them saw and the wedding plans were set.

I often wondered about that first meeting between my great-grandmother and her future daughter-in-law. How did Esther react to the ways of the sharp businesswoman who would obviously rule the house in which she would live? Was she nervous about leaving her family and moving to Bochnia? After all, this was not Mecha's moving from Wisnicka to a town practically walking distance away but a true leave-taking from family whom she would no longer see on a regular basis. Whatever she thought, she obviously kept these thoughts to herself and never shared them with her son, my father. Whether she shared them with her new husband we will never know.

Esther and Yehuda Leib were married in 1896 when he was twenty-two and she was twenty. The young couple moved into the large house on Biala Street along with Mendel and Mecha who gave them the flour warehouse as a wedding present. There was certainly enough room for all of them; by that time Leibeleh's two sisters were married and there were several free bedrooms. In those days it was also quite common for entire families to live together under one roof, particularly if that roof covered a large number of rooms as it did in my ancestral home. True, the equation of two women and one kitchen, even with assistance, can often make for discord. However, bearing in mind Mecha's preference for commerce over housekeeping and Esther's tact in handling her mother-in-law it appears that they found a domestic modus vivendi which suited all involved.

A year after her marriage Esther gave birth to a son but the event ended in tragedy. Yehuda Leib and Esther's firstborn died shortly after birth, even before he was given a name. The young couple was heartbroken, more so when after an additional year of trying Esther had not yet gotten pregnant again. In spite of this ostensibly being a "women's issue" it was Mendel to whom they turned for guidance. Drawing on his Hassidic beliefs he felt it was time for Divine intervention or at least for a blessing from one of his earthly representatives. Mendel therefore requested an audience for his daughter-in-law with the oldest son of the "Divrei Chaim", Rabbi Yechzkel Shraga of Shiniava whose blessings to childless couples were often known to bear fruit. The audience was granted almost immediately; after all Mendel had written a Torah scroll in honor of Yehuda Leib and Esther's marriage – an expensive undertaking for that time – which he had given on loan to the House of Study in Sanz. The Shiniava *Rebbe* indeed blessed Esther, promising that although it would take several years, she would eventually give birth to a son. Before she left, the *Rebbe* asked one thing in return: to name the son she would bear after him.

My father was born on Thursday, October 22, 1903, the second day of the new moon of Heshvan, 5663, four years after the Shiniava *Rebbe's* death. Writing this sentence on my father's birthday, exactly 105 years later, I am filled with a sense of wonder. I do not know whether my father was born at night or during the day, whether it was raining, or possibly even snowing, or if the skies were clear. I can imagine the midwife being summoned to the house, my great-grandmother in residence to assist, the men banished to the synagogue where they would recite psalms for an easy and successful birth. I can imagine my grandfather's anxiety in view of his firstborn's fate and his overjoyed response to hear that his wife had once again born him a son. I can only imagine their

16

hopes and dreams for the child who was to become my father, first and foremost that he remain alive, unlike his older brother. From my father's birth onward his older sibling was never mentioned and like an unfortunate blip in family history was relegated to the past. My father only learned of his existence when he was told shortly before his Bar Mitzvah that he did not have to fast on the fast of the firstborn on the Passover eve as he had not been the firstborn son in the family.

"These kind of things just weren't talked about", my father explained to me when I asked about his older brother. "He must have died very young, possibly at birth. I never asked, my parents never offered information. It was just the way things were done. Death, illness, none of these things were mentioned unless absolutely necessary." When I went through the Bochnia archives in an attempt to find out more about my family there was no mention of my uncle's birth or death, as if he never existed. I found my grandparents, my great-grandparents, my aunt, and my father's first wife and her family, but baby Tydor never even made it into the town records.

The year my father was born was a momentous year in numerous fields. In that year the first transatlantic radio broadcast was made from America to England, the Russian Socialist Democratic party split in a step that would lead to the Russian Revolution and Orville Wright successfully flew an aircraft at Kitty Hawk, North Carolina, the first documented heavier than air flight. My father was one of numerous Jewish children born that year, some of whom came to fame in their various fields. Among them were the literary scholar Nachum Glatzer, the concert pianist Vladimir Horowitz, the mathematician Janos Neumann, and the controversial Jewish philosopher Yeshayahu Leibowitz. My father shared a birthday with Hungarian composer Franz Liszt (1811), actress Sarah Bernhardt (1844), novelist Doris Lessing (1919) and model Catherine Deneuve (1943), but only the first had any impact on his life. A lover of classical music, my father enjoyed all classical compositions but refused to listen to the works of Richard Wagner, the German anti-Semitic composer who Hitler held in esteem.

The dynamics in the Tydor family were clear; everyone had a given role. Zeideh Mendel spent his days learning while Bobbeh Mecha ran the grocery store and the family finances. Yehuda Leib expanded his flour warehouse, traveling to mills throughout Galicia to buy specialty flours and sell them to local mills. Esther ran the warehouse in his absence, returning home in the afternoon when her son would come back from *cheder*. For many years after Chaskel's birth it appeared that the Shiniava *Rebbe's* blessing was a one time event and no additional children were about to follow. Only close to eight years later did Esther become pregnant, this time giving birth to a girl who they named Yehudis, whose family nickname was Ida.

Although it must have been difficult for his mother to live under one roof with such an assertive and strong-willed mother-in-law, my father remembers growing up in a relatively harmonious household. As a businesswoman Mecha could appreciate Esther's intelligence and abilities, giving her space with Yehuda Leib at the flour warehouse. As a natural peacemaker Esther knew how to sidestep her mother-in-law while outwardly granting her the respect she expected. And they had something else in common; a deep love for their son and grandson who would carry on the family name. Only when the two women no longer shared a home after leaving Bochnia could Esther blossom; today we would call it "finding her inner self".

Meanwhile, though, Mecha had found her scholar. Little Chaskel was blessed with an impish streak, but also with a healthy curiosity, a photographic memory, and an unquenchable thirst for knowledge. Soon after starting *cheder* his *Rebbe* began to teach him Bible and within a short time the child could recite entire chapters by heart, along with commentaries. At age six he began to study *Mishna* and by the time he was seven he was moved to the group of older boys who were studying Talmud. From morning to night he would pour over a volume of Talmud almost as big as he was, and by the next day he could recite the entire page he had learned by heart.

We have no family pictures from my father's earliest years, but I imagine him as a small boy in short pants, twinkling eyes and a mischievous smile. He certainly inherited his father's eyes and coloring; from my grandfather's picture one can see that they both had thick straight black hair and jet black eyes, as did my father's sister. My father remembers wearing a velvet *yarmulkeh* to *cheder*, similar to the large black one that his grandfather Mendel wore in the one picture we have of him. In that photograph Mendel is wearing a high buttoned double breasted black coat and has short grey curled sidelocks with a long white beard.

His son, Yehuda Leib, already dressed in a more modern fashion. His picture from that time, probably a passport or identity picture from the time of the First World War, shows him wearing a high black square velvet *yarmulkeh*, but also a modern single breasted coat under which one can see a knit vest, a white shirt and what appears to be a cravat. He, too, still boasted tightly curled black sidelocks in front of his distinctive ears, a family hallmark which my father also inherited.

My father was a normal boy who would often get into trouble because of his curiosity and particularly his sweet tooth. Over eighty years later he told me how his love for sweets caused a family uproar. Once, when he was around six or seven, he decided to sample some of his mother's homemade liquor and wine which she produced for home use and sale. Waiting until she left the house, he broke into her large liquor store-cabinet which she kept in the kitchen, took a sip, and then another and another until he had finished half a bottle. It was delicious. My father recalled: "When my mother came home she looked at me and saw that I had a temperature and that I am somehow not talking the way she was used to hearing me talk. So she called the doctor, Dr. Frankel, a Jewish doctor, who came, checked me from all sides and told mother that I am healthy except that I am obviously drunk. My innocent mother didn't understand how, without a glass around, I could be drunk. Somehow I confessed to her and she let me have a good sleep and apparently I eventually became sober." By the time he came back from *cheder* the next day the bottles had been well hidden and all of his future attempts to find them were unsuccessful.

Another incident involved his love of ice cream. Every week he would get pocket money from his grandmother – "lottery money" they would call it in the family – which he would happily spend at the local *Lody* (ice cream) store run by the wife of a local rabbi who was also the great granddaughter of the "Divrei Chaim" of Sanz. It was a small store, so my father recalled, but wisely located where the children of the town would pass on their way to and from *cheder*. One day he came to the store without money and tried a new tactic, convincing the *Rebbetzin* that she should give him the ice cream now and his mother would pay for it later in the day ("Give me *lody*, my mother will pay"). Passing the store on her way home from the flour warehouse, Esther was called in by the proprietor, and when told of her son's request, she promptly covered his bill. When he saw the success of his strategy he became a frequent customer at his beloved ice cream store, playing on his family's good reputation, his impish charm, and the *Rebbetzin*'s goodwill. Stopping in almost every day on the way back from *cheder*, he would look innocently at the *Rebbetzin* and ask for a portion on credit. The ruse worked for two whole weeks at which point the young store owner presented Esther with a bill for her son's sweet tooth. His mother was aghast. After covering the bill, she sat down with her son, explaining that "credit", a term he had recently learned from his grandmother, was not meant to be used by little boys in ice cream stores. It was his first lesson in the process of loans and banking.

My father's sweet tooth lasted into ripe old age. My daughters remember their grandfather hiding chocolate bars in the large living room credenza, taking one out to share with them. All three – two little girls of four and six and their grandfather of eighty-seven – would lick their lips in delight after "sneaking" a few pieces of chocolate when grandmother's back was turned.

As he grew older my father began showing early signs of a business sense which he combined with a love of faraway places. Noticing the beautiful stamps that adorned his father's correspondence with millers throughout the world, he became interested in stamp collecting, and encouraged his schoolmates to start an underground stamp trade in their *cheder*. Within a short time he had cornered the Bochnia *cheder* market on international stamp trading, and boasted a collection that included the particularly large and beautifully decorated stamps from Bosnia-Herzegovina, as well as extremely rare and valuable ones from countries such as Cuba. Once, an adult even knocked at my grandparents' door in Bochnia asking whether the "stamp trader" lived in that house; he had been told that if he wanted to find a rare stamp, there was a stamp trader who lived at Biala 10 who might have it for him! When my father's *Rebbe* in *cheder* caught him trading stamps instead of learning he chided him, asking why the stamps interested him so much. Stamps, his *Rebbe* reminded him, could never take the place of Torah. "But I want to go and visit all these places *Rebbe*," replied the young boy, "and I can also learn Torah when I get there." Little did he know that forty years later he would begin a third career as a travel agent, and visit most of the countries whose stamps he had admired during his childhood.

Already as a young boy my father was a voracious reader. Although his reading was limited at that stage to Yiddish and a smattering of Hebrew, it was already possible to obtain translations of both classical literature and children's tales into both languages. Like many boys he loved reading adventure stories; his favorites were about two very different cultures: Japanese samurai and the American Wild West. One of the memorable characters who featured in his books was American cowboy "Buffalo Bill" Cody. Like many children of that time throughout the world my father and his friends would often play "cowboys and Indians", and he remembered having remarked jokingly to his friends that he wanted to be the "Buffalo Bill of Bochnia". Fifty years later he would regale me with tales of an adventurous young lad whom he named "Buffalo Bill of Bochnia" who fought either the Indians, the Nazis, or both. I was never sure which.

Whatever my father's intentions were when he told me those stories as a child, the more I learned more about his experiences, the more his image truly meshed with that of "Buffalo Bill of Bochnia", the courageous young boy upon whose stories I was raised. My father went through various adventures during the First World War and a survived a very different set of adventures during the Second World War which would have killed many of the people who experienced them. Did I write many? Such "adventures" indeed killed most of the Jews who underwent them during the Nazi era. The more I learned about his past, the more I realized how unique the moral fiber of his childhood was in forming the man who survived the seven rungs of hell.

Compared to the usual stories of growing up in an Eastern European *shtetl*, and the harsh tales of how young boys in *cheder* often suffered their *melamed's* stick more often than they enjoyed the fruits of his knowledge, my father's childhood appears to have been inordinately happy and secure. Cushioned from hardship by his family's economic status, he grew up in a large house with a beautiful garden, five minutes away from the city center. The only child in the family for close to a decade, he enjoyed the privilege of his own bedroom, and of being loved and cosseted by parents and grandparents who adored him and who he adored in return. His intelligence endeared him to his *melamed*; his charm allowed him to get away with many a childish prank; his trading abilities in *cheder*, whether in stamps, sweets, or other articles, always placed him in the center of a group of schoolmates. Later, his love of Torah and devotion to its study attracted other like-minded boys of all ages. One of them, Shimon Kempler, remained his friend for life. Like him, Kempler escaped with his family to Germany during the First World War; the two were also deported together to Buchenwald twenty-five years later.

While it is easy to dismiss this posthumous evaluation as being an idyllic but unrealistic reconstruction of his childhood, one thing that he continuously told me provides an explanation for many of his tales: his parents believed, above all, in kindness towards children; that they were convinced that if parents wished their children to respect them, they had to grant that child respect in turn. This was certainly not the accepted method of child-rearing in early twentieth century Galicia. Nevertheless, it formed the basis for the unique bonds between my father and his parents and helps solve the riddle of their relationship.

A story that my father recounted to me accentuates this belief. As a young boy my father would *daven* next to his father in synagogue often hiding under his large prayer shawl and playing quietly with its fringes as many children do. Near my grandfather sat another man of the same age whose son was slightly older and more rowdy than my father. In order to keep his son in line, the other man would not spare the rod, and had no compunction in pulling his child's ears or slapping his backside to keep him quiet while *davening*. Seeing this, my grandfather would admonish the other man whose name was also Leib. "Leibeleh", my grandfather would say, "please find another way. Believe me that years from now, when your son no longer remembers the *davening* he will still remember the beatings that he got from you."

When he was eight years old my father took on a new role, that of being a big brother. The large age gap that separated him from his sister Yehudis precluded any chance of rivalry; the gender difference gave them each a different position in the family scheme. The house was certainly large enough for two children; each had their own room and as much as he loved his baby sister, my father remembered being quite happy to still have a bedroom of his own. Not only could he continue reading late at night by candlelight; he would still be able to climb out of his window on to the branches of the old apple tree that reached from the back of the house to the front without anyone seeing where he was going.

At various stages in his childhood this apple tree played a pivotal role in his emotional development. Growing up for so many years as an only child, he would sit for hours reading under its heavy branches. At other times he climbed as high as he could, far above the roof of the house, to glimpse what he thought was a bird's eye view of Bochnia and dream of the world outside. When he wanted a snack, all he had to do was stretch his hand out of his bedroom window and pick one of its tart apples. Apples were indeed among his favorite fruits for all the years to come.

When I visited Bochnia in 1988 it was late at night but I could still make out the shadow of a very large tree at the right side of the house on Biala Street. Examining those pictures on my return, my father smiled at the sight of what appeared to be his apple tree and showed me where his bedroom window had been. Nineteen years later, when I returned to Bochnia during the daytime, my father was no longer alive but the tree was still there. Indeed it was an apple tree whose branches grew far above the roof of the house. In the back garden there were additional apple trees, and I could finally picture my father a hundred years earlier, watching the branches through his bedroom window at night and climbing them as a young boy during the day.

The apple tree featured prominently in two of his childhood stories that shed light on the mores of the Jewish community of Bochnia at the turn of the century. At the beginning of Biala Street, near the *rynek* (town square), there was a large Catholic church whose bell would toll every hour. During certain hours of the evening the priests would form a procession and walk slowly down the street, blessing the houses and returning to the church through a back way. As a little boy my father would lie in bed at night and watch their shadows pass near his window. Although relations between the Jews and non-Jews of Bochnia were peaceful at the time, my father had heard stories from his friends in *cheder* about the priests who would kidnap Jewish children and attempt to baptize them against their will. Every night as the procession passed his house, he would prepare himself to climb out of the window and hide in the branches of the apple tree in order to elude any priests who might suddenly decide to kidnap a little Jewish boy lying in his bed at 10 Biala Street. The priests were his sworn enemies. The apple tree would be his savior.

Another story centered around accepted social behavior for *cheder* boys. Other than his parents and grandparents my father had no relatives in Bochnia. His cousins from his mother's side came from the Chrzanow area and Maerisch-Ostrow; those from his father's side lived in Limanowa and Munich and the more distant second cousins lived in far-away Antwerp. Thus it was a great event when one of his young relatives would come for a visit, something which usually happened during the holiday seasons or the last weeks of summer.

When my father was four his aunt Chatsha (Chaya Bracha) from Munich decided to visit her parents in Bochnia for an extended visit. She was accompanied by her young daughter, Ida, yet another daughter in the family. Chaskel was four at the time, and very happy to have a young cousin around, although she was a girl and a few years older than he. He was even willing to share his beloved apple tree with her, showing her how to swing from its lower branches. One day his grandmother returned from the marketplace and found the two of them sitting together in the front of the house under the shade of the tree, facing the street. "It is unseemly that a big Jewish boy like you should be seen sitting outside next to a girl even if she is a relative", she admonished her grandson. "After all, you are already four and she is almost seven". Not having been raised with female cousins nearby, this was the first time that my father was introduced to the concept of separation of the sexes within the family. It was also his first taste of how straight-laced his grandmother could be when it came to public issues of propriety, a sentiment that his parents did not always share.

By the end of the nineteenth century the gap between religious and secular Jewish society had often become a chasm, and there were noticeable cracks within the framework of the catchall term "Orthodox Jewry".

While it was still uncommon to speak of a "generation gap" within religious Jewish society, its first signs were being felt and would come to a
head after the First World War. Although their outward existence was
almost identical, in many things Mecha and Mendel belonged to a
different generation than their son and daughter-in-law. Mendel had an
unwavering belief in the Hassidic way of life and although he would assist
his wife in the grocery, his life was primarily one of Torah and Hassidic
learning. He lived his life in Yiddish, knowing only enough basic Polish
to speak to the local non-Jews who entered the store. Blessings of the
Shiniava *Rebbe* notwithstanding, his son, Yehuda Leib, was first and foremost a businessman with an eye towards modernity. Although he had
been brought up in Yiddish, he learned enough German from his wife
to read a German newspaper fluently and correspond with other millers
in that language. While he had no skepticism towards observant belief
and practice and accepted many outward trappings of Hassidism to honor
his father, by choice he was moving towards a different way of life in
many things. This would become obvious to his son during their sojourn
in Vienna and later when they moved to Munich.

As long as father, son and grandson lived under one roof, Hassidic
practice was the norm. But after the two families went their separate
geographical ways, only vestiges would eventually be left of their Hassidic
customs. No longer would the younger Tydors eschew kosher meat that
had not been slaughtered by Hassidim and their synagogue of choice was
not always a Hassidic *shteibl* (small prayer house). Their outward clothing
would become westernized; Leibeleh's beard was shortened and Chaskel
did not grow a beard at all. Even in Bochnia, Leibeleh's newspaper of
choice was the secular Viennese *Neue Freie Presse*. Although all men in
the family had been educated in *cheder*, as soon as they moved to Germany
Chaskel received a more modern education combining Jewish and
secular subjects. By the end of the First World War it was uncontested
that he would continue on to university.

Although she was a very modest woman, Esther did not always share
her mother-in-law's strict ideas regarding behavior. I often wondered
how much of my great-grandmother's emphasis on propriety was actually a reaction to her personal inclinations or an attempt to restrain her
own vivacious nature. After all, this was the woman who at fifteen had
the courage to follow a hunch, and to invest all of her dowry and wedding
present money in a lottery ticket!

The only picture that we have of her is her passport picture which
hangs, enlarged, in my parents' home. In it she is wearing a tightly
buttoned elegant winter coat with fur lapels, her hair completely covered

24

by a high turban-like jeweled hat ending in what appears to be a large peacock feather. She must have been in her late sixties at the time; her face is stern and proud with not a hint of a smile. In it, I can see my father's features, his eyes, nose and thin lips which he inherited from his paternal grandmother. Yet I wonder if behind the stern façade were still vestiges of the adventurous girl of fifteen who left behind her family in Wisnicka, taking her young husband to a nearby town and mapping out their life for the next fifty years like moves on a chessboard that had been drafted in advance.

It certainly must have been daunting to live with such a woman, yet it could also be comforting. My father remembered her having not only the answers to everything but the money to come up with solutions. True, being the only grandson at home he was certainly cosseted by her and saw sides of her that his father could only have dreamed of as a boy. It was his mother Esther who must have born the brunt of the physical closeness with her in-laws. Not only my father, but also other friends and relatives who remembered her, described Esther as a saint.

Yet even saints often have other sides to them. Only when my grandmother took my father on trips to visit her family near Chrzanow could she be herself. My father remembered those visits as a time when he was free of so many restrictions which ruled his life in Bochnia. There Esther would frolic with him in the garden in which she had grown up, playing hide and seek and having picnics with him on the grass. Knowing his penchant for sweets she and her brothers and sisters would let him eat chocolate until he couldn't look at another bite. For my father, trips to the home of his Zeideh Sinai and Bobbeh Chaya were ones of pure enjoyment.

There was not much that Leibeleh and Esther could do living in the same house with his parents in order to ease the restrictions of daily life. Life was regulated by the hours of business, the hours of *cheder*, the hours of prayer and the decisions of Bobbeh Mecha. But change was around the corner, even if they were unaware of it. My father remembered no talk of politics at the table as a boy, even during the late spring and early summer of 1914 while all of Europe waited for the Serbian insurgents to meet the Austrian ultimatum. Throughout the beginning of that fateful summer life in the Tydor household in Bochnia continued as usual. Little did the inhabitants of 10 Biala Street know that their days in Galicia were numbered and that their lives were about to undergo a rapid and irreversible change.

2

Munich, 1914–1920

The fast of the ninth of Av (*Tisha Be'av*) is one of the most solemn days in the Jewish calendar, marking the destruction of the Temple in Jerusalem. Similar to Yom Kippur, the five prohibitions of mourning are in effect; one may not eat, drink, wash for pleasure, wear leather, or have conjugal relations. But unlike Yom Kippur which is characterized by a sacred Sabbath-like atmosphere of penitence and hope, *Tisha Be'av* is truly a day of sadness. Exacerbated by the summer heat, it is the fast with the greatest number of daylight hours, usually making it feel like "the longest fast".

Tisha Be'av 5674 was a very warm day in Bochnia, as was much of the following week. Having fallen on a Saturday, the fast was postponed until Sunday as one does not fast on a Sabbath except in the case of Yom Kippur. The fast was not the only thing that had been delayed by a day that year. Equally delayed were the first reports that Germany had declared war on Russia in the wake of Russia's military mobilization in support of Serbia; this declaration followed on the heels of a previous declaration of war five days earlier by Germany's ally, Austria. In addition to the declaration of war on Russia, both Germany and its enemy France had declared a general mobilization and thus, the Great War had begun. It was Saturday, August 1, 1914, the ninth of Av, 5674.

If this sounds confusing to you, indeed it was confusing to many of the participants as well. The Great War, as it was then called, was for many a war of confusion, the result of alliances enacted by various European nations during the first years of the new century. It pitted countries against each other when they actually had no debate between them, placed the children and grandchildren of the late British Queen Victoria on opposite sides of the trenches, and began with bayonets and cavalry but ended with tanks, airplanes, submarines and even chemical warfare. It was a war which would redraw European borders and mark the beginning of the end of colonialism. Political changes would abound: the

Russian Revolution, the establishment of the French and British Mandates in the Middle East, and the creation of the Weimar Republic just to mention a few. There had never been a war of that magnitude in modern history, and after it ended, one hoped that it would truly be "the war to end all wars".

Originally many had thought that the war would be settled in a number of weeks and when the British soldiers assembled at Victoria Station they were sent off with the cry "see you at Christmas". And indeed the troops were home by Christmas. Not Christmas 1914 but Christmas 1918. Four long years later during which sixty million Europeans would be mobilized leading to twenty million military casualties and an equal number of civilian deaths. There are stories of how during Christmas 1914 British and German troops in France took advantage of the temporary cease-fire in order to arrange an impromptu soccer game, showing each other pictures of wives and sweethearts from home in Liverpool and Berlin and reminiscing about those they had left behind. And why not? After all, some British soldiers even remarked, "Kaiser Willy" was a nephew of "King Edward" and the two cultures had so much in common, much more than they had with their allies, "those froggies" the French. But the British and German commanding officers were horrified; how could they continue to wage war in view of such behavior? The next day they laid down the law and outlawed future fraternization with the enemy until the war's end.

My father described the outbreak of the First World War in his usual understated manner. "In the meantime a war broke out between Austria and Russia and the Russians invaded Galicia in order to conquer it." What he didn't mention was the utter trepidation of Galician Jewry in the face of the expected Russians invasion particularly as it was barely eleven years since the Kishenev pogrom and only three years since Mendel Beylis had been accused in Kiev of murdering a Christian child for ritual purposes. The intentions of the Czar's army towards the local Jews were not seen as benign, particularly as the Austro-Hungarian Empire, of which Galicia was part, was Germany's ally and now Russia's sworn enemy. Consequently, many Galician Jews including our family, made plans to flee the Russian invaders as soon as they heard about the official outbreak of war.

At first the family split up. The morning after *Tisha Be'av* Yehuda Leib struck out towards Belgium where his father's sisters lived, joining the exodus of thousands of Jews from Galicia and the Bukovina who were fleeing westward. My grandfather never made it to his aunts. Instead he decided to take his family to his sister Chatsha Tennenbaum in Germany and doubled back towards Galicia in order to find his wife and children.

We have no idea what happened to Mecha and Mendel during those early days of the war, whether they first traveled to Yehidis'l in Limanova or immediately began their journey westward towards Chatsha in Germany. My father never spoke about his grandparents' flight from Galicia to Germany but I assume it was done in a more direct way than his own roundabout escape, predicated by the fact that his grandparents probably decided to refuge at one of their daughters' homes. What I do know from my father is that he, his mother and sister traveled alone until they met his father and that the extended family was only reunited several months later at the Tennenbaum household in Munich.

Meanwhile Esther, left alone with two young children in Bochnia, was feverishly trying to close down the flour warehouse and gather finances and supplies for their future while waiting for word from her husband, which never arrived. During the morning of Friday August 7, reports reached Bochnia that the Russian army was advancing through Galicia. Hearing the news, my grandmother hastily packed up a few things for her two children, hid a large sum of money on her person, locked up the house on Biala Street and made her way with them to the train station. There by a combination of pleading and cajoling, she got them on the train to Krakow, the first step in their journey. Was she planning to take them to her own family in Maehrisch-Ostrau, the area of Moravia near the Austrian border where they owned a chain of shoe stores? Did she contemplate going to her sister-in-law in Munich? Was she actually thinking of traveling to Belgium where her husband's aunts resided and to which ostensibly he had set off? Or did she think that at a first stage they should just join the thousands of Jews fleeing Galicia for parts further west, even without a set destination, all running in terror from the advancing Russian forces? Whatever she thought at the time, she did not share these thoughts with her son, my father, who remembered most of the flight not as one of terror, but primarily one of adventure.

Until then my father had never been on a train, nor had he visited Krakow in spite of its proximity to Bochnia. This time he barely had a chance to see the city from the train windows. Almost as soon as they disembarked from one train they began the next leg of their train journey westward. The second train was packed with refugees carrying bags, satchels, knapsacks and pillowcases stuffed with their belongings.

28

Crossing from carriage to carriage with her children on the moving train, Esther almost lost her grip on little Ida and the two and a half year old child hung in the air over the moving wheels. Seeing his baby sister hovering between heaven and earth, Chaskel lunged and caught her, but the sight of his mother's terror at that moment remained engraved in his memory for decades.

As the heat of the day enveloped the travelers and the din of the refugees combined with the clatter of the wheels, Esther realized that the Sabbath was approaching and that she could not continue to travel. Approaching a railroad official with her little daughter in her arms, she begged him to let them off at a nearby station so that she would not have to desecrate the Sabbath. Touched by her plight he agreed they could disembark at Nikolsburg, a small town in the Hapsburg Empire, located directly on the border of lower Austria in what is today the south Moravian region of the Czech Republic.

Nikolsburg, known today as Mikulov, has a population of about 7,600 inhabitants. At the time it was much smaller with a Jewish population numbering about three hundred persons. My grandmother, father and aunt were not the only Galician refugees to find refuge in the town; at the time they joined dozens and later hundreds of Jews from the east who swelled the local Jewish population, thinking that they would be safer in a location closer to Austria. I do not know why my grandfather decided to look for his wife and children in Nikolsburg of all places – after all, there was no communication between them since he had left Bochnia – but he was successful in his endeavors. Disembarking from the train Esther had met an acquaintance who assisted her in renting a room for the Sabbath; when the same acquaintance saw Yehuda Leib wandering the streets of the town two days later he directed him to the boarding house where Esther and the children were staying. A deeply believing Jew, Yehuda Leib did not see this as coincidence but as heavenly guidance and a sign that they would all survive the war together. And indeed they did.

The family remained in Nikolsburg for two weeks. While Esther attended to her family's domestic needs, Yehuda Leib, free from work, spent a great deal of time with his son, showing him the town and teaching him its Jewish history. Compared to Bochnia, Nikolsburg was a provincial hamlet, so he told Chaskel, and on Friday they would close up the Jewish section with chains to ensure that no transportation would enter on the Sabbath. Taking him to visit some of the older yeshivas in town he regaled him with tales of their founders, the famous Hassidic *Rebbe* Reb Shmelke (Shmuel Halevi Horowitz) of Nikolsburg

(1726–1778) and the Talmudist and chief Rabbi of Moravia, Rabbi Mordechai Banett (1753–1829).

Compared to other refugees in town, the Tydors, who had rented a room in the town center, were living in comparative luxury. In contrast, most refugees were housed in a camp on the town outskirts, as my father learned when sent to find a *shochet* (ritual slaughterer) and purchase a chicken to eat. There was no local *shochet* in Nikolsburg; until then the community had made do with one who made rounds of various towns in the area and had regular days every month when he would visit. My father and grandfather therefore walked to the Galician refugee camp where they found a *shochet* and returned with enough food to sustain the four of them for the rest of the week. It was the first time my father realized how fortunate his family was and under what conditions most refugees were forced to live.

The sojourn in Nikolsburg soon came to an end and the Tydor family continued southward towards Austria on their wartime odyssey. Now they joined tens of thousands of Jewish refugees from Galicia and the Bukovina who swelled the Jewish population of Vienna from 175,000 to over 200,000 during the war years. My father rarely mentioned his escape from Galicia and his experiences during the three and a half months that he and his parents spent in flight. "What do you remember from Nikolsburg or Vienna?" I once asked him. He answered me with a slightly embarrassed smile: "The truth is, not too much. While the few days in Nikolsburg seemed to have had an impact on me, I remember little of Vienna other than my father taking me to see various sites of Jewish and general interest. That's about it." And yet he was already eleven years old, old enough to remember fear and terror if there had been any, and yet it seems that there was none. The only moment of terror was when my aunt almost fell off the train as a baby; other than that, his memories were either neutral or even pleasant, after all he finally spent time with his father who in Bochnia had little time to spend with his young son. For him, that was the "silver lining" of their having to leave home during the war.

From my father's stories of the early days of war one could easily forget the circumstances of their flight and think that his parents had decided to take him and his baby sister on a tour of Europe. War may have been raging in Galicia but it did not appear prominently in his tales. That would only happen when they would reach Germany and Yehuda Leib would be drafted into the Austro-Hungarian army. Even then, his comments were laconic. "In spite of his age, during the Great War my father spent some time in the Austro-Hungarian army and when he came home we heard some horrible stories about what was going on at the front", was all he said about that subject.

Two months later the Tydors began the last stage of their journey, crossing the border westward to Germany. Concluding that it would be futile to attempt to reach his great aunts in Belgium, Yehuda Leib decided to travel to Munich where his sister Chatsha and her family resided. Mendel and Mecha were already there when Yehuda Leib, Esther and the children arrived in early December. Like many refugees they spent their first days living with family, in this case, the Tennenbaums. Soon after, Chatsha found them a room to rent on the floor above them and for a while the extended clan lived in the large building at Klensestrasse 36. Eventually, Esther amassed enough money for them to rent an apartment in a more modern building. Chatsha and her family moved there soon after, bringing the grandparents with them.

The Jewish community of Munich numbered approximately 11,000 persons at that time and was divided into three groups: Jews whose families had lived in Germany for centuries, those like the Tennenbaums who had immigrated westward during the great migration, and refugees such as my grandparents who reached the city during the first years of the war. Six years earlier the community had opened a new Jewish cemetery; three years after that they had finally built a Jewish hospital. The city boasted a large Orthodox Synagogue ("Ohel Jakob") with approximately 1000 seats for men and 800 for women, the third largest Jewish house of worship in Germany. In addition, a number of smaller *shuls* already existed and more were founded by the refugees. Often preferring to *daven* with their refugee brethren many newcomers, such as my own family, were drawn to the smaller, newly created places of worship.

My father recalled only one story about the weeks that the families lived together, in which he expressed surprise at his father's "religious tolerance". Being an extremely religious Jew, my grandfather was careful to observe the prohibition against *kol isha*, of men not hearing women's voices singing other than one's mother, grandmother, wife or daughter. The Tennenbaum family appears to have been somewhat lax in this practice and their three daughters would join in singing the *zmirot* at the Shabbat table regardless of who else was sitting there. When young Chaskel asked his father how they could sit there and listen to the voices of aunts and female cousins, he answered him by saying, "this is not *kol isha*, this is the *kol* (voice) of my *mishpoche* (family)". For my father, used to the strictures of religious life in Bochnia, even this slightly lenient answer was an eye opener.

Unlike in Bochnia, where Bobbeh Mecha had held the purse strings and Yehuda Leib had been the primary younger breadwinner, in Munich, Esther took center stage as family breadwinner, particularly during the short period when Yehuda Leib was inducted into the Austro-Hungarian army. At first she sold various items from home in order to care for little Ida but soon she and her sister-in-law Chatsha entered into a business that flourished in wartime Germany due to the large number of casualties: enlarging, retouching, and framing pictures of fallen soldiers.

Today we have a tendency to view European wars through the prism of the Second World War with its horrific death tolls eclipsing those of the war which preceded it. But at that time, particularly in Germany and France, the death tolls were unprecedented. Two million German and 1,100,000 Austro-Hungarian soldiers were killed in the war. France, with its population of close to 40 million, had suffered close to 1,700,000 military and civilian casualties. Similar to the number "six million" which the human mind fails to comprehend, these numbers were incomprehensible in their entirety. Instead, one began to understand the demographic impact of the war when visiting German high schools in which a large plaque "dedicated to the memory of the entire graduating class of 1914" appears. Not individual students, but entire graduating classes were wiped off the map during the first war years. Among the casualties were 12,000 German-Jewish soldiers, one out of every eight German-Jewish frontline soldiers to fight in the war. There are stories recalling how after battles between German and French forces, Jewish soldiers from one side would stand in no-man's-land reciting *kaddish* over the bodies of their dead brethren. In the distance, they would hear "amen" being answered by their co-religionists on the other side of the trenches, their voices echoing over the smoke still rising from the battlefield.

Someone once said that there are two real possibilities for making money: during the building of Empires and during their downfall. My grandmother and her sister-in-law were among the many who recognized the war's business potential and engaged their acumen and abilities into becoming part of what the late German-Jewish historian George Mosse called the "cult of the fallen soldier". Parents, sweethearts and wives of the war dead would provide them with small photographs that most families had of their sons, often in uniform. The two women would then retouch, enlarge and frame the pictures, hanging black mourning ribbons from the frame. Not only would the bereaved families have a beautiful remembrance of their loved ones; they could also proudly display their contribution to the war effort – their sons, husbands and fathers – on the mantelpiece, proving their patriotism to all who entered their home. Even Mecha entered into the business together with her daughter and daughter-in-law, giving all three families the economic wherewithal to survive during the war.

To succeed in business in Germany one had to speak German. Luckily, Esther was fluent in the language and her authentic accent smoothed her path as she entered Munich's commercial life. Mecha quickly picked up German but never reached Esther's level of fluency. Chaskel began to study German in school and although he had difficulty with grammar, his accent was good and he even began dreaming in that language. Like many immigrant children then and today he lived a linguistically schizophrenic life speaking one language in school and another at home.

School was a sore point in the Tydor family during the first years of the war. There was no *cheder* in Munich and it was unlikely that Yehuda Leib and Esther would find one for Chaskel anywhere in the country. But unlike other cities which boasted Jewish schools combining both religious and secular education, Munich did not even have a Jewish school. Jewish schoolchildren received no privileges and were required to study on Saturday. For religious Jewish children there was the problem of not being able to write on the Sabbath or carry their books to school on that day.

Yehuda Leib knew that at least one Jewish family's children in town had received an exemption from carrying their books to school and writing on the Sabbath, those of Rabbi Dr. Chanoch Heinrich Ehrentreu (1854–1927), the chief rabbi of Munich. He therefore requested Ehrentreu to submit a similar application for Chaskel and later for Ida, and he made an arrangement with the school custodian to keep their books there over the Sabbath studies. Throughout the months of 1915 the arrangement continued; nevertheless, Yehuda Leib was troubled when he saw his son, and later his daughter, make their way to school each week after the end of the Sabbath morning services. How could he let his children attend school on Shabbos and receive their Jewish education only from their parents and grandparents? His heart grew heavier as he began to prepare his only son for his Bar Mitzvah which was to take place in the coming year.

Yehuda Leib berated himself over his son's truncated Jewish education, and at one point even shared these worries with his family physician, Dr. Levy, who was an acquaintance of Yehuda Leib's brother-in-law, Aaron Tennenbaum. Discussing his emotional and not only physical health with the doctor, Yehuda Leib confided to him about his misgivings regarding his son's Jewish education, or lack thereof. Levy immediately suggested a solution. His brother-in-law, Rabbi Ben-Zion

Ellinger, lived in Fürth in northern Bavaria where he taught in the Israelitische Realschule, an Orthodox Jewish boys' high school founded in 1869 which combined secular and religious studies. Many of the students who attended the school later became famous; among them were composer Jacob Schoenberg and former American Secretary of State Henry (Heinz) Kissinger whose family emigrated from Germany in 1938. Levy suggested that young Chaskel could possibly be accepted to the school, thus solving the problem of Sabbath observance and Jewish education in one fell swoop. The only issue was money. School fees were high and as it was an out of town school with no dormitory, Chaskel would be required to board with a family in town.

The money was found. Yehuda Leib was delighted at the thought of his son having both a religious and secular education. As Chaskel had done well in his Munich primary school neither language nor his grades were a problem. Dr. Levy arranged for him to receive a letter of recommendation from a teacher in the school and for his sister, Mrs. Ellinger, who ran a pension for students from out of town, to accept Chaskel as a border. His education was now set. Initially he was accepted into the Israelitische Volksschule (Jewish primary school) of Fürth and the following year he was permitted to enroll in the Realschule, the academic Jewish high school.

My father described almost everything about the school in glowing terms. He recalled: "The school's program included *shmiras Shabbos* (Sabbath observance) and *shmiras mitzvos* (keeping the commandments) which after Munich was a delight." The curriculum was rigorous. Religious lessons in the elementary school included Hebrew reading and writing, Bible and Biblical history while secular lessons included penmanship, composition, German, arithmetic, history, geography, science and singing. In high school one added Talmud, the study of two foreign languages, English and French, mathematics, physics, chemistry, art and gym. Chaskel had a great desire to make up for the months when he had gone without formal Jewish studies and requested extra hours with his teachers after he finished his secular lessons to be able to study Bible with commentaries. At the same time he was also busy completing preparations for his Bar Mitzvah which would take place at the beginning of the next school year.

My father's Bar Mitzvah took place on Shabbat *Rosh Hodesh Heshvan* (the new moon of Heshvan) October 28, 1916, precisely on the Hebrew date of his birth. Keeping the occasion a family one, it was held in a small *shul* which a relative, Yidel (Yehuda) Rosner had started in Munich, called "Shomrei Shabbos" ("The Sabbath Observers"). The *shul's* name was a somewhat ironic reminder of Yehuda Leib's previous misgivings regarding his children's enforced Sabbath activities and of his fortune in finding a solution, at least for his teenage son. My father remembers a small celebration in the *shul*; cake, schnapps and for the children, candy. Apart from receiving his own set of *tefilin* (phylacteries) from his grandparents, the entire event was low keyed in view of the family's circumstances and the fact that the war had entered into its third year.

Had the celebration taken place in Bochnia before the war, my father would have been fêted by family and friends alike for an entire week, receiving not only *tefilin* but a new set of Hassidic clothing and a *gartel* (ritual belt). In Munich, the family still kept to most Hassidic customs but had already abandoned the special dress; other than the fact that he had a beard and sidelocks and covered his head at all times, Yehuda Leib's mode of dress was indistinguishable from his surroundings. Chaskel, on the other hand, no longer even sported the sidelocks and was on his way to becoming an Orthodox German Jew. Just as the spelling of the family name had been changed from the Polish "Tydor" to the German "Tider", even his pronunciation of the Hebrew prayers had become Germanized. No longer did he begin his blessings with the Galician *burich atu* ("blessed art Thou") but rather with the German *bauruch ato*. This ability to rapidly adapt linguistically followed him throughout his life. As a child I remember him using the general *Ashkenazi* pronunciation common among Orthodox American Jews but in Israel he immediately adapted to the ubiquitous *Sefaradi* (Oriental) pronunciation. When I once asked him what Hebrew pronunciation was in his mind during the silent prayers such as the *Amida ("Shmoneh Esreh")* he immediately replied "the one from my childhood, of course". Having myself moved to a different continent as a teenager, I fully understood what he meant.

Yet there were Hassidic customs and trappings which the family continued to observe in Germany, and which my father maintained throughout his life. When praying privately he continued to use the Hassidic liturgy and his personal prayerbook was always of that version. On Friday nights, he sang *Sholom Aleichem* to a Hassidic melody that one of their ancestors was reported to have composed for R. Elimelech of Lizhensk. *Eishes Chayil* ("A Woman of Valor"), the chapter of Proverbs 31 which Jewish husbands sing to their wives before *Kiddush*, was sung to the tune attributed to R. Naftali of Ropshitz (1760–1827), a crucial figure in the development of the Galician Hassidic movement, known for his profound wisdom, sharp sense of humor, and musical gifts. On Passover the family kept the Hassidic tradition of not eating *gebrokts,* eschewing anything that combined flour and water including dunking

Matzo in soup in case even the tiniest piece of leaven would ensue from it. But in spite of all these Hassidic customs, after moving to Germany my father definitely no longer considered himself a *hassid*, unlike my grandfather Yehuda Leib who remained torn between the two worlds, German and Galician.

Now that he attended a religious Jewish school away from home, Chaskel also had little opportunity to speak Yiddish. His spoken German grew better almost daily as did his written command of the language. His favorite subjects were mathematics and languages, particularly Latin which he took as an elective, and Greek which he studied on his own. But his true love was French, which he wanted to learn in order to understand the foreign words found in *Rashi's* Bible commentary. To assist his fellow students in French, he even composed a long rhyming poem in German delineating the major points of French grammar. Years later he heard that the Realschule French teachers would use this poem to teach their first-year students the rudiments of the language.

Although the school itself was destroyed, the school archives, including copies of students' report cards, survived the war as they had been sent to Palestine in 1939. Among them are my father's school reports from 1915 to 1921 which show his progress in all subjects. By the time he graduated in early 1921 he was a straight A honor student in every subject but gym. He excelled in running and carrying weights, something that would later save his life in Buchenwald and Auschwitz, but being both short and slightly built he had trouble with the climbing exercises and fell behind the boys with longer legs. Beloved by both the headmaster and teachers, they decided to release him from matriculation in gym during his senior year, so as not to ruin his perfect report card. His matriculation certification from April 1921 therefore reads *"sehr gut"* ("very good") in every subject, while next to the line for "gym" it states *"befreit"* ("exempt").

Apart from the academic side of his schooling, the most vivid memories of his school years were his relationships with his teachers, and particularly Rabbi Ellinger, and the friendships that he made with his fellow students. Already during his first year in Fürth, he befriended a number of pupils from out of town who attended school with him, one of whom, Robert (Ya'akov) Felsenstein, became his closest friend of that time. Fifty years later, Felsenstein sent my father a picture of their school class, the only picture we have of him in his youth which was probably taken towards the end of the First World War. In it, you can see a thin, pensive teenager with piercing dark eyes, a special look that would accompany him for the next seventy-five years.

The student population of the Israelitische Realschule was not homogeneous and included German-born students, a few Eastern-European refugees, and even a number of charity cases from the local Jewish orphanage whose director, Dr. Deitsch, taught at the school. The difference between the orphans and the other students was obvious both in their mode of dress and in the food they ate. Every morning the young pupils would bring a snack to class to eat during the morning recess. Chaskel and his fellow boarders at the Ellinger household would usually receive a flask of coffee or chocolate along with two thin slices of bread with marmalade from Mrs. Ellinger before leaving for school. These were the war years, food was scarce, but on principle the Ellingers refused to buy on the black market. Yet compared to what the children from the orphanage brought for recess and were being fed in general, two slices of bread with marmalade was an unheard of bounty.

Once when my father took out his bread, he saw the hungry eyes of a fellow student from the orphanage following him. He recalled: "I tried to give him a slice, at first he was too bashful to take it, the second time he took one of the slices, and it became a habit between us that every day each one of us took one slice of bread." In addition, as Chaskel was not used to eating vegetables from home, he would leave over his lunchtime vegetables at the Ellinger household and a short time later his friend from the orphanage would come over and surreptitiously transfer them to his bag. Eventually the director of the orphanage learned of the arrangement and Mrs. Ellinger wrote about it to Esther, concerned that Chaskel wasn't eating enough food for a growing boy and was growing pale and weak.

Esther immediately traveled to Fürth to see her son's condition with her own eyes. The young boy was indeed pale and thin, much more than when he had lived in Munich. Hearing from Mrs. Ellinger about the food shortage and the fact that her husband refused to supplement what existed with black market purchases, Esther agreed to send her son additional food to the boarding house. Soon after, a large package arrived for Chaskel with home baked cakes and cookies, chocolates and whatever other tasty treats that his mother could clandestinely purchase. It seems though that even then a socialist streak ran deep in his blood – something that later in Buchenwald would save his life more than once – and he immediately gave the package to Mrs. Ellinger stating that he would not touch its contents unless she divided it among the others at the *pension*. Esther was not happy with the result; after all she was spending her precious hard-earned wages on her son and not the entire boarding house. But Chaskel was adamant and after not touching the food on his plate for two days, Mrs. Ellinger gave in to his demands. From then on, any food that Esther sent was shared among all the children in the boardinghouse.

Although Chaskel desperately missed his parents, the Ellinger boarding house soon became his second home. Shortly after arriving he asked Rabbi Ellinger if he could stay up a bit later than the other boys in order to learn with him in the study. Seeing the young boy's hunger for Torah, the Rabbi agreed. Chaskel had never seen a study like that of the Ellinger house except in a yeshiva. The large room had no furniture other than a small table, two chairs and a stove for warmth against which he and Rabbi Ellinger sat; every wall had a floor to ceiling bookcase overflowing with *seforim*. Asking his teacher to see some of the *seforim* up close, Ellinger took out a copy of the "Schach", the *Siftei Cohen* written by the seventeenth-century Talmudist and halachist, Rabbi Shabbati ben Meir Hacohen (1621–1662). Opening it he showed the young boy where the margins of pages were covered with handwritten remarks and told him that the Schach had been his great-great-great-great-great grandfather and thus he had this original copy.

My father's love of Jewish learning had been born in his childhood but his years in the Ellinger household cemented it as a central part of his being. Every day after school he would spend hours in the Ellinger library, pouring through antique *seforim* which were still bound with wooden plates and strings. In the evening after the other boys were asleep Rabbi Ellinger would devote an extra hour or two to learning with him and even filling him in about current events. Ellinger was not the only teacher to take a special liking to my father; he was also quite close to his mathematics teacher, Dr. Krause, who was known for his dislike of Polish Jews but appreciated my father's excellent command of the German language. When one of the other pupils, possibly jealous, pointed out Chaskel's origins to this teacher, Krause answered with a paraphrase of the famous statement regarding "who is a Jew" made by the anti-Semitic former Mayor of Vienna, Karl Lueger (1844–1910): "*Wer Ostjude ist, bestimme ich*" ("Who is an *ostjude?* That I decide!).

My father's memoirs make little note of most events of those years; the war is mentioned only in passing regarding the difficulty in obtaining food; the Russian Revolution and end of the First World War are not mentioned at all. Only one major political event stood out in his memory during my father's school years as it had a direct impact on his family: the socialist revolution in Munich headed by Independent Social-Democrat Kurt Eisner, in which he overthrew the Bavarian monarchy in November 1918. Following the German defeat at the end of the war,

Eisner was one of a number of German communists and socialists, many of whom were Jews, who attempted to overthrow the various local governments throughout Germany, encouraged by the Russian Revolution of 1917. Unlike the unsuccessful Spartakist uprising in Berlin headed by Jewish communist Rosa Luxemburg and her partner Karl Liebknecht, Eisner remained in power for over two months. However his defeat in the February 1919 elections and subsequent assassination made the members of his Bavarian Socialist Republic flee Munich and had disastrous consequences for the Jewish refugees of that city.

My father learned about the revolution by chance. "It was December 1918 and I was on my way home from Fürth to Munich", he told me "When I disembarked from the train, I saw large red notices throughout the city declaring the establishment of the new Bavarian Soviet." Six weeks later, when he returned home once again, he was told that Eisner had been assassinated and that the new government had declared that all Jewish refugees who had come to the city after the war's outbreak in 1914 had three days to leave. In the eyes of the new Bavarian government the equation between *ostjude* and communist was clear and thus, all Jewish refugees were suspect. Unlike the Tennenbaums who had lived in Munich for decades and could therefore remain there, the Tidors had to leave immediately. Luckily, a relative of Esther's, Chaim Klausner, his wife Gusta and their four children, lived in Frankfurt and they helped the family find a suitable apartment in the city. The next time my father came home for vacation, it was no longer to Munich but to Frankfurt and the role that the Tennenbaums had played in the Tydor family mosaic was taken over by the Klausners. In time, my father became quite friendly with his distant cousins, Chaim's children Hermann, Nelly, Mali and Freida. Only Hermann and Nelly managed to escape with their families to England right before the Holocaust. All the others perished.

Looking at the bottom line in my father's report cards, one notices the jump in the number of sick days during 1919. From the usual one to three days a semester, they grew to eleven in the spring of that year, with an additional twenty-one – almost an entire month – in the fall. The year had been one of upheavals with the move from Munich to Frankfurt acting as a trigger to his not particularly robust health. Having devoted most of his waking hours to intensive studies for several years, he had overworked his mind and body into a state of constant tension. A local doctor examined him, and suggested a period of recuperation in the mountains where the rarified air would help his body and spirit. Worried about her only son, Esther came to Fürth and took young Chaskel to Garmisch-Partenkirchen, a German Alpine resort. The beauty of the mountain region and lake entranced the teenager. "I was in love with this place", he told me, a very uncharacteristic remark for him. The kosher restaurant in the town where they were staying was under the rabbinical supervision of Rabbi Ehrentreu from Munich as were several of the resorts in the area. Ehrentreu and his daughter would make unannounced visits to these places, going directly into the kitchen to spot-check that the requirements for kosher food were truly being observed. Leaving the restaurant's kitchen and entering its dining room, Ehrentreu saw Chaskel and Esther eating lunch and came to greet them. "*Rebbe*, it gives me a good feeling to see you are eating here", my father remarked. The Rabbi answered him with a heartfelt sigh and made a remark which alluded to the spiritual nature of Kashrut certification: "You are eating on my *neshome* (soul), but on whose *neshome* am I eating"?

The Rabbi's words and sigh made a great impression on my father. Years later, long after he received *semicha* (rabbinical ordination) he would tell me how careful one had to be when making decisions of Jewish law. "If you err when you give someone advice, the sin is actually then yours, not his."

Chaskel never forgot the four lessons of his stay in Garmish-Partenkirchen. The first was one of accountability which he learned from Rabbi Ehrentreu, not only about the responsibility of Rabbis towards their congregants but of all leaders to their followers. He would feel that lesson personally after the war as one of the founders and the leader of Kibbutz Buchenwald, composed of liberated Holocaust survivors on their way to Palestine.

The second was one of balance and equilibrium, the lesson that one cannot study or work non-stop without any type of other outlet. Even during his years of backbreaking labor in Nazi camps, he would always try to maintain his inner spiritual life as an internal outlet, even if no external one was then possible. Later on, although there were years where my father would work very long hours, he always broke it up with Torah learning and travel to clear his mind.

The third was a love of the great outdoors and an understanding that the greatness of the Almighty can often best be felt through the wonders of nature. Walking the paths of Garmish-Partenkirchen he learned to reflect on the magnificent creations of the Lord and the deeper meaning of the first verse in the Torah, "In the beginning the Lord created the Heavens and the Earth".

The fourth, most important lesson was of belief and faith; that when one door in your life closes, you must believe and hope that another is being opened. Even when his family was forced to leave Munich almost overnight, a new door opened in Frankfurt which would ultimately lead him to community, marriage and his own family.

These lessons, learned during the four weeks of his stay in the German Alps, were to guide him during the years to come and form his personality into that of the very unique man who he became.

3

Frankfurt–Lodz–Bochnia–Frankfurt, 1920–1939

"As one door closes, another opens", was one of my father's favorite sayings and it epitomized his perception of the many transitions that he underwent throughout his life. A chapter of my father's life came to an end in the spring of 1921 when he completed his high school studies in Fürth and returned to Frankfurt. Not only was this the first time in five years that he would be living with his parents for an extended period; he was also returning to a relatively unfamiliar city in which he had few friends and relatives. At the same time it was a transition between his childhood and adulthood. Now that he was eighteen he faced the question of his future. What profession should he train for? How should he continue his Jewish education? Where should he live in the future?

Soon after the war's end Mendel and Mecha returned to Bochnia, moving back into the house on Biala Street which had stood empty for half a dozen years. Although she was over seventy, the indefatigable Mecha was still working as a picture enlarger and developer. Would Chaskel remain in Frankfurt with his parents and sister or would he return to Poland like so many Jewish refugees, in order to live with his grandparents? Would he train for a profession or go into business like his parents and grandparents before him?

The summer and autumn of 1921 was indeed a period of transition when my father would make a number of decisions that would affect the rest of his life. The first was to remain in Germany, and particularly in Frankfurt. Chaskel was greatly attached to his parents and their physical absence from his life during his school years in Fürth had weighed heavily upon his heart. True, the apartment in Frankfurt was small; Chaskel slept on a pullout bed in the living-dining room and little Ida still shared their parents' bedroom, but it was "home". As for his grandparents in Bochnia, even before the war they had one child living in Germany. Now it was two. Only Yehidis'l remained in Poland and her children spent much time with Mendel and Mecha during their final years. One of her sons eventually inherited the house on Biala Street after their death in the late 1920s as Yehuda Leib did not want to take over its upkeep from Germany.

The second decision that Chaskel made was to continue his religious studies at the Breuer yeshiva in Frankfurt which belonged to the Frankfurt *austrittsgemeinde*, the separatist Orthodox Jewish community. The Frankfurt Jewish community was large and illustrious, punctuated by separations and schisms. By the middle of the 19th century it had become a center of the Reform movement with less than 10 percent of the city's Jews considering themselves Orthodox. This situation changed when Rabbi Samson Rafael Hirsch (1808–1888) moved from Hungary to Frankfurt and revived the city's Orthodox Jewish community which grew in numbers and wealth. Ultimately Frankfurt boasted two Orthodox communities, the general Orthodox Jewish community and the separatist community headed by Rabbi Hirsch and later his son-in-law, Rabbi Shlomo (Solomon) Breuer (1850–1926).

One of the first things Rabbi Breuer did upon succeeding his father-in-law was to found a yeshiva in the city in 1893, the same yeshiva which my father decided to attend. Rabbi Breuer continued the tradition of *Torah* and *Derekh Eretz* which epitomized Rabbi Hirsch's teachings, combining a full acceptance of modernity with an uncompromising belief in Torah precepts. Having enjoyed the fruits of both religious and secular study during his years in Fürth, Chaskel was naturally drawn to a community which espoused a philosophy that did not see the two as being mutually exclusive. Chaskel's growing closeness with Rabbi Breuer would soon determine much of the direction that his life would take until the outbreak of the Second World War. Although he would eventually pay dues to both the regular and separatist communities he was without doubt a staunch member of the Breuer *kehilla* (community) during both the Weimar Republic and the Hitler years.

I often wondered what attracted my family to the separatist community instead of the regular Orthodox Jewish community of Frankfurt. Was it because of a negative attitude towards *ostjuden* in the general Orthodox community? When I asked my father he explained that the choice of community was solely because of the strict religious nature of the *austrittsgemeinde*. As the general Orthodox community had many members who were not Orthodox in practice, it had adopted more lenient religious attitudes which were unsuitable for the Tiders. Yehuda Leib Tider was looking for a fully Orthodox community in which he

43

would not stand out in his beard and sidelocks although he had adopted western European dress. His son was happy to find a community which encouraged yeshiva study along with preparing oneself for a white-collar profession. The Breuer community and its philosophies were therefore a mainstay in my father's life throughout the years that he would reside in Frankfurt and for long after.

The third decision my father made was to simultaneously enroll in university and begin pre-medical training while continuing his yeshiva studies. Although his *Rebbe*, as he always referred to Rabbi Solomon Breuer, considered this to be *bitul zeman* ("a waste of time"), Chaskel was adamant about becoming a doctor and his dream was to study home-opathy and combine the two. To appease his *Rebbe* he enrolled in yeshiva while attending university as a "guest listener" for his first year, not registering as a full-time student. As a first step in entering the German university system he also chose a German name – Heinrich – which he used in his public dealings. His future was now mapped out. While preparing for *semicha* (Rabbinical ordination), Chaskel-Heinrich would begin training as a doctor and like many in the Breuer community, would combine his future knowledge of medicine and religion to ultimately serve the Jewish community.

My father would indeed serve the Frankfurt Jewish community in various capacities however it would be as neither doctor nor rabbi, two professions requiring years of study and extensive financial support. After a short burst of optimism at the end of the Great War, the economic situation in Germany deteriorated rapidly, as did my father's family's financial situation. Having given up her wartime photography work, Esther and Yehuda Leib had entered into the textile business, selling sheets, towels and other household goods to Jewish families on the installment plan. No longer did they run their financial enterprises out of a large warehouse and store as they had in Bochnia; instead they became traveling sales-people, journeying by bus and train to Jewish areas in the environs of Frankfurt, carrying packages of textiles on their shoulders while trudging the streets in search of new business. They had indeed come a long way from the days of the lottery money which had eased the family's economic existence for over half a century.

The Tider's of Frankfurt were among millions of Jews and Gentiles alike, who were beginning to feel the economic upheavals that plagued Germany during the early 1920s. The looming scepter of war reparations that Germany had agreed to pay hung heavily over the country that had been forced by the terms of the Versailles treaty to accept sole responsibility for the devastation and consequences of the Great War. The result was a galloping inflation, the likes of which had never been seen in Germany. From a relatively stable 60 marks to the dollar during the first half of 1921, the exchange rate dropped to 330 marks to the dollar by November of that year. By July 1922, when the first reparation payments were supposed to be made, the German economy was put into a state of artificially induced hyperinflation, created primarily to show the world that the Weimar Republic was incapable of continuing to pay out such sums. In January 1923 the exchange rate reached 9,000 marks to the dollar; by November of that year one dollar was worth an unbelievable three trillion marks. The paper that the banknote was printed on was worth more than the banknote itself and people with torn shoes would use wads of million mark notes to pad the soles; after all, it was cheaper than buying a new innersole. A person sitting down for a cup of coffee at 10 a.m. at the cost of 5,000 marks a cup would pay the bill an hour later and find it at 8,000 marks – that was the hourly inflation rate in the middle of 1923. To many, it was a world gone mad.

Like most Germans, my father's family was affected by the economic crisis in several ways. Although they often used a barter system, it was still necessary to utilize currency at a basic level, such as when purchasing food at the local grocery. For years Ida's would go down to the bakery every morning and buy bread for the family. By mid-1923 she needed her big brother to help her carry the two suitcases full of banknotes necessary to pay for one loaf of bread. My father remembers lugging knapsacks full of money down the stairs in order to do their daily bread-shopping; when he was in the store he would see workers, now being paid twice a day, rushing to purchase food with their wages. They, like all Germans, knew that the price of foodstuffs would have more than doubled by the time they would receive their evening pay.

Far more worrisome than the technical aspects of inflation was its impact on Chaskel's education. In an attempt to stabilize its budget the German government decreed that all non-citizens would have to pay for their university education in gold value. This was impossible for many, including the Tiders, who had no resources to find the necessary gold currency and had no way of obtaining German citizenship. Consequently, Chaskel had to leave university, putting an end to his dream of medical studies. More troublesome to him was the fact that he would have to leave full-time yeshiva studies in order to find work and supplement the family income. Although he was good at French, Talmud and mathematics, none were professions and so he turned to the director of the Breuer Yeshiva to ask his advice.

The meeting rapidly brought my father down to earth. "It was as if he held a mirror to my face with the word 'Galicia' written on top". Looking at him with a sad smile, the German-born director stated that although Chaskel's command of German was quite good, it had to be excellent to succeed in business. Knowing that both his accent and grammar were perfect, he was surprised to encounter this prejudice against *ostjuden*. The same prejudice did not exist among the Breuer family who considered him a prize student and a worthy candidate to assist. Knowing that he had studied bookkeeping, Rabbi Dr. Yitzhak Breuer introduced him to the Feuchtwangers, distant relatives who owned scrap metal factories and were looking for an assistant bookkeeper. The nineteen year old Chaskel was interviewed by Feuchtwanger nephews, Max and Yaakov Bollag from Basle, Switzerland, and was immediately hired as an assistant bookkeeper in the Frankfurt metal factory. For the first time in his life Chaskel brought home a steady paycheck helping make ends meet in the Tider household.

Although he was relieved that he could help his parents, even more than he missed his medical studies, he was distraught over leaving the yeshiva. "When I left the Breuer Yeshiva I did it with tears", he stated. Although he could learn on his own at night or with his father, he sorely missed the yeshiva atmosphere. The solution came from an unexpected source – Rabbi Shlomo Breuer himself. On one of his last visits to the yeshiva my father was called over by Rabbi Breuer who said that he had a problem which Chaskel could possibly help him with. His eyes had gotten weak and it was difficult for him to read the fine print in some of his *seforim,* particularly a number of the Talmudic commentaries. Would it be possible for Chaskel to come over one evening and read some of the commentaries aloud to him?

What began as a one time attempt soon became a nightly occupation. These were the years after Rabbi Breuer had lost his wife, and his lonely evenings were soon filled with hours spent with his young *vorlearner* ("reader") pouring over volumes of the Talmud and commentaries. Night after night Chaskel would go home after work, eat a quick bite with his parents and sister and hurry to the Breuer household where he would read texts aloud to the elderly Rabbi. What began as "reading" soon turned into much more. Chaskel became a member of the Breuer household and even began tutoring Rabbi Dr. Yitzchak Breuer's young sons in Hebrew; in addition to his *vorlearner* and tutoring positions, his knowledge of Hebrew also earned him the position of Rabbi Shlomo Breuer's Hebrew secretary.

My father recalled several incidents which stood out during his years in the Breuer household. The first was his introduction to the more difficult Talmudic tractates and particularly the Tractate *Eruvin*. Starting each evening by reading out the text to Rabbi Breuer, the two progressed to in-depth learning in which my father was taught the intricacies of Talmudic reasoning. From this he learned that understanding the reasoning behind Talmudic debates was often equally important as understanding the texts themselves.

The second was his introduction to broader Jewish knowledge, beginning with the Septuagint, the non-canonized books of the Bible. Although my father wished to concentrate on his *semicha* studies towards ordination, heavily weighted towards Talmud and Jewish law, Rabbi Breuer gently suggested that he broaden his general knowledge of Biblical literature, Jewish philosophy and other subjects. In his opinion, a well rounded Jewish education consisted of more than knowledge of Talmud and Jewish law, something he tried to impart to his young *vorlearner*. It was during this period that my father became interested in Ecclesiasticus, the Book of Ben Sira, a second-century collection of ethical teachings which was often quoted in the Talmud and in Rabbinic literature. From his foray into the non-canonized texts my father progressed to Jewish philosophy and particularly to the study of Rambam (Maimonides). During those years he developed a deep appreciation of the Rambam's rationalist teaching and his writings would eventually be his among his favorite topics of study.

Already during his late high school years Chaskel had been fascinated by philosophy, an interest that grew when he was introduced in university to the great philosophers including Spinoza. Fearing that his father would consider it heresy to bring such books home, he made sure to read Spinoza's "Ethics" only late at night when everyone else was certain to be asleep. Once, however, he fell asleep while reading and when his father came in to switch off the light, he found his son deep in slumber with Spinoza's writings open on his chest. Noting his son's choice of reading material, Yehuda Leib closed the book and put it on the night-stand. When Chaskel awoke in the morning he realized what had happened and waited for the explosion – but it never came. Only later that day did Yehuda Leib comment about what he had seen: "I could not help but notice what you were reading last night", he mentioned gently to his worried son. "You obviously have a need to read these things so I will not stop you from doing it. But one day you will realize that it all comes from Torah and that anything worthwhile has already appeared in our Jewish sources."

"Only when I got older and had greater knowledge of Jewish teachings did I realize that my father had been right all along", stated my father to me once about this incident, "but his understanding my young mind and not stopping me from learning philosophy stayed with me for years." That openness along with the education to Torah and Jewish ethics that he received both at home and in the Breuer household reinforced his belief that there was no contradiction between secular and Jewish studies, and that to fully understand Jewish teachings it was imperative to have a working knowledge of other fields.

The third incident had to do with the parameters of Orthodox Jewish belief. At some point before his death in 1926 Rabbi Breuer asked my father to deliver a personal note to another rabbinic figure of stature living in Frankfurt, Rabbi Jacob Rosenheim, insisting that it be handed to him and no other. Rosenheim, known as "*Morenu*" (an honored title used from the 14th century for Rabbis and Talmudists), was ill at the time, and the Rabbi's wife ushered my father into the bedroom where the great Rabbi rested on a couch. As he waited for the Rosenheim to pen an answer, Chaskel glanced around the bedroom, noting a small framed inscription over the bed. Rosenheim motioned that he could go closer and my father realized that he was looking at an amulet written by the eighteenth-century kabbalist, Rabbi Yonathan Eybeschutz of Prague. A controversial figure in his day, Eybeschutz had been accused of Sabbateanism by his contemporaries and most notably by Rabbi Ya'akov Emden. Although exonerated by some, others still considered him a heretic whose son had been excommunicated for Sabbateanism.

Chaskel was taken aback; he couldn't conceive that a rationalist of Rosenheim's stature would have such an amulet in his home, no less above his bed. Unable to contain his surprise my father turned to Rabbi Rosenheim. "*Moreinu*, I do not understand!" he exclaimed. Rosenheim looked steadily at the young man and then gave a small smile. "One never knows", he answered. "Even if it doesn't help, it surely won't do any harm . . . in spite of what they say." It was a lesson that my father never forgot regarding the degree to which people, including the most rational and Orthodox Rabbis of German Jewry, would go in order to fulfill their inner spiritual needs.

The months after my father began working as an assistant bookkeeper for S. Feuchtwanger & Co. Metals were an unremarkable period in his working life except for one incident. In 1924, during one of their visits to Frankfurt, the Bollag brothers found a major discrepancy in the book-keeping which would cost them a small fortune. All eyes were on the new assistant bookkeeper who was accused of having made the costly error. In response, my father spent days examining the records, going back to the years before he joined the firm until he finally uncovered the culprit, the former chief bookkeeper who had doctored the books for his own financial benefit. Not only did Chaskel find the error and exonerate himself; he also suggested to the Bollag brothers ways of rectifying the financial loss which they put into action. After less than two years in the firm Chaskel was promoted to the rank of chief bookkeeper and later general manager where he continued to sharpen his business acumen and suggest innovations to the owners on each of their trips to Germany. Impressed by the ambitious young man, in April 1929 the Bollag brothers agreed to let him buy out the company of which he now became owner. Chaskel's financial future appeared to be set.

Nineteen twenty-six was both a memorable and transitional year for my father. On the spiritual level he lost his *Rebbe*, Rabbi Solomon Breuer, who passed away after a difficult illness. Although he became close to his sons and particularly Rabbi Joseph Breuer who became Rosh yeshiva in his father's stead, the void in his spiritual life that was left after Rabbi Solomon Breuer's death remained unfilled.

Another transition had to do with his father's health. The early 1920s had been a financially difficult time for the Tider family and the stress had taken its toll on Yehuda Leib who began showing signs of illness. Becoming thinner and weaker by the week, he unsuccessfully attempted to hide his infirmities from his son, but Chaskel soon realized the extent of his father's incapacity. One of the Breuer sons, the pediatrician Dr. Joshua Breuer, directed him to a number of doctors who examined his father and diagnosed him with stress induced diabetes. Chaskel realized that he was now the family breadwinner until his father recovered. This was his true "coming of age", so he told me, when he ran with his father from doctor to doctor and realized that the cushion of his childhood and youth had now ended. Indeed, as one door closed so another door had opened, and his promotion to chief bookkeeper of the factory ensured a steady and rising income for the Tider family.

Looking back at my father's stories from the 1920s, two people seem to be missing: his paternal grandparents. Unlike his maternal grandparents who he rarely saw during his early years, Mendel and Mecha had been pillars of his childhood. Why then do they disappear from his narrative sometime after the end of the First World War? I am not even sure of the exact dates of their death as my father never referred to the subject and I never thought to ask. Did my grandfather travel to Bochnia for their funerals? I assume that had my father gone along to such an event he would have mentioned it to me. Did my grandfather's ill health at the time prevent his being there? It might even be that the stress of one of their deaths was an additional cause of my grandfather's illness. I will never know. On the other hand, as neither my grandparents in Frankfurt nor my great grandparents in Bochnia had a telephone, news of a death would have had to arrive either by telegraph or by letter. It could be that Yehuda Leib only learned of his parents' deaths weeks after the fact when a letter reached Frankfurt with the sad tidings. That, after all, was the way of the world in those days.

But it gets even more mysterious. Before visiting Bochnia during the summer of 2007 I obtained a list of all graves in the Bochnia Jewish cemetery, most of which were reconstructed after the war. Using every possible spelling of their names I could not find a gravestone for either Menachem-Mendel or Mecha in that cemetery. And while I found listings of their birth, marriage and moving from Wisnicka to Bochnia in the Bochnia archives, along with the births of their children and grandchildren, I could not find any listing of their deaths. Does that mean that they were buried elsewhere? Did they possibly spend their last months with their daughter in Limanova? Were they buried with their parents in the old cemetery in Wisnicka? There is no longer anyone from that generation in the family who I could ask.

The third transition my father underwent during the late 1920s was in his personal life. Having reached his twenty-fourth year and in view of the fact that he now held a steady financial position, it was time for Chaskel to consider marrying. Like many Orthodox matches of the time this would be an arranged marriage to a girl who Chaskel's parents found suitable. Yehuda Leib had maintained contacts in Bochnia and turned to a Bochnia matchmaker to find his son a bride from their home town. Bearing in mind that Chaskel was an educated young man, the bride had to be educated. In view of the secularization of Polish Jewry following the war, she had to come from a fully observant family and be observant herself. And although the Tiders were no longer wealthy, Chaskel was at the beginning of what appeared to be a promising career and the bride's family should be able to offer a suitable dowry that could assist the young couple during their first years.

The choice fell on an attractive young woman, almost a year younger than Chaskel, whose family had lived in Bochnia for many years, Bertha (Beile) Greiver. Bertha was the only daughter of Ruchel Leah and Zvi Hirsch Greiver, a men's clothing manufacturer, whose house was situated at the south-east corner of the Bochnia *rynek* only a few minutes walk from the house on Biala Street. The two families had been acquainted before the war and Chaskel and Bertha had even played together as very small children. During the war the Greiver family had taken refuge in Holland and even after their return to Bochnia, Bertha and her younger

50

brothers, Salo and Yosef, would often speak Dutch to each other. The Greiver family was well to do, strictly Orthodox, and Bertha was a food chemist by profession. Hirsch Greiver offered a large dowry to the potential suitor including a possibility of going into business with him in Bochnia. It appeared to be a very suitable potential match.

After inquiries had been made on both sides, Chaskel traveled to Bochnia and the two young people hit it off immediately. Chaskel was taken with the slim attractive dark haired and energetic Bertha; Bertha was entranced by the intelligent young man with the small dark German moustache. Both families were satisfied. Hirsch was adamant that the couple have an official engagement and in spite of the fact that no wedding date had been set, the two families arranged a party where they wrote *tenoyim*, an officially binding engagement contract listing the large sums of money and promise of future employment in his factory that Hirsch was offering the bridegroom. In their engagement picture Chaskel is wearing a black suit and a striped tie; Bertha is wearing a black dress with the gold necklace that Chaskel had given her as an engagement gift. In spite of the fact that this was an arranged marriage, the young couple looked very happy with each other, Bertha more exuberant and her future bridegroom slightly more serious looking. Little did they know that it would be almost three more years until they would marry, years that would be filled with economic worries, long-distance travel, broken promises and the constant threat of having the engagement broken by one set of parents.

Although the economic worries of the first half of the 1920s were behind them, Chaskel considered it imperative to strengthen his position in the Feuchtwanger factory before actually getting married. Bertha agreed with this reasoning, particularly in view of the political and economic situation in Germany and Poland during the late 1920s. Hirsch Greiver constantly offered his future son-in-law a position in his Bochnia firm and at one point Chaskel even considered it seriously. But Bertha, who used to meet him at the train station in Krakow so that they could travel together to Bochnia, wept bitter tears when he mentioned this and implored him not to agree to her father's offer, reminding him that he had already invested so much in his professional future in Feuchtwanger and Co.

I always wondered how much her tears were the result of her own fears that Chaskel would ultimately give in to her father's offer in view of her burning desire to leave Bochnia and move to Frankfurt. Although this was a favorable period for Polish Jewry under the leadership of Marshall Jozef Pilsudski, life in Weimar Germany during these years of political stability and economic prosperity was still considered a more attractive prospect. Another possibility for those tears was Bertha's familiarity with her father's business practices and the fear that her fiancé would become caught up in his questionable promises. She was unfortunately correct in her appraisal, as shortly after the *tenoyim* were signed, Hirsch Greiver reneged on a number of his financial promises regarding Bertha's dowry. The Tiders of Frankfurt were aghast and even looked into the possibility of dissolving the engagement. However the *tenoyim* that had been signed were legally binding, and Hirsch Greiver's conditions that had been included in their wording made them almost impossible to break. It would be easier for the couple to marry and divorce rather than to dissolve the engagement, so stated the Rabbis with whom Yehuda Leib had conferred.

Chaskel reassured his father that his love for Bertha had grown to the point where a dowry was not an issue; he would marry her without one altogether if necessary, but the marriage would then have to be postponed until he could augment his savings. With a sigh, Yehuda Leib and Esther gave their approval to this turn of events. They, too, were impressed by their future daughter-in-law; slightly less with her father in spite of the fact that Hirsch Greiver once again was offering financial incentives for the young couple to marry according to schedule.

The Greiver–Tider wedding took place in Bochnia more than two years after the engagement had been concluded, on a Friday afternoon on the 9th of *Shevat*, the 7th of February 1930. Europe was just beginning to feel the pressure of the economic events that had taken place on Wall Street three months earlier and neither Chaskel nor Bertha could guess the extent to which the economic crisis would affect their lives. On that day, though, all thoughts of money were set aside in order to celebrate the happy event. It was a Hassidic custom to marry on Friday afternoon, inviting the entire Jewish community to a festive celebration later in the evening. Being of Hassidic stock the men in the two families dressed in full Hassidic regalia. Chaskel, however, adamantly refused to wear a *streimel* (Hassidic fur hat) in view of his loyalty to the Breuer German tradition; instead he was married in a top hat which he wore with as much pomp and dignity as his five foot two inches would allow. It is unfortunate that no wedding pictures survived the Holocaust; from my father's descriptions they would have shown a seemingly incongruous mix of guests, some in Polish Hassidic dress and others in German Neo-Orthodox attire surrounding a modest and beaming bride next to a much more serious looking groom, attempting to keep his unfamiliar top hat from falling off his head.

For Chaskel, one of the more moving moments surrounding his wedding had actually taken place the previous day when he received a hand-delivered envelope from Rabbi Joseph Breuer containing his *semicha* and an official statement that after his marriage he was entitled to use the title *"Morenu"*. Chaskel was to have received his rabbinical ordination from Rabbi Solomon Breuer in late 1925, but the Rabbi's illness that year and subsequent death postponed the ceremony indefinitely. Although he continued to learn with his son, Rabbi Joseph Breuer, Chaskel never mentioned the technical matter out of modesty. Breuer, however, knew of the young man's engagement and wished to present him with the ordination before his wedding; the wedding's many postponements enabled him to further get to know Chaskel and discover his unique abilities including a photographic memory and his breadth of Jewish scholarship. He, together with a number of other scholars who were acquainted with Chaskel, concluded that the young man was entitled not only to his long awaited ordination documents but to a public acknowledgement of his Talmudic scholarship. Although extremely moved by the gesture, Chaskel never used the title *"Morenu"*, and rarely publicized his rabbinic ordination. Only years later, during and after the Holocaust, did it come up when he was asked to determine points of Jewish law under situations that no one could have imagined in February 1930.

Chaskel and Bertha initially moved into a spacious apartment in Simonstrasse in Frankfurt and then to an even larger apartment in Habsburger Allee, not far away from his parents. The entrance hall led into a long corridor, off of which were two bedrooms joined by French doors, a living room, a large kitchen and a study. One bedroom was already set aside as a nursery; Bertha was expecting a child in early December, almost ten months to the day of their wedding. The study was something Chaskel had dreamed of for years since learning with Rabbi Ellinger in Fürth. Similar to the room in which he had spent many hours during his boyhood, this one was covered with floor to ceiling bookcases, some holding *seforim* and others containing secular books. Many of his relatives remembered sitting in this library as children, enjoying being able to read for hours. One of them was Chaskel's second cousin Bernie, Ida's young son who, after his parents' divorce, was sent to England to boarding school. On school vacations he and his mother would often come to Frankfurt to visit Chaskel and Bertha and would spend hours curled in the library, reading and enjoying the quiet. It was Bernie who gave Chaskel his only nickname – "Chatch" – which he began calling him as a child before he could pronounce his older cousin's full name.

Finally feeling financially secure Chaskel also indulged his love of astronomy and purchased a Zeiss telescope which he kept on a terrace off the study. This was the telescope with which he would later teach his children about the stars and other celestial bodies; it was through this instrument that he discovered another facet of the natural word that he had learned to appreciate during his stay at Garmisch-partenkirschen, an additional proof of the wonders of nature that the Lord had given mankind to study and enjoy.

The sense of economic security that the young Tiders felt was fleeting. Within months Germany felt the full weight of the Great Depression. Like most firms Feuchtwanger and Co. suffered great losses to the point where Chaskel, as a new partner, despaired of being able to support his family, a fear that heightened after the birth of his daughter Zipora Camilla, on Thursday, December 11, 1930. The baby, born at home, was named for Bertha's grandmother. Years later Chaskel remembered standing over his sleeping daughter's cradle, thinking about how his world had turned upside down and wondering whether he would be able to provide for her future.

Chaskel's economic fears were also accompanied by political worry. The German elections of September 1930 in which the Nazi party received 18 percent of the total votes had been a first shock to the family; even Yehuda Leib began speaking about the hooligans with the swastikas who were spouting nonsense against the Jews. How lucky that they were not in power and still considered a radical fringe group.

Life continued as usual in the Tider household with periodic trips to Bochnia to visit the Greiver grandparents. Several months after Camilla's birth Bertha found herself expecting again and on March 18, 1932 she gave birth to a boy, this time at a Frankfurt hospital. Menachem Manfred, was named for Chaskel's paternal grandfather. Despite the economic upheavals the family was still on its feet and although he often went to work by bicycle, Chaskel eventually purchased a large black car for the family. It appears in the background of one of the few pre-war pictures that survived in which a young Bertha in a stylish dress and wig is bending over little Camilla sitting on her tricycle in front of the car.

Hitler's rise to power in early 1933 was a watershed event for all of German Jewry, including the Tider family. Although he had been content during his nineteen years in Germany, the fifty-nine year old Yehuda Leib realized that Germany had changed and it was time for the Jews to leave. The question was, to where? He had little contact with his aunts' families in Holland, and no relatives in Europe except in Poland. Hirsch Greiver had even made him an offer to work with one of his clothing manufacturers in Lodz. Yehuda Leib and Esther debated the offer; they knew Greiver's tendency to offer financial opportunities that never came to fruition but felt that in view of the situation in Germany they had little choice in the matter. Thus, scant months after Hitler came to power, the elder Tiders, who once again became Tydors, returned to Poland, this time to Lodz, to escape the Nazi specter. Although she didn't want to leave Germany, Ida, now a young woman of twenty-two, felt obliged to accompany her parents. Her father's health was fragile and her mother needed another pair of hands around the house. Although she had developed a large circle of friends in Frankfurt, the only home she truly remembered, she followed her parents to Lodz, remaining a dutiful daughter.

Nothing, however, turned out as planned. Yehuda Leib had been right to distrust the Greiver offer as it never materialized. Instead of moving into a spacious apartment the family ended up in a small flat in an old building on Sienkiewicz street. As they were no longer self supporting, Chaskel sent his parents a monthly sum to pay for the family's upkeep during the next five years, until he was deported from Germany in October 1938.

Chaskel was not oblivious to the worsening situation of German Jewry, but for the first years of the Hitler regime he immersed himself in family and community. Like most self-employed Jews in Germany, he was relatively untouched by many of the economic restrictions. His wealth provided him with a cushion that allowed him a period of time to weigh his possibilities and as he was neither an active Zionist nor a communist, he did not think of immediately leaving for Palestine or Paris as many did during those years. Instead he became a member of the volunteer Frankfurt *chevra kadisha* (burial society), a staunch supporter of the Breuer community institutions, and although not an active Zionist, even a supporter of Poalei Agudath Israel, originally the trade union branch of the ultra-orthodox Agudath Israel political party in Poland and ultimately a settlement movement in Palestine, later headed there by Rabbi Dr. Yitzchak Breuer after his immigration in the mid 1930s.

One of those active Zionists making their way to Palestine at that time was Chakel's young brother-in-law, Yosef Greiver from Bochnia, who would be instrumental in his future. Greiver had been a religious Zionist from his youth and dreamed of moving to Palestine but his father threatened to cut him off if he made a move in that direction. Yosef was an adventurer, bold and good looking, and refused to bow to his father's dictates. Around the same time that Yehuda Leib and Esther were on their way to Lodz, Yosef set off to Palestine, partly by hitching rides with peasants and partly on foot, practically penniless as his father made good on his promise to disown him. It took him almost two years to travel from Bochnia to Tel Aviv, a journey that included a six-month stop in Salonika, Greece where he collapsed and was taken in to the home of the city's Chief Rabbi whose family nursed him back to health and assisted him in finding passage to the Holy Land. Yosef's Zionism and natural tenaciousness were his salvation; he was the only member of the immediate Greiver family to survive the war.

Chaskel had always been close to his young brother-in-law and kept in contact with him after the latter reached Palestine. Hirsch refused to have anything to do with his son until he heard of his upcoming marriage to Yaffa Meyer, daughter of the religious Polish Zionist Rabbi Alter Meyer who had left Sanok with his family to open a small kosher laborer's restaurant on the shores of Tel Aviv. It was there that Yosef, soon to found the Palestine Travel Agency (Patra), met the vivacious Yaffa and fell in love. Hearing of the impending nuptials Hirsch penned a letter to his son and future daughter in law, offering them a partnership in one of his factories if they would come back to Bochnia. Seventy years later Yaffa spoke about the letter in which Hirsch had offered his congratulations to the young couple and made his offer which the young couple politely declined as they had no intentions of returning to Poland. Hirsch apparently had a tendency to offer this partnership to family members – his son-in-law, his son-in-law's parents, and now his son – and renege as soon as it appeared that the offer was seriously being considered. Yosef and Yaffa eventually moved to Jerusalem where they began to raise a family and develop the travel business. Their home would be Chaskel's first permanent residence after the war when he would move to Palestine.

Yosef was not the only member of Chaskel's intimate circle to move to Palestine. Another was his boyhood friend Moshe (Moni) Wexler. Chaskel had known Moni from his first days in Germany; their background was similar and their birthdays were only ten days apart. Moni's older sister had come from Galicia to marry Rosi's widowed father and Moni followed in her wake. He fell in love with Rosi at first sight and they shared everything . . . except Moni's desire to move to Palestine.

The couple married in Germany. However Hitler's rise to power impressed upon Wexler that it was time to act on his Zionist leanings. In order to obtain a British immigration certificate from the Mandatory Government in Palestine Wexler had to learn a new profession, auto mechanics; Rosi greatly feared the primitive Middle Eastern conditions which she expected to find in her new homeland. In spite of her fears Moni, Rosi and their baby son Menachem left Germany living first in

Haifa where Moni worked as a bricklayer and then in Ramat Gan where he found a job in an automobile garage. Soon after, the Wexler family moved to Jerusalem where Moni became a publisher of religious texts in the Levin–Epstein publishing enterprises while Rosi, who had hebrai-cized her name to Roni, raised their four children and became involved in the cultural life of Jerusalem. They, too, would play a major role in Chaskel's future after the war.

Despite the Nazi regime, the Tider family in Frankfurt was flour-ishing. Camilla began to attend the Breuer kindergarten and was soon joined by her brother Manfred. Although both children left Germany while still young, each of them retained memories of their life in Frankfurt. Manfred recalled that his mother was quite strict in house-keeping and that she willingly embraced the traditional Germanic educational dictates for child rearing. Once, when he was recovering from illness and his mother had to be absent from the house, Chaskel came home early from the factory to spend time with his son. Manfred remembered the two of them lying on the floor at the end of the long entrance foyer, launching a toy airplane with a rubber catapult down its length and watching it crash into the great wooden doors at its end time and again. "Don't worry, we won't tell Mutti!" Chaskel told the little boy as they laughed in glee with each "smash" of the airplane on the immaculate doors.

Camilla's memories were not always as pleasant. Although she recalled good times with her parents she also remembered the increasing restric-tions placed on the Jews of Germany. Once when Bertha took both children to have their hair cut, they found a notice stating "*Juden Verboten*" (Jews forbidden) hanging in the shop and they were forced to leave. Another time she took them for swimming lessons in the local pool and as Camilla wrote in her memoirs, "again the ill-fated words *Juden Verboten* gleamed back at our faces and we could no longer continue our swimming lessons". She remembered coming out of *shul* one Saturday morning to see a group of Nazi storm troopers standing guard outside the building ready to pounce. Chaskel and Bertha whisked the children away before anything could happen.

Camilla also remembered periodic visits to her grandparents in Bochnia and Lodz. Although she was no more than five or six, she was appalled by the poverty which she had never encountered in Germany. For the first time she saw veterans of the Great War without limbs sitting on the sidewalks in Poland; she was also horrified by the old cramped building in which her grandparents lived in Lodz. Coming from a priv-ileged background with a spacious apartment and constant household help it was an eye opener for her to see members of her own family living a very different life.

Luxurious living conditions notwithstanding, by early 1936 Chaskel realized that the Jews in Germany had no future and he began to make arrangements for the Tider family to leave Germany. Unlike his parents he had no desire to return to Poland and thought that it would be safer to travel westward, either to France or England. During 1936 and 1937 he made several trips to Paris with Bertha, each time checking out employment possibilities. At the same time he attempted to begin liquidating his assets in Germany and sent valuables such as jewelry, leather-bound first edition books, and *Leica* cameras to two of his most reliable and trusted friends in Holland and Switzerland for later recovery. In addition, he decided to send a small box of books to Moni Wexler in Palestine; except for three *seforim* which he would find in Frankfurt after the war, these would ultimately be the only books that would return to his possession from the thousands of volumes that had lined the walls of his pre-war library. Of all his other possessions, he would only get back a small package of jewelry that he had managed to send to England; the rest of his valuables and assets either disappeared en route or were confiscated and destroyed before reaching their destination.

While Paris held few employment possibilities for Chaskel, the situation in England was more hopeful. Already in 1937 he had contacted an old friend from Frankfurt, Eli Hackenbruch, who had moved to England, in order to assist him in finding employment and pursuing the technical aspects of obtaining visas for the entire family. Chaskel managed to obtain a first set of papers for the family and began to make definite plans to leave Frankfurt and relocate to England; however this was not to be. While Chaskel realized the urgency of the situation for Jews in Germany and was even ready to leave his parents in Poland as he knew that his father's medical condition would make it impossible to obtain an immigration visa for him to England, Bertha refused to immigrate without her parents. The Greivers, on the other hand, refused to leave Poland, certain that Hitler was a temporary aberration and that the fate of Polish Jewry would have no connection to the actions of the madman running Germany. The months passed, the family's immigration papers passed their expiration date, and thus the Tider family found itself still in Frankfurt at the beginning of October 1938.

Chaskel may have lived in Germany for almost a quarter of a century however he, like Bertha and many Jews from Eastern Europe, were not German citizens. In early September 1938 the Polish government passed a law stating that any citizens abroad who had not returned to Poland during the past five years would lose their citizenship and property. The German government decided to use this opportunity to rid themselves of the Polish Jews who had moved there during the Great War. On October 27, 1938, over 17,000 Jews in Germany with Polish passports were given deportation orders by the Gestapo and forcibly taken to the German-Polish border. Chaskel was in one of the first groups to be arrested. Bertha, being the mother of two small children, was given an additional few hours to make provisions and she and the children were slated for a transport later that evening.

Over 8,000 Polish Jews succeeded in crossing the border that night, while the other half found themselves stranded in the small border town of Zbonszyn (Zbaszyn) next to no-man's-land as the Polish troops closed the border and the Germans refused to let the Jews return to their homes in Germany. Having heard what was going on at the border, the group Chaskel was in bribed the train conductor so that the train would not stop at the border but would go directly towards Lodz where a large number of passengers including Chaskel had family. Bertha and the children were supposed to be sent to the border separately from Chaskel but at the last minute the transport was delayed. Bertha was lucky. Sometime during the night the German authorities decided that mothers of small children would be permitted to remain in Germany, at least temporarily. Camilla and Manfred had no knowledge of the entire potential upheaval from which they had been saved.

Chaskel reached his family in Lodz and immediately sent word to Bertha in the hope that she would still be home. He had no idea of the reprieve that she and the children had been given, but knew that as Polish citizens, their fates hung in the balance. During the weeks that followed Chaskel began working for his father-in-law both in Bochnia and Lodz while Bertha tried to find paid employment for herself in Frankfurt so that she and the children would have enough to live on. Although Camilla and Manfred had no memories of the carnage, they experienced the trauma of *Kristallnacht* – the orchestrated Nazi pogrom of the night of November 9, 1938, which the Nazis claimed was the spontaneous response to the murder of the German Third Secretary at the Paris embassy by a Jewish teenager, Herschel Grynspan, whose family had been deported in late October. During that pogrom more than 100 Jews lost their lives, over 1000 synagogues, yeshivas and Jewish communal buildings in the Reich were burned by the Nazis, and 20,000 Jewish men were incarcerated in concentration camps.

The next step was a series of additional restrictions on Jewish life in Germany and a surge in popular anti-Semitism. Coming home from school in late December, someone threw a stone at eight year-old Camilla and knocked her unconscious. To Bertha, this incident emphasized the need to get the children out of Germany as soon as possible, even before she and Chaskel could follow them to safety. These were the days of the *kindertransports* – groups of Jewish children from Germany which were being sent out of the country, primarily to England – and Chaskel urged Bertha in his letters from Poland to find such a framework for their children and get them out of the country. Bertha preferred to send the children to her parents in Bochnia but even from the distance, Chaskel's will prevailed. From Poland he managed to contact friends in Frankfurt who informed Bertha that in February the Breuer community was arranging a children's transport to Brussels and she requested that Camilla and Manfred be allowed to join. In March 1939 Bertha placed eight year-old Camilla and seven year-old Manfred on a train to Belgium with a group of Jewish children from the Breuer *kehilla* with the promise that they would be resettled together in a Jewish children's home in Brussels; meanwhile she and Chaskel would attempt to obtain English entrance visas for the entire family so that they would soon be reunited. Little did she know how events would evolve and that she would never see her children again.

Despite these promises the children were separated after reaching Belgium and would only be reunited two and a half years later. Camilla was placed with a Catholic family in Brussels and Manfred was sent to a Jewish children's group home in a different area. The two children were not in touch with each other for months on end, had minimal contact with their mother in Germany, and no contact with their father in Poland. During the German invasion of Belgium in May 1940 Camilla's foster family fled with her to Southern France, turning her over to the Jewish children's aid service, the OSE (*Oevre de Secours aux Enfants.*) At the same time Manfred was also evacuated to southern France and after Camilla learned that her brother was in an OSE children's home nearby she demanded that the two be reunited. During the spring of 1941 Camilla had been chosen as one of the fortunate children to be sent to safety in the United States under the auspices of a Quaker organization, the American Friends Service Committee but she refused to leave without her brother. Finally, during the summer of 1941 the two were reunited in Chateau de Masgelier, the OSE children's home in which Camilla had been living. A short time later they were both included in a transport of Jewish refugee children who were sent to America from France.

All of this, of course, would only be far in the future. Meanwhile, from his exile in Poland, Chaskel corresponded with his friend Eli Hackenbruch in London and with various manufacturing firms in England in order to obtain an offer of employment; such an offer would, in turn, enable him to apply for an English entrance visa for the whole family. During the spring and summer of 1939 weekly letters went back and forth from Lodz or Bochnia to London, France and Switzerland where Chaskel's former employers, customers and associates provided him with glowing personal and professional recommendations that would allow him to obtain the desired visa. From Germany Bertha submitted the necessary forms to receive a domestic visa as a housekeeper, proving that she would be self supporting in addition to the five pound a week salary offer that Chaskel had received from an English firm which the British government did not find enough to support an entire family.

During these months, Bertha had been approached by a Nazi representative of the metal industry to sell him the Tider shares in Feuchtwanger and Co. at a fraction of their true value, a ruse which Bertha resisted until threatened that she would not be allowed to leave the country if she did not comply. The use of threats and terror was a common tactic used as part of the Nazi "aryanization" plan to force Jews to sell their businesses to Nazis at much less than their real worth. Bertha did not yet give in, but after the war began, in her terror of not being permitted to leave Germany, she became one of many who succumbed to this scare tactic and received a pittance in return. At the time the shares were of little value to her or to Chaskel who was already incarcerated in a Nazi jail. However, after the war's end her signature on the deed transferring the shares would prohibit Chaskel's from being able to claim compensation from the German government for his stolen property.

Throughout the months in Poland Chaskel felt as if he were living a twilight existence. He, who had experienced the Nazi terror, felt that he had to convince his friends and relatives in Poland that they, too, would not be safe if Hitler would carry out his threats to invade the east. As he related to me years later, it was as if he were speaking to a brick wall. No one wanted to listen. He recalled the Passover *seder* in Lodz, where he told friends of his parents about what had occurred in Germany. Laughing at his insinuation that such things could happen in Poland they stated firmly that although Polish Jewry was also experiencing a wave of anti-Semitism, it was the "usual" type of thing and not what the Nazis were doing to the Jews of Germany. "That can never happen to us here", they stated categorically, similar to what he had heard in Bochnia from his in-laws.

Meanwhile his parents' and sisters' life continued as usual and Ida became engaged to a young man whose parents owned the building in which the Tydors who had resumed the Polish spelling of their surname in Lodz, lived. Yehuda Leib knew that in his state of health and fortune he would not be allowed into England and also hoped that Polish Jewry would come through any future ordeal unscathed. Only Chaskel felt that he was in a mad rush against time, trying to escape from Europe before some uncertain date in the future when the apocalypse would begin.

In late July 1939 the younger Tiders in Germany and Poland received word that their English immigration visas had been approved and were en route to Frankfurt. Bertha, still living in Germany, would have no trouble obtaining hers but Chaskel had to apply for permission to enter the country in order to pick his visa, liquidate the last of his assets and finally leave the country for good. The request was approved and in mid August Chaskel returned to Frankfurt for the first time in over nine months to wait for his visa and prepare for immigration. If the months in Poland had been a twilight existence for him, the weeks in Germany were indescribable. Although he was once again united with his beloved wife, so much else in his life had changed. His children were no longer in Frankfurt; many of his friends and acquaintances were gone, having scattered to the four corners of the earth. His cousins from Munich had left for England. Ida, who had been like another sister to him, had immigrated to Palestine together with her new husband Paul. The Breuer *kehilla* as he knew it had ceased to exist. Rabbi Joseph Breuer was in New York; Rabbi Dr. Yitzhak Breuer was long in Palestine. Even the impressive *shul* at the Freidberger Anlage had been burned down during *Kristallnacht* as had the general Orthodox *shul* of Frankfurt. Decades later a colleague of mine who had witnessed the carnage as a fourteen year-old in Frankfurt remarked that he would never forget the sight of flames leaping from the tops of the two *shuls* which the Nazi storm troopers had set on fire almost simultaneously although they were situated on opposite corners of the main city park. His thought at the time was that although the two Orthodox communities in Frankfurt never managed to unite during their existence, they were finally "united", now burning together in their dissolution.

As the month of August came to an end Bertha and Chaskel became more and more anxious about their visas. A day or so before the end of the month Bertha's visa arrived from London but for some reason Chaskel's was delayed in transit. Refusing to leave without her husband and knowing that only after both of them would reach England could they apply to have the children transferred there, she remained in Frankfurt in spite of her husband's pleas.

On Friday September 1, 1939, Adolph Hitler informed the Reichstag that Poland had tried to invade Germany and in retaliation German forces had been returning fire since 5:45 a.m. Today we know that the "Polish invasion" was a German hoax perpetrated in order to legitimatize Hitler's expansion plans towards the east. Two days later the United Kingdom declared war on Germany and the British embassies in Germany were closed. Although Bertha and Chaskel, being Polish and not German citizens, were still permitted to enter Britain, Chaskel's visa had still not arrived. Their citizenship, however, was a two-edged sword. What could save their chances to enter England now put them in danger as enemy citizens living in Germany.

The first week of the war passed with incredible tension, although daily life in Frankfurt had not yet undergone any massive change. The change was to take place for them at the end of that week on Saturday evening, September 9, 1939, when the Gestapo knocked at the door to arrest Chaskel, along with hundreds of other Polish Jews still living in Germany, for being an enemy of the State in wartime. Bertha tried to explain that they had not yet left the country for technical reasons; the embassy was closed and the ambassador had not yet come in to sign the necessary papers, and she was promised that as soon as Chaskel's papers would arrive, he would be set free and the couple could leave the country. Chaskel packed a small bag with *tallis* (prayer shawl) and *tefilin* (phylacteries) and parted from his wife with words of comfort; soon they would be reunited. Little did they know that those were the last words that they would ever exchange and that they would never see each other again.

4

Buchenwald – Auschwitz – Buchenwald, 1939–1943

Part I: Buchenwald

When Chaskel Tider was arrested by the Gestapo in September 1939 he was almost 36 years old, entering early middle age by the yardstick of his time. In the concentration camp world, unless he was in excellent physical condition, he had only a small chance of survival. The odds that he could exist for five and a half years in Nazi camps were next to nothing. And how many German-Jewish businessmen of that time were in excellent physical condition? Religious Jews were even less fit, spending their free time learning Torah and caring for communal affairs. At most they would walk in one of the few parks still permitting Jews to enter. Although he bicycled to work, my father was no exception to this rule. Looking at his pre-war pictures one would not have put odds on his survival for more than a year under the conditions of Buchenwald or Auschwitz. Did I write a year? Three months at most.

Yet Chaskel – *"Bihasdei Hashem"* – "by the grace of the Almighty", as he would say, survived that entire period in Nazi prisons, camps and extermination centers. "Why did I survive while others did not?" he would often ask. "The Almighty must have his reasons, but who can understand them . . . "

Although this chapter tells the story of his wartime years, much of it is written in my words and not his. Had he written it himself it would certainly be more understated. My father was a modest man, sometimes excessively so, and would often brush off my incredulous reactions to stories I heard from others about his wartime feats with the words "it was nothing". But his twinkling eyes belied how "something" it really was.

His words might have been measured and precise, a residual legacy of his years in Germany. But the truth could usually be seen in his eyes which burned with the passion of his Galician Jewish heritage and his Hassidic forbearers.

My father was a quiet and unassuming man and throughout my childhood he often quoted the words of Rabbi Levitas of Yavneh, *"Meod Meod heve shefal ruach"* ("One should be exceedingly modest", *Avoth* 4,4), reminding me how rarely our sages used the work *meod* (exceedingly) and how in the case of modesty it was repeated twice to emphasize the need to fight excessive pride. But at moments when he came face to face with injustice or a slight to others, though almost never to himself, he would indeed burn, raising his voice from its usual soft pitch and becoming a different person. This was the Chaskel Tydor of Buchenwald and Auschwitz, the one who in spite of his five foot two stature and modest build, was always referred to by his friends as "a giant of a man".

As in many survivor homes, we almost never used the term "Holocaust" to describe the horrors of the Hitler era. For the protagonists in Adolf Hitler's macabre production of the "Final Solution", these were "the war years", "in camp" or just "there". At the Shabbos table my father would tell stories about "there", often pertaining to Jewish belief and practice, but almost nothing about the horrors of the war itself. Only when he got together with his *chaverim*, his camp friends, and particularly on the 28th of Nissan, the Hebrew anniversary of their liberation from Buchenwald, did I hear "real stories" of what happened "there". Many such stories are included in this chapter. Others I learned of later when I interviewed him before his death. Realizing that his time on earth was short, he decided, as did many survivors in their later years, to "bear witness", and not to let these stories disappear with him. When speaking about his childhood he would often interject with "Who in the world could ever be interested in these stories?!" but the question never came up when speaking of his experiences in Buchenwald and Auschwitz. It was as if he knew that these stories finally had to be told, and it was now or never.

Writing this chapter was one of the most difficult parts of putting together the story of his life; only the chapter about his death was harder. When I initially re-read what I had written it was obvious that something was missing. The facts were there, often in his words, but the picture was two-dimensional. Only when I gave it to my husband to read, the man who had never met his father-in-law but had heard much about him, did he ask "But where is his soul? Where is the burning that was his essence?" And indeed the words were there, but they could only express part of the story. The rest was in my father's eyes, in his tone, in the way he held his head when talking to me about it. None of that can be captured in mere words. I have attempted to include the spirit and tone of those words through my own interjections and comments at various points in this narrative. I know that if my father would read it, he might appreciate the additions but to me he would say only one thing: *"meod meod heve shefal ruach"*.

As Bertha sat alone in their Frankfurt apartment, Chaskel was taken to a prison where he met Jews arrested by the Gestapo in the same area. None knew why they had been arrested, how long they were to be incarcerated for, or what the Nazis had in store for them. A small group of prisoners was put into each cell sharing sleeping and washing space and twice a day the entire group would eat together in a larger cell which served as a prison "dining room". None had ever been in prison before.

Three days after being imprisoned the Jewish prisoners realized that Rosh Hashanah would begin the next evening. Still not comprehending the abrupt change that their lives had undergone a number of them approached the German police guards, mentioning that the next day was the Jewish New Year and they wish to recite their prayers as usual. In order to do so, they explained, they needed *machzorim*, special holiday prayer books. Would it be possible for the police to supply them with *machzorim* so that they could pray on the holiday? Just as the Orthodox Jewish leaders in Germany of 1933 had believed that they could cause the Nazi regime to alter decrees by submitting petitions, here, too, the Orthodox Jews appeared to be under the naïve impression that the German tradition of "law and order" would compel the Nazi police to supply them with the necessary Rosh Hashanah accoutrements. And just like the Orthodox leaders of 1933, they were greatly mistaken. "Were they crazy?" I asked my father, "Didn't they realize where they were, who they were talking to?" He looked at me with a sad smile. "We were German Jews. We were taught to believe in a system of law. I personally thought it nonsense to ask the policemen for *machzorim* but I expected that at worst the request would be refused."

Naturally, no *machzorim* were provided. When a number of Jewish prisoners reminded their guards of their promise they were met with a blank stare. A few minutes later a policeman entered the dining room and with a smile that only later they realized was meant to ridicule them, asked "Who among you can ride a bicycle?" Most answered positively.

"How many can drive a car?" – a number said yes. The next question dealt with driving a truck and here, too, there were several positive answers. The policeman left the room without explanation. "Maybe they want a driver to get *machzorim*?" asked one of the Jews. Most looked at him as if he was out of his mind, but a few still lived in hope.

On Rosh Hashanah eve Chaskel and the rest of the Jewish prisoners assembled in the prison dining room, where they recited as much of the holiday prayers as they remembered by heart. "It was a very sad *davening*", my father recalled. "We stood together but in truth everyone was alone with his thoughts, missing his family and loved ones." The next morning they were awakened at six a.m. and the police called out to all those who knew to ride a bicycle to come out of their cells. Then came the call for those who drove cars and trucks and finally the policeman turned to the group with a mocking smile and said that they were all going out to the courtyard to wash the police cars. "This was the 'surprise' that they had in store for us", my father told me, his voice flat. "How did you feel at the time?" I asked him, unable to comprehend the dispassionate tone in which he told me this story. Now his voice picked up in timbre and volume. "Of course we were upset, angry in that we had been tricked, cheated. But this was exactly the problem of German Jews. Even under the worst of circumstances there was this underlying belief in what was proper, acceptable behavior. Some who could not understand that those days were over, rarely survived for long. The rest understood that we were now helpless, totally at the mercy of our captors, and that there was no law or justice that could help us anymore".

The Jewish prisoners were forced to clean the cars until noontime after which they gathered again to recite the day's prayers from memory. And what prayers they were! Although the prisoners attempted to remain unobtrusive, fearing more scorn on the part of their captors, the usual disciplined *yekkish* form of *davening* gave way among many to heartfelt tears. This was Chaskel's first taste of being treated as a Nazi prisoner; a person with no rights. When he was deported to Poland in October 1938 he had little contact with the Gestapo and like most Jewish prisoners in the Frankfurt jail he was slowly beginning to understand that to his captors he was no longer a human being. This was to be the framework of his existence for the next five and a half years.

It was also his first taste of the Nazi approach towards Judaism. In their desire to mock the Jewish prisoners and desecrate anything they considered sacred, the Frankfurt prison guards singled out Saturdays on which to force them to perform the dirtiest and most uncomfortable tasks of the week. "It was horrible and degrading", my father said. "A few of the

Orthodox prisoners even protested, saying that this was their holy day of rest." "Rest?" roared the policeman on duty, "prisoners are not entitled to any day of rest!" ordering them to clean latrines on the Sabbath mornings. "It wasn't even necessary to beat us to get us to carry out orders", my father continued. "After all, we were German Jews . . . " he sighed, belying their naïveté at the time.

Chaskel and the other prisoners did not yet know that this was typical Nazi behavior: mocking Jewish symbols such as the Sabbath and Jewish holidays even without comprehending their deeper meaning. Throughout the Nazi regime, these days were often chosen for incarcerating, punishing or deporting Jews, not only in Nazi camps but throughout occupied Europe. The Warsaw ghetto deportation began on *Tisha Be'av*; the deportation of Danish Jews was to begin on Rosh Hashanah. The massacre of the Jews in Babi Yar near Kiev began on Yom Kippur eve. It was almost a "Nazi tradition".

From the Frankfurt prison the Polish Jews were transferred to a penitentiary in the Kassel area where they remained for Yom Kippur. A few in the group knew of Chaskel's religious background and turned to him in a matter of Jewish law: Should those with heart ailments fast in view of their condition? Realizing that those questioning him were not only looking for *halachic* (Jewish law) assistance but a listening ear and human guidance he decided to give all those who posed this question the same response: as they were incarcerated in a Nazi prison for an indefinite amount of time, anyone who felt that their health would suffer was under no circumstances to fast as it might endanger their life. This answer would set the tone for similar *halachic* responses that he would give throughout his years in concentration camp: One had to do everything within the boundaries of moral propriety in order to stay alive and survive the Nazi imprisonment.

Several days later the Jewish prisoners were loaded on to truck and brought to a nearby railroad station. There was no need to herd them onto the train by force as they stood in orderly rows and waited their turn to enter the freight cabins. When I asked whether any of the prisoners attempted to ask where they were being sent and for how long, he looked at me in the same way that one regards an innocent child. "We were German Jews", he answered with a sigh. "We were used to the concept of not questioning authority. In any case, by then I think that most of us realized that we would not get an answer if we asked."

The prisoners were loaded into the long freight train. Settling down silently onto the cold floor of the cabin, each man was initially alone with his fears. After a while they began to voice their thoughts, questions which they could not ask their captors but which festered in their minds, poisoning their bodies. Where were they being taken? How long would the journey last? How much longer would they remain in prison before being released? No one could begin to guess. One man suggested that such a release might occur within the framework of a cease-fire agreement between the Polish and German governments. Others told him that he was a fool, reminding him that no such agreement could take place as the Polish government had unconditionally surrendered. The journey continued as the group settled into silence once again.

Several times during the day the train stopped to pick up loads of prisoners, appearing to double back on its route and travel in circles. The physical conditions in the cars became more and more uncomfortable as they were packed with additional prisoners. Although the men had been given food and water earlier in the day no sanitary facilities were provided other than a bucket which was difficult to reach under the crowded conditions. Finally, after a lengthy and winding journey the train arrived at its ultimate destination: the Nazi concentration camp of Buchenwald.

Buchenwald had been founded near the city of Weimar in July 1937 as a Nazi detention and later concentration camp. Taking its name from the nearby beech forest, its famous landmark was the "Goethe oak tree" which stood inside the camp's perimeter. Over 250,000 prisoners passed through the camp during its almost eight-year existence; these including Jews, Poles, political prisoners, Gypsies, criminals, and prisoners of war. Until 1942 most of political prisoners in Buchenwald were communists and they were instrumental in the camp's internal administration.

When Chaskel's transport entered Buchenwald he and the other prisoners were given the usual reception for new inmates. "The Nazi guards stationed at the railway roughly pulled us off the train and we were forced to run through the gate while they rained truncheon blows down on our heads and backs." Those who could not keep up the pace were kicked and pummeled until they lay in the dirt. Chaskel had no time to look at his surroundings as he ran into the camp; he and the other new prisoners were herded into a large hall where they were received by a high-ranking SS (*Schutztaffel* – Nazi elite corps) officer. The room was packed with the newcomers who were suddenly ordered to stand at attention. Facing the rows of prisoners, the officer began his "welcoming speech" with the pronouncement: "You should know that this is your last station. From here no one will come out alive. The best that you can do is to hang yourself". After a few more sentences the officer left the room and the prisoners were ordered to undress. Allowed to keep their underwear, belts, shoes and glasses they were forced to relinquish the rest of their clothes and any personal possessions they still had.

"That was our entrance into the hell of Buchehwald, our new world", my father said. "A world turned upside down. This was not just a prison; it was a dreaded Nazi camp. Most of us had heard about these camps before the war. But who would believe that we would end up in one of them, torn from our parents, our wives, our children?! We moved like robots, from one station to another, following commands being barked at us and trying not to feel anything, not to think."

Chaskel's head was shaved and he was handed a striped shirt and trousers, the usual concentration camp uniform. Forced to relinquish his few possessions, he was ordered to leave his *tallis* and *tefillin* behind, his last tangible link with normal Jewish life. Along with the other members of his transport, he was sent to group B which was headed towards block twenty-nine. Entering the block he met friends and acquaintances from other German cities such as Munich, Nuremberg and Aschafenburg who had also been imprisoned as *ostjuden* and they spoke with each other about their experiences since the beginning of the war. "You can't imagine how comforting it was to be among friends", my father explained. "After weeks of being separated from the outside, I was finally with people who knew me, who knew my family, just as I knew theirs. We were each other's family now, and that's how we acted with each other."

My father learned the danger of the communist leadership on his first day in camp. As the sun began to set, he stood at his assigned place near the window and began to *daven mincha*, the afternoon prayer. Just then the supervising *Stubendienst* came over to him, administering a hearty slap to his face. Throwing Chaskel's cap to the ground, he told him the Buchenwald "facts of life": "You are not in a synagogue and you should forget all this nonsense". My father then realized that he would have to fear not only the Nazis in the camp but also the anti-religious communist functionaries.

Life in Buchenwald followed a set routine. Prisoners were awakened at five-thirty, allowed a short time for washing, dressing and putting the block in order, and then marched to work. Woe to he whose bunk was not arranged in a precise manner or to those responsible for cleaning the barracks table who had left a spot of dirt on the wood. All this had to be carried out in a few minutes every morning and like the other inmates, Chaskel soon learned to do everything with speed if he wished to survive.

Chaskel's group was assigned to a work detail that carried stones from the quarry to build installations throughout the camp. All labor was performed at a running pace. Prisoners caught moving slowly were beaten by the Nazi guards. Everything in a prisoner's day was regulated: how much time he had to get up, use the toilet facilities, wash, eat, march to work, run with each load of stones, and return to camp. Prisoners who could not keep up the pace would be punished, even killed.

The absolute scheduling of all time in Buchenwald also meant that there would be no opportunity for daily organized prayer. With the rigid camp schedule it was almost impossible to find a private moment to be alone with one's thoughts. Like many of his fellow observant Jewish prisoners, Chaskel recited his prayers while marching on the road to his labor battalion. If he was lucky, it was sometimes possible to put together a *minyan* (quorum) in a barracks corner in order to recite *maariv* (the evening prayer) together.

Life in a Nazi concentration camp turns into a never ending triangle of work, food and sleep. In order to survive at work Chaskel and his fellow prisoners learned how to always appear as if they were working. It was a lesson which he later taught prisoners in Auschwitz who had been sent to hard labor and would collapse from exhaustion: work only while being observed but during those times, labor with all your might. Make up for it by taking a respite when the Nazi guards would turn their backs for a smoke.

Food was another issue of life and death importance. What could Orthodox Jews eat in Buchenwald? Food consisted of a small portion of bread with margarine, artificial coffee, and later in the day, a bowl of soup that usually contained bits of what prisoners claimed to be either salami or horse meat. Although Chaskel had decided to be stringent for himself and eat only the bread and margarine, he told all who asked him that they should be lenient and eat the soup and meat. "One could not know how long it would take until the enemies of the Jews would be vanquished," he stated, "and therefore until then, everyone had to do whatever he could in order to stay alive." When a number of observant Jews who subsisted only on bread alone collapsed at work and were brought back on stretchers, attracting the SS's attention, Chaskel stated categorically that it was a situation of mortal danger and they must eat everything they could to stay alive. Despite his advice to others, he refrained from eating the soup for a number of months until one day he, too, collapsed from malnutrition. Only then did he eat the soup as well as the bread.

By the time he reached Auschwitz Chaskel had become an authority on the relative value of the soup and its connection to the previous issue: work. Everyone knew that it was better to be later in line when the soup would be ladled from the bottom. Then one had a chance to receive a piece of meat or potato in the soup instead of only getting the watery mixture which floated on top. But Chaskel also realized the danger of attempting to rejoin the line for a second serving, as some of the starving prisoners were wont to do. Warning a new inmate about this practice he explained that the blows that he would have to ward off when trying to obtain a second portion would cause him to expend more calories than he would gain in a second bowl of soup. Instead, he told the prisoner, it is better to live on one bowl of soup and not have to expend extra energy shielding oneself from blows, while saving calories at work by slacking off the minute the guards would turn their backs.

Finding a decent place to sleep could also make or break a prisoner. Most prisoners slept in three-tiered bunks that lined the walls of the barracks. Those who slept on the top bunk could fall while climbing up or down, but did not have other prisoners climbing all over them, giving them a drop of privacy. The lowest bunk was the easiest to get in and out of, but it was closest to the floor and easy prey for lice and other vermin. The middle bunk was at eye level and easy to steal from. My father never mentioned which tier he slept on; only that as time passed the barracks became more crowded and there was less room to even turn over.

Prisoners in Buchenwald usually had no contact with the outside world but could often ascertain the war's progress from the treatment they received at the hands of the SS; the bloodier the war became, the more brutality they showed to the prisoners. At the same time, in response to the cruelty and feelings of isolation, small groups of prisoners banded together in the camp and thus the concept of "camp brother" or "camp sister" – someone you were in camp with who was often closer to you than a biological brother or sister – was born.

"I was never a natural leader before the war", my father one remarked to me, "but something happened in Buchenwald." During his first months in Buchenwald Chaskel became the leader of a group of young men, many just boys in their late teens who were looking for a father figure. A number of them were Orthodox; others were far removed from Jewish practice. Their common denominator was a need to be with others as the first rule of survival under the Nazis was that one could rarely survive totally alone.

The first test of this group's solidarity occurred in December 1939. This was one of the first Buchenwald stories that my father told me as a child and I recall the backdrop to his tale. One evening we sat at the table while he peeled an apple, giving me a quarter to eat. My father loved apples and as a child I was mesmerized by his ritual for eating them. He would never just bite into one; it would first be washed and then peeled in one long winding strip from top to bottom. "Let me tell you a story about apples", he suddenly said, "and how they can save a person's life."

During the early war years Buchenwald had a canteen where prisoners sent money from outside could purchase foodstuffs and a few boys in Chaskel's group bought a sack of apples in the canteen. Noticing the division of apples taking place in the block corner, Chaskel chided the boys, reminding them that they were now part of a group. How could they purchase apples and eat them at the table while other boys in the group had nothing? They should remember the common good, he stated. Under such circumstances either everyone gets some, or no one should have any. "We must always remember that we are responsible for each other here", he concluded. "Otherwise the Nazis will have won in taking away our humanity."

The boys understood. The apples were put on the table, divided into quarters, and everyone ate some. The boys learned a lesson which would stand them in good stead in Buchenwald: it was incumbent upon everyone to help their fellow prisoner. Equally important was that the incident had been observed by the Block leader, a prominent communist named Erich Eisler who had risen in the camp's interior administration. Hearing Chaskel's short speech Eisler was sure that despite his religious background, he was "one of them". This erroneous belief that Chaskel was a secret communist was instrumental in saving his life more than once during his years in both Buchenwald and Auschwitz.

If work, food and sleep were the triangle in which a prisoner's body functioned, there was no parallel framework to nourish their spirits. Each prisoner had to find his own emotional or spiritual solace according to his beliefs. The Communist comrades maintained contact and there was even an underground communist library in Buchenwald. The Orthodox prisoners, Chaskel among them, eventually developed their own methods of meeting their spiritual needs.

From their early days in camp religious prisoners kept a *luach*, a Jewish calendar to know when holidays would occur. The first festival which Chaskel celebrated in Buchenwald less than two months after his arrival was Chanukah. As the first night of Chanukah approached, a number of Jewish prisoners spoke to him about the upcoming festival. "They came to me and said how wonderful it would be if a few of us could get together and light candles to celebrate the event." As much as the thought appealed to them they knew that in the context of a Nazi concentration camp it was fraught with danger.

The days passed and Chanukah grew close. Once again the men approached Chaskel, asking if he could think of a way to put together such a gathering. One evening after work Chaskel approached Erich Eisler and mentioned that it would soon be Chanukah and a few of the prisoners wanted to put together some kind of clandestine celebration. Would this be possible? The *blockeltester*'s initial answer was a resounding "no". "But I wouldn't accept that as his final answer", my father recalled. "I appealed to his communist spirit, explained that by not doing so he was collaborating with the Nazis. The Nazis were trying to break down our spirit. Anything that could lift up the Jewish spirit should therefore be deserving of support on the part of the communist leaders in an attempt to fight Nazi tyranny." In addition, my father remarked, Chanukah was not only a religious holiday but one of Jewish heroism, and celebrating it would awaken the fighting conscience of the Jews in Buchenwald and act as a morally uplifting event.

Eisler looked at Chaskel in dismay. Did he really think that it would be possible to put together a Chanukah celebration in Buchenwald in December 1939, almost four months after the war had begun? Eisler mulled over the idea and recalled Chaskel's arguments about supporting any event that would keep the prisoner's spirits from breaking. Later in the day he sought out my father and informed him of that he would close a blind eye to any goings on if several conditions could be met. "First," Eisler said, "you are responsible that the event will not be discovered by the guards. Second, none of the block functionaries will be involved. Third, the event has to be totally on your own initiative." If it works, Chaskel should let him know how it went. In any case, Eisler would make sure not be in the block at that time.

Chaskel and his friends went into action. Mobilizing the Jewish prisoners, they opened supply lines to the camp workshops. Prisoners in the carpentry commando constructed a wooden menorah; those from the cleaning department "organized" a tablecloth and paper towels. The shoemakers and tailors obtained candles and wax while those in the kitchen hid food that would round off the celebration: apples, cookies and even a bit of chocolate. On the afternoon before Chanukah the prisoners began preparing a wing of block 29 for the event and word went out that after nightfall all Jewish inmates who wanted to celebrate Chanukah should gather discreetly in the block. Finally, the prisoners set up a warning system if SS men should enter the area.

My father described the event in glowing terms. "The hall was filled to the top and people were still climbing on each other and through the window to get in." Before the candle lighting ceremony Chaskel delivered encouraging words about the history and significance of Chanukah. Just as the Jews who were slaves in Egypt felt hopeless and only a minority held out, thus the Jews in camp should consider themselves such a minority and know that they will hold out in the exile of Buchenwald. "This is the purpose of Chanukah and these lights", Chaskel concluded. "A hope in the darkness, giving us courage and strength to survive this evil decree."

As the inmates in the packed block stared at the flickering lights in the makeshift menorah, some even with tears in their eyes, Eric Eisler's face appeared at the doorway. The block elder looked around the room, taking in the prisoners' faces, the food, the menorah, and then he disappeared once again. For a moment, everyone in the room dreamed that they were free. What did Chaskel think of as he looked around at the group gathering in block 29? Could he even imagine that five years later he would still be a prisoner in a Nazi camp, secretly lighting Chanukah candles in a camp in Poland that did not yet even exist – Auschwitz-Buna?

The Jews in block 29 continued eating fruit and cookies, encouraged for a few moments to believe that one day they would again be free. It was a most memorable Chanukah, one they would recall years later, both during and after the war. Even Eisler remarked to Chaskel that he had been brought up in an assimilated home and until then he knew of Chanukah only by name as a "festival of lights" which he imagined was like Christmas. But what he saw in the block made a deep impression on him and his communist friends as it reminded them of communist solidarity. Still uncertain of Chaskel's political leanings, a number of Jewish communist functionaries in Buchenwald attempted to "convert" him by giving him communist pamphlets from their secret library which he later discussed with them, using the opportunity to teach them about Judaism. While he did not try to convert the communists to the Orthodox Jewish way of life, he did engender a respect for Orthodox Jews in more than one communist who had previously been rabidly anti-religious.

"Actually I did live in hope of freedom for a while," my father once said, "especially during my first months in Buchenwald." As they had a permit to enter England, Bertha knocked fearlessly at the door of every embassy or consulate which might grant them a transit visa that could expedite Chaskel's release from Buchenwald. Chaskel knew little about these endeavors except from cryptic messages Bertha sent through various channels. However he had another way of knowing what she had been up to, one that had serious repercussions on his health each time it happened.

Whenever Bertha completed the paperwork for a transit visa, she would apply to the police in order to obtain Chaskel's signature on the necessary forms. The police would inform the Gestapo office in Frankfurt which would contact the concentration camp authorities to let them know that documents were being sent for a prisoner's signature. When the documents arrived, they were handed over to the Buchenwald Gestapo who would order Chaskel to immediately appear at a central camp office.

"The first time I received this order my heart leaped in hope," my father recalled. "Was I finally going to be released?" The events that unfolded were a far cry from his hopes. Told to stand at attention and remove his cap in the presence of a Gestapo official, the officer began to shout. What connections does your wife have that enabled her to obtain these documents?! How did she manage to get the necessary funds to do so?" Over and he roared the questions and Chaskel answered that he had no clue; indeed Bertha was resourceful beyond human imagination. In response, the officer beat him on his shoulders, back and limbs but even after such "encouragement" Chaskel could not supply him with an answer.

Beatings aside, as this was Germany, orders were orders. The Gestapo had been ordered to photograph Chaskel for his visa and each time the beating was over the Gestapo covered up his prisoner uniform and photographed him. This explained why the officer had not beaten him on his head or face. He was then required to sign the photograph and forms that had been sent to the camp which were returned to Bertha in Frankfurt. In spite of the indefatigable Bertha's efforts, months passed and nothing came of any of these attempts, particularly after Germany's invasion of the west during the spring of 1940. Nevertheless, Chaskel still lived in hope.

At unguarded moments he thought of Bertha, still in Frankfurt, and of little Camilla and Manfred, far away in Belgium. Oh, how he missed her, and how he missed both of his children. When the Gestapo came to take him away in late October 1938, he couldn't imagine that he would not see his children for over a year. He had hoped they would be safe in Belgium but now that it was overrun by the Nazis, what would happen to them? Would he ever see them again? Were they even still alive? And what about Bertha, how was she managing in Frankfurt? What about his parents and sister in Lodz? What had happened to them since Germany invaded Poland over a year ago? How was his dear father's health faring? How was his beloved mother managing? His little sister had been about to get married when the Germans invaded Poland. What had happened to her and her fiancé or husband? When he would begin to think about his family his heart would fill with longing and dread, but it brought him close to them, at least in his thoughts. He would imagine his children's faces, how they must be growing up. He would try to picture his sister getting married, even in wartime. The one thing that he tried not to think about was his own fate.

To be a prisoner in a concentration camp meant living from day to day, not thinking about how long one is going to be imprisoned but always hoping that liberation was around the corner. This is how my father and his comrades survived their incarceration. His only personal calendar was the Jewish *luach*, and he lived from holiday to holiday, from fast to festival. Whenever possible, he attempted to observe Jewish holidays, for example, by sending his friends in Buchenwald *mishloach manos* (presents of food) on Purim, using a slice of bread which he had saved or a dab of artificial honey or margarine. As there was no *megillah* scroll from which to read the Purim story, those observant Jews who remembered parts by heart recited them for the others.

Passover raised a number of difficult questions as the prisoners' main daily food was bread. During the days preceding Passover a number of prisoners approached Chaskel with questions. Should one eat the bread? If one eats it, should it be eaten in a special way? Seeing how many inmates' health had deteriorated, he refused to prohibit eating bread under the circumstances. But once again he was strict for himself, making deals with non-Jewish inmates, exchanging bread for potatoes during most of that week. When it was impossible to exchange bread for potatoes, he gave away his bread to a prisoner who looked as he was obviously in a very bad state of health, subsisting only the ersatz coffee and soup.

Passover 1940 was also a spiritual watershed for Chaskel and his religious comrades as it marked half a year that they had been in the camp. Occasionally he asked himself how he had already survived so long in Buchenwald. Before the war, he had heard of Jews who had been imprisoned in German camps but they were usually released on the condition that they leave Germany. He and his friends had already been there for six months with no end in sight.

That, he reminded himself, was as far as his body was concerned. But what about his soul? Passover, also known as the festival of redemption, had reminded Chaskel and his friends that although their bodies may not have been free, their souls certainly were. But how had they been nourishing these souls? The occasional clandestine holiday celebration was not enough; now they felt the need for something more constant. It was time for them to return to a regular practice of learning Torah, even once a week. How could they do this with no books, no sources and almost no opportunity to meet outside of marching to and from work?

My father came up with an idea. On the first Sabbath after Passover it is customary to begin learning *Pirkei Avoth* (Ethics of the Fathers) until the festival of Sukkot (Tabernacles) in the autumn. Why could they not do this in Buchenwald as well? On Saturday afternoons when work officially ended by 2 or 3 p.m. they had a bit of unsupervised time when prisoners would tidy their blocks and clean their clothing. After completing their chores, some prisoners would walk between the barracks or even towards part of the Buchenwald forest that lay within the camp's perimeter, keeping watch for the SS. Maybe it could be done then?

The few Orthodox prisoners with whom he raised the possibility responded with alacrity. From the Sabbath after Passover onwards Chaskel and his friends used some of the time in the afternoon to walk around the camp and learn *Pirkei Avoth* together. "It was suddenly important that I had a good memory", my father remarked while telling me about this incident. "I would begin by reciting the chapter of the week aloud to the group, and then everyone would discuss it." The men would walk towards the trees, learning Torah and discussing commentaries, winding their way around the barracks and into the open areas of the camp near the forest. It must have been an incongruous sight: a small group of prisoners in striped uniforms, caps on their heads ostensibly shielding their faces from the spring and summer sun but actually serving as a religious head covering, walking through the woods of Buchenwald as they discussed the intricacies of *Pirkei Avoth*. As a child I did not understand why my father expected me to learn every religious text I was taught in school by heart; after all, he said, you never knew when you would be without a *siddur* or a *sefer* and would have to rely on memory. Only after hearing stories such as this did I fully comprehend what he was trying to tell me.

From week to week the study group grew, but the walks were kept short so as not to attract attention. At some point my father was joined in Buchenwald by a member of his extended family, Yidel Rosner in whose *shul* he had his Bar Mitzvah almost a quarter of a century earlier; Rosner became a member of this study group throughout its existence. A few more study groups grew out of this one, one which studied *Parashat Hashavua* (the Torah portion of the week), another headed by a Gerrer *hassid* who remembered the teachings of the Gerrer *Rebbes*.

My father recalled this as one of the spiritual high points of his years in Buchenwald. He and his friends saw it as a triumph against the Nazis, a small victory in their ongoing battle for spiritual survival in the concentration camp. Throughout the long summer Saturdays the groups continued to walk and learn, even when some of the participants were taken out of Buchenwald and deported to other camps. But the Nazis were not the Orthodox prisoners' only enemies. "At one point we were the victims of 'Jewish anti-Semitism'," my father recalled, "when we were persecuted by a number of the more fanatic communist camp functionaries, some of whom were Jewish." The groups were forced to go underground but even then they refused to give up their moments of spiritual freedom, continuing the momentum of Torah study under such abnormal conditions.

A main rule of survival in a concentration camp is to become invisible. To do your work, to slack off when you aren't being observed, to eat, sleep, and keep out of sight of the guards as much as possible. If you put yourself out for your fellow prisoner you risked being harmed; if you requested someone's assistance for a third party you were marked as a "do-gooder" and liable to be punished for your efforts. And yet, there were those who did not lose their spark of humanity and continued to protect others. My father was one of them, and as a result he paid a high price for his actions.

During the summer of 1940 my father was singled out several times for punitive exercises as a result of his attempts to protect observant Jews in the camp. This was a favorite punishment used in Buchenwald as it did not require the SS to expend their energy. Instead, inmates were sent to perform repetitive exercises that were meant to sap their strength and worse. While the prisoners chosen for punishment were forced to climb, run and jump, the other camp inmates were made to stand at attention and watch. Often, my father and the other prisoners were ordered to run up to the top of huge gravel hills and roll down again and again. This punishment went on for hours until the prisoners would collapse or the SS would tire of watching them climb.

One time after rolling down the gravel hill my father lost consciousness, something that usually brought a beating from the SS in its wake. Risking his own life, Erich Eisler walked out of the line of those being forced to observe the punishment, picked up the emaciated prisoner and carried him to the hospital. There he informed the chief orderly, also a communist, that Chaskel was a "comrade" and was to be kept alive at all cost. And indeed he was; the orderly made sure that my father remained in bed, tended his wounds and fed him warm soup until he could stand on his feet. A strong sense of solidarity existed among the communists in Buchenwald, and they would often risk their lives for each other. This solidarity usually did not extend to those who were not considered communists. Obviously my father's actions regarding his group of boys in block 29 were enough to make him a communist or at least a welcome fellow traveler in the eyes of that group.

When it came to keeping his own comrades alive, Chaskel, too, went to great lengths in order to help them. Once he tried to transfer a friend to a different work battalion and was told that it could only be done through the battalion's kapo, a former owner of a large house of ill repute in Frankfurt. My father never frequented such places, but had once accidentally been in the area of this brothel during his yeshiva years. Walking along the streets of Frankfurt while going over his lessons, he made a wrong turn and lost his way through the city's back streets. At one point he suddenly looked up, finding himself in an unfamiliar area, the Frankfurt red light district. Making his way home he saw a familiar face, a neighbor, standing on the street. "What in the world are you doing here Chaskel?" the neighbor asked. "This is the biggest brothel in Frankfurt, do you even know what that is? Go home!" he stated as he pointed to the building at the corner, its name glowing in lights.

When my father learned that this kapo was indeed the owner of that brothel he decided to try a different tactic. Coming over to him, he put his arm around the kapo's shoulder, gave him hearty a slap on the back and said "Don't you remember me?" When the kapo looked at him blankly, my father, drawing upon his best acting abilities, remarked "Benno, it's Heinrich, how could you forget me just like that?! After all, I was your best customer at the house on X street for years!" Slightly embarrassed at having forgotten a seemingly long-time customer Benno returned the slap with camaradie, asking what he could do for his old friend. Chaskel, in turned, asked him for a favor, to get his comrade into the labor battalion in return for "all those good years of girls that we shared together". Benno granted him the favor and every time they met in the future, he would go over to my father and wink, saying "Ach, did we have a wonderful time in those days . . . ". When my father told me this story he almost doubled up in laughter but I can only imagine what it took for my father, a former yeshiva student and Orthodox Jew, to put on such a performance in order to save a friend's life.

And indeed he remained an Orthodox Jew, in both belief and practice. During his first year in Buchenwald he observed both major and minor fasts but after his health deteriorated, he fasted only on *Tisha Be'av* and Yom Kippur. The Nazis knew when it was Yom Kippur and the day before the fast they would give almost no food but on Yom Kippur they would put out food that hadn't been seen since the beginning of the war to mock the Jews who wished to fast. "How could you fast like that?" I once asked him, knowing that even *Tisha Be'av* and

Yom Kippur were a danger to his health. His answer was simple: "Everything is connected", he said. "There were times that I felt that my spiritual health was what kept my physical health intact, and fasting on those two days reminded me of who I was and gave me the strength to continue." Nevertheless, when approached by prisoners asking whether to fast, he always answered that under the circumstances no fast was obligatory for those who felt that their health or life would be endangered. As usual, he was lenient for others while still attempting to be strict in his own observances.

Chaskel missed his family tremendously. Between 1939 and 1941 Bertha sent him several messages, one informing him that their children had escaped from Belgium to France and there was talk of sending at least one of them to America. What did he think? Should she give them permission to send a child to America, not knowing if she and Chaskel would even be able to trace them after the war? Using a week's ration of bread as barter, Chaskel managed to send a message to her in Frankfurt: under no circumstances should the children stay in Europe, he responded. They should take any offer and any chance to leave for America as soon as possible.

Bertha's cryptic message about sending one or both of their children to America was the only clue he had regarding Camilla and Manfred's whereabouts after the war. It was also the last communication he received from Bertha. After the war he learned that she had received his message but it seems that she did not manage to send any message to the children in France after receiving Chaskel's note. Neither Camilla nor Manfred remember any contact with their mother after escaping Belgium to France.

Apart from the hope that his children might be saved, the months of late 1941 and early 1942 were a particularly difficult period. During these months the Nazis built a crematorium in Buchenwald to save on costly transportation of bodies elsewhere. "They built it very close to the center of the camp", my father recalled, "Every time we came to the *appelplatz* (roll call square) we would see the small grey building reminding us about what the Nazis intended as our end." The demoralization it caused led to a wave of suicides among the prisoners.

Chaskel too was slowly sinking into the abyss. From new prisoners entering the camp he had heard that the Nazis had established ghettos in Poland and that Jews there were being sent to forced labor. No one yet knew about the Final Solution which had begun in the Soviet Union and which was slowly being implemented in the rest of Europe but it was obvious to Chaskel, as it was to the other Polish Jews in the camp, that the situation of their families in Poland was tenuous. Chaskel had not heard anything from his parents or sister and despaired for their lives.

Sometime in late 1941 a pocket-size book of *tehilim* (psalms) appeared in the camp, missing some pages and having been at one time immersed in water. Nevertheless, the little book was a comfort to many Orthodox prisoners who would pass it from hand to hand silently reciting chapters late at night. My father found particular solace in chapters seven and seventy-three which spoke of how the forces of evil would not triumph. "O Lord my G-d, in thee do I put my trust: save me from all those who persecute me, and deliver me, lest he tear my soul like a lion, rending it in pieces while there is none to deliver. (Psalms 7, 2–3)."

In September 1942 a pair of *tefilin* came into the camp through the hands of a nonbeliever who said "I have no use for these here, if you would like them . . . " and showed them to Chaskel. Not having any way to check whether they were kosher *tefilin* my father nevertheless embraced the opportunity of putting them on a number of times during that month. "My hands trembled when I held this pair for the first time, even though they were grey and worn in places." Earlier he had heard rumors that there was a pair of *tefilin* in Buchenwald but no one he knew had ever seen them. This time the privilege to don them was his.

It was during this period that my father suggested a scheme to give the "boys" of block 29 a better chance to survive the war: to have them trained as skilled workers. Chaskel knew that the Nazis had no need to keep unskilled manpower alive. "There were new prisoners coming into the camp every week who could take the place of old or sick prisoners in carrying lumber, cement, or cleaning the barracks. But this wasn't true in terms of locksmiths, metalworkers, electricians and other skilled labor. I hoped that if the young boys would be trained as skilled laborers, the Nazis would want to keep them alive as their skills were always needed in the camp."

Chaskel first broached the idea to the head of the locksmith commando, a "green triangle" prisoner (professional criminal) who had the ear of the *arbeitsdienst*, a high-ranking SS Officer who commanded the labor services. He made the same approach to the Kapos in charge of the electrical and shoemaking commandos and thus the training scheme was launched. Eventually it encompassed three commandos that trained close to 250 boys and young men in skills that would ultimately secure their future in the camp as desirable prisoners. As a next stage he suggested that they would need to keep the trainees separate from the other prisoners, so that no additional men would try to join the group. In practice, the idea was to separate the group and grant them privileges such as additional food under the excuse that they would need it to become skilled workers and better serve the Germans.

As soon as the scheme was implemented the "boys" were transferred to barracks 42 and 44 and kept separate from the other camp inmates while they were being trained. In addition to receiving larger food portions during this time they were also exempt from appearing in the *appelplatz* during the prisoner selections which began to occur regularly in mid 1942. This move eventually saved their lives when most of the Jewish section of Buchenwald was liquidated and sent to Auschwitz in the autumn of that year. When my father returned to Buchenwald in early 1945 he was amazed to find that apart from those who succumbed to illness or were killed in accidents, most members of these special commandos, such as his good friend Leo Margulies, had survived the rest of the war. The scheme had worked.

Although Margulies was much younger than my father, from the first time they met in Buna the two had become kindred spirits. He, like my father, was by nature a quiet, and deeply believing Orthodox Jew. He, too, learned quickly to adapt to his surroundings in a Nazi concentration camp, at first blending into the background and becoming anonymous. Later, after my father was sent to Auschwitz, he took over my father's role, becoming a guiding figure among the young men of the special training commandoes which my father had been instrumental in creating. In spite of his unassuming nature, when it was necessary he, too, turned into a natural leader. When my father suffered from typhus in Buchenwald right after liberation he helped secure oranges to give him vitamins as there was no medication available. When my father awoke from his coma sometime during the epidemic, he saw Margulies sitting at the foot of his bed where he had sat for days, reciting *tehilim* for my father's recovery. He was one of my father's "camp brothers" and felt the responsibility to save my father's life through any means at his disposal, physical or spiritual.

I remember Leo Margulies and his family from my youth, especially at the festive dinners marking the anniversary of their liberation from Buchenwald that we held either in their home or ours. Years later, when he lay dying, Margulies' last words to his sons were the same as my father's: to bring him a *tallis* and *tefilin* so that he could *daven* one more time. I am still in awe of how both men, at the final moments of their lives, could have the same thought. To praise the Almighty one last time for his grace and kindness to them. *Bihasdei Hashem.*

"What was the most important lesson that you learned in Buchenwald?" I once asked my father. His answer surprised me. "That you can never know how a person will react in a given situation and you should never expect something from someone just because he comes from a particular background." The years in Buchenwald and Auschwitz – those he called "the bankruptcy of Western civilization" – taught my father a lesson regarding the value scales of human beings. Not only of Nazis, but of the prisoners as well. "One never knows a person until seeing him under stressful circumstances", my father would say. "There were prisoners from educated backgrounds who turned their backs on basic human decency while others, simple people, showed tremendous kindness towards their fellow prisoners."

The war progressed and with it, the destruction of European Jewry. In early 1942 the Nazis built a series of extermination camps in Poland including enlarging two pre-existing camps – Auschwitz and Majdanek – to which they added gas chambers and crematoria. By the spring of that year they began liquidating Polish ghettos and sending their inhabitants to their death. During the summer of 1942 the Germans opened a military offensive against Stalingrad and a new stage in the war began which became a major turning point leading to an Allied victory. However at that time, Germany was still the unvanquished king of Europe and the Nazis decided to cleanse Germany of its remaining Jews.

The Jews of Buchenwald were no exception. During the second half of 1942 a wave of selections took place in Buchenwald and five transports numbering up to a thousand prisoners each left the camp "for the east". Prisoners were told that they were being sent to textile factories in Poland to sort clothing and would be given good living conditions. In fact, all transports were slated for immediate extermination in Auschwitz.

My father was included in the last transport of about 500 prisoners from Buchenwald that left the camp in October 1942. Along with him were many prisoners that he knew, including Erich Eisler. For several days they were kept in a freight wagon near Auschwitz and given neither food nor water. Many died as a result. None understood the reason for the delay. I never asked my father what he felt during those few days, what he feared, how he survived the hunger and thirst while so many others did not. But had I asked, I know what he would have answered. When I spoke to him about tricky situations in normal life his eyes would twinkle and he would usually give me a smile and say "One usually needs ninety percent *siata dishmaya* ("assistance from heaven") and ten percent good luck". But when I would ask him how he survived impossible situations during the Holocaust, he answer was always the same, three simple words that contained his entire core of belief: "How? *Bihasdei Hashem*".

Only later did the group learn that while their transport was en route to Poland, the SS Economic and Administrative Main Office in Berlin, responsible for forced labor in extermination camps, issued an order not to gas the entire transport upon arrival. Earlier that month a typhus epidemic had broken out in the area killing hundreds of prisoners and causing a shortage of unskilled workers. The acute labor shortage was felt most in a small satellite camp of Auschwitz then being set up in the nearby town of Monowitz, nine kilometers away. The new labor installation known as Buna and later as Auschwitz III was to supply the I.G. Farben factory in Monowitz with slave labor and an agreement to that affect had already been signed between the SS, responsible for the camp's administration, and the I.G. Farben industrialists. The factory was central to the German war effort; it was supposed to manufacture synthetic rubber (whose chemical symbols were BuNa, hence the camp's name) and methanol gasoline for the German army. During its peak in 1944, it would make use of over 83,000 slave laborers but now, at the end of 1942, it urgently needed a few hundred prisoners to help complete its immediate construction. How could the Nazis suddenly come up with enough slave laborers to take the place of those who had died in the epidemic?

My father's transport was their answer. Instead of sending the Buchenwald prisoners to extermination in Birkenau their train was kept on a siding for three days until the final order arrived from Berlin to quarantine them in Auschwitz and prepare their transfer to Buna. My father, who right after the war almost lost his life in a typhus epidemic in Buchenwald, was now saved by the fact that one had broken out two and a half years earlier in Auschwitz. How? *Bihasdei Hashem.*

Part II: Auschwitz

Like his entry into Buchenwald, my father's arrival at Auschwitz was unforgettable. "From a transport of 500 men only 300 survived", he told me. "We marched from the railway station into the main camp, but I didn't see the *Arbeit Macht Frei* sign over the entrance because I was too exhausted to look up." The prisoners prepared for their first selection in Auschwitz; being camp veterans they knew what to do. "We tried to make ourselves look strong and healthy", my father recalled, "which wasn't easy considering that we were after three years in Buchenwald and several days of sitting without food and water in a freight car". The selection, however, was cursory; the Third Reich desperately needed slave labor to build Buna and most prisoners survived this first round.

The Buchenwald transport was placed in block six in the main camp near the infamous execution block eleven. The new inmates were informed about the nature of that block by the veteran prisoner who distributed food to the newcomers. He also told them that they were the only transport from Buchenwald to survive; the four preceding ones had been sent directly to the gas chambers without selection. Chaskel thought of Yidel Rosner who had been in a previous transport, the only living relative he had seen in three years. Hearing the tragic news, he asked a few of his fellow prisoners to join him in a *minyan* to say *kaddish*, the memorial prayer, for Rosner who had officiated at his Bar Mitzvah ceremonies. This was the first *kaddish* that my father recited in Auschwitz, followed by many others during the next two years as he lost friends and learn of other close deaths. For days the group remained in Auschwitz without knowing what was in store for them. As veterans they understood that until they were officially listed as Auschwitz prisoners their fate still hung in the air. This occurred only two weeks after their arrival; until that time they remained the object of a power struggle between two factions in the Third Reich, one demanding their immediate extermination and another which believed in working Jews to death, meanwhile using them as slave labor. Only after they received their Auschwitz numbers on October 19th were they reassured that they would be sent to forced labor and not to the gas chambers.

The Buchenwald prisoners who were transferred to Buna received numbers in the 68,000 series; these were the relatively "low" five-digit numbers of which few survived the war. Unlike arrivals from late 1943 and 1944 who were tattooed with tiny numbers on the inner part of their arm, the groups arriving at Auschwitz in late 1942 received massive tattoos on their outside forearm. As my father one stated ironically, at the time Germany appeared victorious and could therefore be generous with its use of ink. Chaskel became inmate number 68715.

I never asked him how long the tattooing took, whether it hurt, but I can imagine what his answer would have been. Years later, when a friend of his from Buna, Siegfried Halbreich, passed away in Los Angeles at the age of 98, his obituary included the following story. One day after the liberation, when Halbreich was acting as an interpreter for General Dwight D. Eisenhower, the Allied Commander noticed the numbers 68233 on his skin and he asked him whether it hurt when the Nazis tattooed this number on his arm. Halbreich was stunned and at first he didn't know what to say. His only thought was "What kind of people are these Americans? They see what is going on here, full of bodies, dead people . . . and he asked if **this** was hurting?"

While it was more common to see people with concentration camp numbers when I was a child, as the years past and the survivors died, it was no longer a regular event. But the 68,000 series was never commonly seen; few Buna prisoners from the autumn of 1942 lived to see the liberation. Once on a Tel Aviv bus I noticed an elderly man with a number from the 68,000 series. I immediately asked him whether he had been in Buna. "Yes I was", he answered in a shaky voice. I told him about my father and it turned out that they had known each other in the camp, but had no contact after the death march. Little did they know that they would end up living only a short distance from each other in Israel during their latter years.

Two weeks after arriving in Auschwitz the transport survivors were sent to Monowitz. The camp had barely been established, the prisoners were living in tents as they built their own barracks using mobile carts drawn by prisoners. There was no electric fence yet; instead it was surrounded by chains, guarded by guards with guns. Some prisoners were marched daily to the nearby I.G. Farben factory, the one where Italian Jewish chemist Primo Levi (1919–1987) was later forced to work when he was a prisoner at Buna. Levi's memoirs, entitled *If This be a Man (Survival in Auschwitz)* describe life in Buna and his forced labor in the I.G. Farben laboratory. Having become one of Italy's famous postwar literary figures, Levi's poignant story of his months as a prisoner in Auschwitz III introduced the world to the camp's existence and the life of a Buna inmate.

As the camp itself was still being built, a large number of prisoners, including Chaskel, were chosen to remain there and work in construction. Not being a professional bricklayer, glazier or electrician, he was sent to do menial labor, carrying large bags of cement. At the time Chaskel weighed little more than ninety pounds. Day after day he staggered under the weight of the sacks he carried on his shoulder, often collapsing as he carried out his work. Once during my childhood I asked my father why his shoulders were uneven. "It is a 'souvenir' from the Nazis", he remarked sardonically. Until the end of his life one shoulder was lower than the other, a reminder of the forced labor that almost cost him his life.

For two weeks Chaskel worked outdoors, growing weaker by the day. Under later camp conditions the average life expectancy of a Buna inmate was less than three months; in the conditions of October 1942 it was not even than half of that. Just as he was nearing collapse his life changed once again, this time to the better. Although the camp was nowhere as politicized as Buchenwald, Buna had a strong communist contingent and within days after his arrival, Eric Eisler had been given the position of infirmary block leader. Through his assistance and that of the communist functionaries Chaskel was transferred to an indoor job, physically protecting him from the elements. But this new job would not only save his life; it would enable him to save the lives of many others.

My father spoke little about the position he held in Buna. In his customary modesty he mentioned that in late 1942 he became a *schreibdienst*, block secretary, responsible for work details and registrations. But from other sources I learned that my father's position was much more prominent. In a condolence letter after my father's death his friend Arthur Tennenbaum referred to him a *Blockaelteste*, or *Blockovi*, one who commands an entire block, and stated "I guess you know that he was one of the few Jews in a position of great responsibility in Buna". From the memoirs of Bernard (Boruch) Merzel, a Buna inmate from Antwerp, my father appears to have been one of the main work dispatchers in the camp. Merzel writes: "He was the chief work dispatcher of the entire camp of Buna Monowitz, and everyone who was there remembers him favorably. He was of the most honorable people in the world – I didn't come across even five people like that in my entire life. He was a man with incredible ethics who saved the lives of many prisoners and particularly those who were young. A man who saved my life time and again".

Unlike most Jewish prisoners then in Buna who were Polish and knew little German, my father was fluent in German and could write in flowing German script. However his capabilities went far beyond those of language. His organization skills were known already from Buchenwald; The communists "suspected" him of being a "comrade", one of them, but knew that he was an Orthodox Jew who tried to help everyone he could. Equally important, he was an "honest broker", willing to jeopardize his own life for his friends as he had shown more than once.

Chaskel initially refused to accept the position of work-schedule supervisor but finally acceded to the request. Not only because it would keep him indoors permanently, something any forty year-old concentration camp inmate needed to stay alive in the inclement weather, but because it would give him the opportunity to ameliorate some of his fellow prisoners' plights. Merzel's memoirs described how Chaskel's position enabled him to save many prisoner's lives. He used his connections to transfer prisoners from difficult jobs to easier ones; from dangerous outside labor to safer indoor positions. He sent wounded prisoners to Eisler to be protected in the communist-run infirmary until they recovered; he was asked by fellow *schreibdiensts* to save ill prisoners' lives by passing on erroneous or incomplete lists to the Nazi overseers, thus protecting prisoners too ill to report for work or in the infirmary. Within time his name was known among the Buna inmates not only as someone with a broad network of powerful friends to which one could turn in need, but as one who had not lost his humanity; a man with a listening ear and a desire to assist his fellow prisoner. This assistance was not only extended to people in his block or to other religious prisoners in Buna but also to non-Jewish prisoners in the camp. Many remembered his intervention as something that saved their lives at a critical juncture and attempted to recompense him in some way both during their time in Auschwitz and after. Although it appears to be an exaggeration, Merzel writes that "Even the SS treated him with *derekh eretz* (respect)."

During the spring and summer of 1943 transports of Jews began arriving from labor camps in Galicia. One included survivors of the Bochnia ghetto, most of whose inhabitants had been deported to their death at the end of August 1942. My father feared what he would hear from these new prisoners. "I trembled at the thought and alternated between hope and despair a thousand times that night. Finally I had the possibility to find out what had happened to my family in Poland", he told me. And indeed he did. From one of them he learned the news of his family's tragic fate. All were dead.

Sometime in early 1941 Bertha encountered an SS officer who she had known as a young boy. There is about to be a roundup here, he told her, get out immediately. Don't even go home. Just go anywhere and fast. Bertha had a sum of money on her person and without going back to her apartment, made her way out of Frankfurt. Hoping that her children were already safe in America, she decided to go to her parents in Bochnia, arriving there sometime in the spring of 1941, just as the Jews were being forced out of their homes into the ghetto. The ghetto was situated in a poor section of the city near the railway station which the Nazis closed off with a boarded fence through whose gaps one could see in and out of the ghetto. Forced to live without electricity and in minimal sanitary conditions, Bertha, like the rest of Bochnia Jewry, existed from day to day, hoping to survive the war and be reunited with her beloved husband who was still in Buchenwald. At the same time she still dreamed of getting to the United States, having obtained the necessary papers although she had no foreign currency with which to pay for her ticket. In August 1941 she corresponded with family in New York, hoping that an aunt there would be able to assist her. But the money could not be transferred to Europe and Bertha's dream of being reunited with her children in America disappeared.

Bertha was not the only family member who had thought that her chances of survival would be better in Bochnia. Yehuda Leib and Ida had also come to that conclusion after Esther's death from a typhus epidemic in the Lodz ghetto during the harsh winter of 1940–1941. Making contact with a local Pole who agreed to smuggle them out of the ghetto for a fee, they hid in a wagon driving south and made their way to Bochnia sometime during the spring of 1941.

Yehuda Leib had several reasons for wanting to reach Bochnia. The Lodz ghetto was the second ghetto to be established in Poland and Jews of other cities, particularly those in the south, were still living in their homes. Yehuda Leib hoped that this would be the case in Bochnia. He also wished to be with his family. From what he knew, his sister's son was still living in the house on Biala Street and the Greivers, lived nearby. When he and Ida reached the city they learned that Yehidisl's son was no longer in Bochnia, the house on Biala Street was closed up, and the Jews of Bochnia were in the process of being moved into a ghetto. But they soon found that it was extremely advantageous to be related to the Greivers who became one of the most influential families in the inner ghetto workings.

Hirsch was no longer the wheeler-dealer of the Greiver family. Now the title belonged to Bertha's brother Salo who had connections with Wehrmacht personnel in Krakow. Realizing that a Jew who produced a vital product for the German war effort had a better chance of surviving the war, he suggested establishing workshops in the ghetto for the Wehrmacht, providing them with goods. At the same time he planned to employ Jews who otherwise would have been marked for expulsion, keeping them alive for longer. This way everyone would profit. The Wehrmacht agreed as did the town mayor who was chosen to oversee the ghetto administration and received a cut of the workshop profits.

"Salo was a special type of person", recalled his cousin Menachem (Mundek) Greiver after the war. "He had tremendous courage to face the Nazis and make demands. He also knew exactly how far he could go before losing his advantage with them and that's how he survived for as long as he did." Salo Greiver became an important ghetto functionary as the workshops employed more than 2,000 Jewish workers. Some workshops produced uniforms for the German army. Others manufactured underwear, shoes, brushes, handkerchiefs, toys, motor cars and electrical apparatus. German firms would supply the ghetto with raw material and the manufactured goods were shipped out to the army or the civilian market by the truckload. Almost everyone but the Gestapo benefited from the enterprise and this absence of Gestapo profit would ultimately be the workshops' end.

Chaskel heard only one story about Bertha's activities in the Bochnia ghetto. When the Wehrmacht stopped providing the uniform factory with material, Bertha almost magically managed to find large bolts of cloth which they could use in order to continue their work; she, too, realized that if the factory would cease to be productive, they would all pay with their lives.

During the spring and summer of 1942 the mood in the Bochnia ghetto grew tense as the Jews heard rumors about mass deportations throughout Galicia. Although Salo Greiver reassured his workers that they would come to no harm, families began constructing underground bunkers in which they could hide during an upcoming Nazi *Aktion*. In late August 1942 the SS and Gestapo began liquidating the Bochnia ghetto and as the *Aktion* progressed, Salo Greiver contacted the Wehrmacht in Krakow for assistance. In retaliation he was immediately shot to death by the SS. Later that day the Gestapo rounded up members of his family, including his parents, who were to be taken to a prison in Krakow. Bertha came running after her parents trying to save them; listed as Bertha Tider and not Greiver, her name had not been on the family list. She, along with her parents, were thrown into a truck by the SS and taken away, never to return.

Bertha and her parents were probably shot in Krakow or en route to the city. Ida was caught in the August *Aktion* and sent to Belzec with the majority of Bochnia Jewry. Yehuda Leib, who had been hiding in a bunker with a group of Rabbis, so Chaskel had been told, was caught on September 9 (27th of Elul), three days before Rosh Hashanah, and the group was shot on the spot. The Greivers and Tydors of Bochnia were no more.

From then on, the 27th of Elul was the only memorial day that my father had for any member of his family killed during the war. He would later commemorate all the others on the fast of the 10th of *Teves*, a traditional fast day which the Israeli Chief Rabbinate declared in 1949 as a memorial day for those killed during the Nazi era whose date of death remained unknown.

The stories he heard about his family's fate pushed Chaskel to the brink of despair. "For several days I refused to eat and could barely sleep. During the time in Buchenwald I still lived in a naïve hope that my family was alive and well. Now that hope was gone forever." At one point it looked as if he were on the verge of "going to the fence", camp parlance for approaching the camp perimeter which would cause one to be shot by the Nazi guards. His friends never left him alone, talking to him and telling him that he still had a reason to live. He had to survive the war, so they told him, in order to go to *Eretz Yisrael*, the Land of Israel, the Jewish homeland. Suicide was not an option. It was forbidden to help the Nazis murder the Jewish people. Over and over they spoke to him about the future, telling him that he had a task and that he could not choose to abandon them. Slowly he began to listen and understand. Of all his family members he had been chosen to live for a reason and still had a purpose on earth. What was that purpose?

"Two things kept me alive during this period", he once recalled. "My faith and my friends." Even when he was in such deep despair that his faith was on the way to suffering, his friends – men such as Erich Eisler, Ya'akov Zilberstein, and Chaim Tyson (who received the Auschwitz number after his, being listed alphabetically after Tydor) who he knew from Buchenwald or Freddie Diament, Sigi Halbreich, Arthur Tennenbaum, Leo Seigel, Boruch Merzel, Norbert Wollheim, Artur Poznansky, and Ernst Michel who he met in Buna – kept him strong and would not let him give up. Merzel reminded him of what Chaskel has said to him during his early days in camp when he despaired of surviving. "There is a verse in *Tehilim* that states *'Basru miyom leyom yeshuoso'*, ('Announce His salvation from day to day', Psalms 94, 2). That is how one has to live. If you think about tomorrow, you are already dead today. In the morning when you get up to work think only about that day and do the same when you come back at night. Live from day to day. One day after another. That is the only way that one can survive here". This had become Merzel's motto in camp and for the rest of his life; it was later the title of his autobiography. Now he reminded his friend of it until he could regain his emotional strength.

Faith and religious practice were central points in Chaskel's life, in Buna as well as in Buchenwald. In Buna there was no internal suppression of religious practice because it was not a politicized camp run by communists; one could *daven* whenever time permitted. Prisoners had been warned that it was strictly forbidden to gather in any numbers so one had to pray unobtrusively at the workplace before or after work. There were no *siddurim* or *tefilin* that Chaskel knew of; those who had a fraction of one usually kept it hidden for their self.

"But there were other ways to keep our spirits up", he recalled. Just as he had in Buchenwald, Chaskel tried to form an occasional "learning group" on Shabbat afternoon in Buna. On Chanukah he arranged a clandestine candle lighting using candles bartered from Polish forced laborers who worked in the I.G. Farben factory. A number of the inmates at that ceremony had come from Buchenwald, some even remembered that first Chanukah celebration in December 1939. But as my father said: "We got together and remembered but the spirit was not the same." The Buchenwald prisoners had gone through a lot since December 1939. Most had lost friends and family. All had heard about the mass extermination of hundreds of thousands of Jews taking place in Birkenau during that period. The combination weighed heavily on their hearts.

Nevertheless for a few of the newer inmates in Buna, just the fact that someone remembered the Jewish holidays was a reason to keep on living. Boruch Merzel recalled his first meeting with Chaskel. "One night, less than two months after my arrival, I find myself woken up by someone holding his finger to his lips in a 'hush' sign, and motioning me to follow. I got down from my bunk and followed him as if in a dream." The man led him towards the front of the block behind the curtain of the 'elite' where Merzel saw two candle stubs and a towel on a table. "'Cover your head and wash your hands", the man said to him. The astonished Merzel realized that it was the second night of Chanukah and that he was being given the opportunity to light Chanukah candles. He quickly did as he was told and lit the candles with a blessing. Within seconds the other prisoner had extinguished them before they could be discovered. Looking at Merzel's injured leg the man shook his head and said, "This is no good; you can't go on this way. Tomorrow morning after selection go to Erich Eisler in the infirmary. Tell him that you come from Tydor and that he should take care of you". And indeed Eisler did. Chaskel had heard of Merzel from two of his students who said that their teacher, an Orthodox Jew from Antwerp, was in the camp and would be grateful to have the opportunity to light Chanukah candles. Thus, a lifelong friendship between the two was born.

I met Boruch Merzel, or "Burich" as my father called him in his Galician inflection, for the first time when we visited Israel in the early 1970s. A thin man of medium height with grey hair, horn rimmed glasses, and a large black yarmulkeh, he was a fascinating man, one who could go from melancholy to laughter and back in moments. He was also a unique raconteur; to understand him, you had to understand five or six languages. In an average conversation he would begin a sentence in Hebrew, peppering it with words in French, Flemish, Yiddish and occasionally German and finally make his point at the end with an English expression. He was a "character", but of the best kind. Warm, generous in spirit, he was a born teacher even though he made his living as a businessman and diamond dealer. He was also a man of deep mystical faith.

After we moved to Israel he and my father would learn Torah together several times a week either in our home or his. On each occasion he had another camp story to tell me about my father's past. When he first spoke to me about my father's wartime exploits, my father would stop him and say "Oy Burich, what does she need to know that for", but as time went on he added stories of his own about those days. Years later, when Boruch Merzel's daughter Lillian and I were at a meeting of the "Second Generation" at which many complained about how their parents had never told them anything about the war, she and I looked at each other until she finally burst out laughing and said, "And what about those whose parents never stopped talking about it?" Indeed, though, I am grateful to him for filling in the gaps of much of what I know about my father's life during the war.

Merzel recalled how during Purim 1944 when he was lying in his bunk after an operation, someone entered his barracks and called out his number. The messenger, a young Romanian boy of seventeen, was brought to Merzel and climbed up to the highest of the three bunks where he slept. Handing him a piece of bread and a tiny jar of preserves he said: "Your friend Tydor sent you *lishloach manos.*" The prisoner had obviously repeated the phrase several times in order to remember it, but had jumbled the first word *"mishloah"*. Chaskel had saved Merzel's life several times before then, but it was this incident which remained etched in his memory; the fact that Chaskel could remind him that in spite of the conditions in which they existed, their souls were still free and they could act as Jews.

Even among the most apathetic, a spark from their previous life occasionally remained. My father recalled: "Once a religious prisoner came back from work saying that under normal circumstances he would have needed to *bench gomel* (recite a prayer of deliverance)." Of course, as my father interjected in an aside, under "normal circumstances" such an incident wouldn't have happened at all, but by 1943 long-time prisoners rarely thought according to those lines. A heavy construction barrier had fallen a hairbreadth away from the prisoner's head and it broke to pieces; he was saved by a millimeter. The prisoners began discussing whether one was permitted to say the prayer without a Torah; for a moment, while quoting sources to each other, it almost appeared to be a normal pre-war *halachic* discussion. Chaskel found a solution. "I told them that that just as one recites a particular blessing when passing a place where a miracle happened to you ('*boruch hamokom sheoso li nes bamokom hazeh*' – 'blessed is the Lord who made a miracle happen to me in this place') – he should recite that blessing when he passes the place where the incident occurred." The importance was to mark the occasion as Jews, free in spirit, able to still praise the Lord even in the Nazi abyss.

Chaskel's friends were a great source of comfort for him during the dark days of 1943. Not only those from Buchenwald who were still alive, but also a few of the new inmates such as Merzel, who he met in Buna and who were his "camp brothers". Yet it was a very different prisoner who gave him the most unexpected comfort. Among the prisoners whose lives he had saved was a gypsy. Seeing his benefactor looking more and more haggard after hearing about the murder of his family, he offered the only comfort he could: to read his palm. Time and again Chaskel thanks him but gently refused; it was against Jewish belief, he explained. One day the gypsy suddenly took hold of my father's palm and stared at his benefactor's lines. Before he could pull his hand away, the gypsy said to him: "You will survive and live a very long life". Chaskel stood there as the gypsy told him what he had seen: "You will first move across the sea and then you will move again across the ocean where you will find members of your family (Chaskel had never spoken to anyone about the possibility that his children had been saved by managing to get to America) and will start another family. You will have one more child and will move across the sea one last time, and live long enough to see grand-children from all your children." Chaskel looked at him incredulously. True, he hoped and prayed to survive the war, but how did he know about his children? And what was this story of having one more child? Or of moving across the ocean? The gypsy's words appeared to be an impossibility, "and yet they gave me comfort at the time", he concluded. Little did he know that they would all come true.

From each group of incoming prisoners the Buna inmates learned about the advances on the war front. Germany had been defeated at Stalingrad and supplies were being sent to the German soldiers still at the Russian front. Once during the winter of 1943–44 a transport of rotting onions was dumped at the camp gates; despite the food shortage at the front these appeared too decayed to send to the German soldiers serving there. In their hunger, some of the prisoners peeled away the rotten layers and began to eat the onions, becoming violently ill from their sharpness. "I remembered that onions become sweet after cooking", my father told me, "and I threw some of them into the fire we had burning to ward off the cold." Taking the charred onions out of the embers he peeled away the outside and was delighted to taste their sweetness. Other prisoners followed suit and for the next few day they managed to augment their meager rations with burned onions.

As a child, I remember my mother preparing tiny boiled or grilled onions for my father to eat and telling me that they were a special deli-cacy for him. I could never understand how boiled onions were a delicacy for anyone, least of all for my father who was definitely not a lover of cooked vegetables, except possibly for carrot *tzimmes* (a sweet traditional Jewish carrot dish) or the traditional German boiled cabbage. But one day he told me the story of the onions in Buna and explained that from that time on they were always a reminder of the incident that symbolized both a German defeat and the inmates' ingenuity to utilize everything they could towards survival. They were a delicacy that reminded him of life, he said, and every time he ate them he gave thanks for his survival. *Behasdei Hashem.*

During the spring and summer of 1943 transports of Jews from Salonika were brought to Buna. Selected from the 45,000 Greek Jews who ultimately reached Auschwitz, these were the lucky few who were not sent immediately to their death. Understanding neither Polish nor German they could barely communicate with their surroundings or understand the German orders. Chaskel remembered their pitiful condition and how he tried to help some of them but to no avail. "I communicated with a few in Hebrew, but as they knew no Polish, Yiddish or German, they couldn't understand the Nazi commands fast enough. Sometimes they were killed just for not standing to attention at the right time." Another problem was the new inmates' footwear. "They were given unsanded wooden clogs in camp. As a result many had deep splinters in their soles which became infected, and they died from these wounds." Used to a more temperate climate, even the hardy ones who managed to understand the language and survive the clogs barely survived the harsh winter of 1943–44. "They dropped like flies", my father recalled, still heartbroken at his inability to help most of them before their premature deaths in Buna, "and there was nothing we could do to help them".

Nineteen forty-four was a test of Chaskel's ingenuity. On Passover he again traded his bread for potatoes in order not to eat leaven. Indeed, he told me, during the six Passovers that he observed in Buchenwald and Auschwitz never once did he eat bread. On Rosh Hashanah and Yom Kippur he arranged to work at the *schreibstube* and *davened* with a *minyan*. Five days before Rosh Hashanah the factory at Monowitz had been bombed by the Allies; a previous bombing mission had taken place in July and two more would follow. Chaskel remembered the inmates' jubilation. "While the SS hid into bunkers during the bombing some of us ran outside and stretched out upraised fists towards the Allied bombers willing them to destroy the camp even if it meant destroying us as well." Why did the Allies not bomb the Auschwitz gas chambers, many would ask after the war? Ordered to bomb only war industries such as the Buna factory, they left the camps themselves untouched and reconnaissance pictures of the area from the same period did not even identify the Auschwitz III camp as being what it was.

Nineteen forty-four also brought a new group of prisoners to the camp, those from Hungary. Hungary had been invaded in March of that year, and from the end of May to early July more than half a million Hungarian Jews were deported to Auschwitz. While most were immediately sent to the gas chambers, certain groups were selected for forced labor and sent to Buna. Among them were Elie Wiesel and his father. At the time, the man who would become a famous writer and political activist was a fifteen and a half year-old boy who claimed to be older in order to survive the selection and accompany his father to Buna. Similar to Primo Levi's autobiography, Wiesel's autobiography of the war years, *Night*, gave readers throughout the world an inside view of life in the camp.

Twenty-five years after my father and Elie Wiesel met for the first time in Buna, my father sent him a copy of a book report that I had written in junior high school about Wiesel's book and the concentration camp experience. In his letter, my father asked Wiesel what he thought about my understanding of what they had gone through during the war. Wiesel answered with alacrity. Complementing my work, he commented to my father that I had an "unfair advantage": "After all, she knows about it not only from the book but also from you. One day she will write about it herself and make you proud." I remember his words as I write this chapter.

Chaskel remembered the anger of so many of the Hungarian Jews who in mid 1944 had never heard of Auschwitz and the mass murders taking place there. "There had been Jews from Poland who escaped to Hungary and told the local Jews stories of what was going on, but they were told to be quiet and not spread unfounded rumors", he was told by a few of the Hungarian newcomers. Now these Jews learned that the truth was far more frightening than the stories they had been told. Chaskel attempted to help them adjust to the camp conditions; among them were Hungarian rabbis and scholars. "You couldn't tell from looking at anyone who they were", he told me. "After all, we were all with shaven heads and no beards." Nevertheless he soon identified the rabbis and attempted to place them together so that they could at least be among their own for prayer.

Throughout the year, Chaskel used his connections to help prisoners in Buna. He took ill and emaciated prisoners off work rosters send them to Eisler for various "operations" on their feet, head or the like which never took place, while giving them time to recuperate and eat better food. When he heard of an upcoming selection at the infirmary Eisler would get these prisoners out immediately, even if they were still too weak to stand on their feet. "It was amazing where we found the strength to do certain things", Boruch Merzel remarked in his memoirs regarding one time when my father had sent him to the hospital for recuperation from foot sores but Eisler warned him of an upcoming selection, forcing him to leave and stand outside and walk upright to show the Nazis that he was healthy. "The pain was so excruciating that I was sure I was going to pass out, but I managed to do it and stay alive."

One of the main things that kept the prisoners in Buna alive was their solidarity and mutual assistance and the knowledge that they would never betray one another. This feeling of solidarity received an abrupt shock in October 1944 when three prisoners in the small Buna resistance move- ment – Nathan Weissman, Janek Grossfeld and Leo Diament – were betrayed and caught by the SS while making contact with Polish parti- sans. For six weeks they were tortured in Auschwitz's infamous block 10 but refused to break. Finally they were sentenced to death.

Diament's younger brother Freddie was one of the young boys in Buna who my father had tried to protect. He, too, had been instrumental in the small Buna underground movement as he worked as the Nazi commandant's personal servant, allowing him to eavesdrop on conver- sations and pass on information to his brother in the resistance. But there was nothing that anyone could do to save the three prisoners. As the younger Diament could not bear to witness his brother's execution my father and another friend, Siegfried Halbreich, who worked in the camp infirmary, arranged for young Freddie to be with Halbreich in the infir- mary until the hangings were over. On October 10, 1944 the three were hung in front of the entire camp as an example to all of the fate they would meet if they would try to escape. Leo Diament was the last of the three to be killed. Just before the hangman pulled the crate from under his feet he shouted out to the other prisoners: "Courage comrades. We are the last victims. Long live liberty!" Elie Wiesel describes the incident in his book, remarking "that night the soup tasted of corpses".

By January 1945 Chaskel was one of the older prisoners in the camp in terms of both age and seniority. He was already over 41 years old and had been in Buna almost since its construction. He could also gauge subtle changes taking place around him which led him to guess that the Russian forces were advancing and that the Germans were planning to evacuate the camp. He was correct. On the afternoon of Wednesday January 18, prisoners working in the I.G. Farben factory were marched back to Buna. All afternoon and evening they remained at the *appellplatz*, being counted for hours while standing in the snow. Eventually they were sent back to their barracks. Very few of the prisoners could sleep that night; it was obvious that their fate would be sealed within a short time.

The next day all prisoners were told to appear at roll call with their blankets. Early in the morning those able to walk were marched out of the camp towards the main road and from there westward. Most were in rags. Some marched in wooden clogs or torn shoes with rags tied around them. As they continued on their journey they were joined by thousands of prisoners from Auschwitz-Birkenau and from satellite camps; guarding them were hundreds of SS men whose numbers swelled; marching prisoners back into the Reich was undoubtedly better than being sent to the Russian front. All in all more than 63,000 starved prisoners set out from the various Auschwitz camps on the death march of January 1945 into the unknown.

Chaskel and his comrades marched long into the night, faltering and holding each other to keep from falling. He recalled: "It was freezing cold. I put one foot in front of the other until I could no longer walk. At that point two of my comrades picked me up, one on either side, and continued marching while holding me up until I regained my strength." All saw the fate of those who collapsed at the side of the road or in the middle of the procession – a bullet in the head or a beating from an SS man followed by a bullet. Just as he had saved his comrades lives over and over, now they held him up and kept him from falling throughout the long night's march. After walking in the snow for over 24 hours the survivors of what was later called "The Auschwitz death march" reached the Silesian town of Gleiwitz where they were allowed to rest. There was no place for them to lie down; the few empty barns were already packed with prisoners. Many collapsed in the snow where they were standing and slept, some freezing to death after surviving the inhuman march.

Chaskel wondered about the fate of those prisoners left at the Buna infirmary, unable to work. Had they been killed by the SS on their way out of the camp? Only later did he learn that they remained in the deserted camp for over a week, until liberated by the Soviet forces on January 27th. Among them was Primo Levi.

That night Chaskel learned that the next day a number of transports would be taking the prisoners deep into Germany and one would be heading towards Buchenwald. "Better the devil we know", he stated, and came to Boruch Merzel, Artur Poznansky and a few friends from Buna, asking if they wanted to join him on this transport. While some like Poznansky decided to join, Merzel declined as he hoped to hide in Gleiwitz and be liberated by the Soviet troops. He was sent to Germany on a different transport, and ultimately liberated in Bergen Belsen only three months later.

Part III Buchenwald

In his diary, *"As a Human Being in Buchenwald"*, Avraham Gottlieb, a young Polish Jew who Chaskel would soon meet, described camp life during those days: "Every few days transports of inmates reach Buchenwald from different camps. How pitiful is the state of the new arrivals! The Auschwitz inmates were in transit for nine days, on foot and by open boxcar, with 130 people sandwiched in each car. Many froze to death . . . food was distributed only three times . . . many corpses were removed from the cars and many are ill. The healthy are painfully thin. They have no flesh on their faces or bodies, they walk slowly on unsteady legs and die, daily they die."

Chaskel's transport arrived in Buchenwald where he was greeted by many of his old comrades and particularly those who he had placed in the "training commandos" in 1942. "I couldn't believe that they were still alive", my father recalled. "It was miraculous, seeing people after more than two years who I had helped get into the locksmith and electrical commandos and were still alive." The "old Buchenwalders" caught up with their friends about the events of the two and a half years during which they had been separated, and were given privileged treatment and accommodations.

Many things had changed in the camp during the previous years including in the role of the administration. As the Germans knew that they were losing and war and their forces were retreating, they paid less attention to the internal situation in the camp and left the inner administration more and more to the high-ranking prisoners. There was more religious freedom for those who wanted to *daven* but many of the younger prisoners who Chaskel had known before being deported to Auschwitz were no longer interested in religion. "It was understandable", he recalled. "Several years in a Nazi camp with a communist inner regime where it was dangerous to be religious had turned many of them apathetic towards *Yiddishkeit*."

During the death marches Buchenwald had become a refuge for invalids and sick prisoners from other camps who the Nazis had dumped at the camp's gates. Invalids were sent to the newly established *kleines-lager* (small camp) in Buchenwald, where barracks had been erected to accommodate the sick, locking them up with insufficient medical treatment until they died. At some point there was a call for medical help in the *kleineslager*. Chaskel recalled how his instinct to help his fellow prisoner was still alive. "I was among those who volunteered to work there with the sick prisoners. How could I see this happen and not try to help them?" Within a short time he also volunteered to work in the *revier*, as the Buchenwald hospital was called, cleaning the barracks and washing the sick inmates while trying to give them the little medication available to ease their pain. Day turned into night and night once again turned into day and the weeks passed almost without Chaskel realizing it. "I would spend my days in the *revier* and the *kleineslager* and would go to my own barracks only to sleep." On his way outside he would notice the bombers who flew over the camp towards the front which was getting closer every day.

Passover came at the end of March. For the first time in his entire five and a half years in Nazi camps Chaskel managed to trade his bread for flour from which he and a few friends could bake matzo. "Who could have believed it", he remarked. "There we were, huddled around a fire in a distant part of the camp. We could almost hear the Allied guns booming in the distance, and we were baking matzo for a seder, hoping to be liberated before we would use them."

As the holiday came to a close there were rumors that something was about to happen in the camp. These rumors were confirmed on the bleak day of April 3 when hundreds of Jewish inmates were shipped off from Buchenwald to an unknown destination. Such transports became a daily occurrence, punctuated by the approaching American artillery fire, which could be clearly heard throughout the camp. "We lived in daily hope of being liberated by the Allies", Chaskel recalled. "Some prisoners placed large signs reading SOS, BUCHENWALD in the camp's empty lots, hoping that they would be spotted by American planes bombing the area." And indeed they were.

Chaskel described those days: "We hoped that something will happen. A load of bags, sacks and cartons with food were dropped about the camp so we were that aware that the signs had been noticed." Transports out of the camp increased. At the time Buchenwald had approximately 52,000 inmates.

Nightly, the camp inmates fell asleep to the sound of the approaching American artillery fire. On the night between April 10th and 11th, Chaskel and the remaining inmates were able to discern the sounds of machine-gun fire, a sure sign that the front was moving even nearer. Sometime that night an order arrived from Berlin that the camp should be evacuated the next morning. Those prisoners who could not walk were to be shot on the spot and the entire camp was to be set on fire. It was especially emphasized that no inmate should be allowed to fall into Allied hands alive.

At dawn, before this plan could be carried out, many inmates including Chaskel, decided to go into hiding. Hearing shooting coming from the watchtowers, he took refuge in a man-sized sewage pipe where he hid for the entire day until emerging to freedom. Sometime during the morning the Germans left the camp and for a number of hours the communist underground took over Buchenwald. My father recalled the shouts he heard at about four p.m., when the first American tanks arrived. Fearing that it was a cruel trick, he and other prisoners nevertheless decided to take their chances, rather than rot in their hiding places, and slowly they emerged, embracing one another. From every corner of the camp the prisoners could hear the announcement over American loud-speakers – *"Ihr seid frei"* – You are free. After almost two thousand days in Auschwitz and Buchenwald, Chaskel Tydor was once again a free man. How? *Bihasdei Hashem.*

The five and a half years that my father spent in Nazi camps changed his life in many ways. He went in as a husband, father, brother and son and came out a widower and orphan. When he was taken away to prison in September 1939 he was a wealthy factory and homeowner. When he was liberated from Buchenwald 68 months later he owned nothing but the disintegrating concentration camp uniform which he was wearing at the time. One of his eyebrows was slightly higher than the other, the result of a blow that he had received at the beginning of his stay in Buchenwald. One shoulder was lower than the other; the result of the cement sacks that he had to carry during his first weeks in Buna. He had seen mankind at its worst and human kindness at its highest levels. He went through experiences which made many turn their backs on G-d and religion but in spite of the despair that he underwent at various stages, in the long run, his faith only became strengthened by these experiences.

Decades later he would try to explain to me how he could remain a believer after everything he saw and experienced. To do so, he explained, one has to learn the true meaning of Psalm 73, one of those that he used to recite in camp during his moments of despair. As verse 22 states: *"Va'ani baar velo eida, behemos hoyisi imoch"* ("Then foolish I am and igno-rant, I am as a beast before thee"). "There are times when one can not understand the evil surrounding us. At those times we almost lost our minds, like animals, looking for self preservation at any price and not looking towards the future. And yet, only when we reached that kind of despair could we truly understand the simple meaning of belief as the next verse continues: "*Va'ani tomid imoch, ochazto biyad yimini*" ("But I shall be continually with three, Thou hast held me by my right hand"). So it was with me. I hoped and prayed that we would all survive, but only when I reached the depths of despair after hearing that most of my family had been killed did I stop thinking, knowing that the only way that I could continue from day to day, would be to believe that I feel G-d's hand holding mine. No intellectual explanations of faith could comfort me. Only a simple belief that if G-d intends for me to live, I shall live, and so I must continue on, helping where I could and making sure that I would never lose my humanity."

It was only after his death, when I began speaking to some of the people he saved during those years and hearing stories about his valiant actions, that I began to realize the depths of what he meant.

5

Geringshof, 1945

When one imagines watershed events, they are often perceived in stark primary colors. Total transpositions after which nothing is the same. This is how many people imagine what the moment of liberation must have been like for the fifty thousand Jews freed from Nazi concentration camps in Germany during the spring of 1945. But it is far from correct. From Ohrdruf, the first camp liberated on April 10 to Stutthof, the last camp captured on May 9, tens of thousands of prisoners found themselves "free", but without many of the trappings of freedom. Everything had changed, and yet so much remained the same.

Certain changes were massive. In one fell swoop the world moved "from darkness to light and from slavery to redemption", as states a prayer recited on Mondays and Thursdays. But the rehabilitation process from that slavery lasted for months, and in some cases, much longer. Camp inmates had to recover from years of physical deprivation, disease and starvation, and the psychological after-effects of their imprisonment often manifested themselves only much later. For many, the ordeals they experienced under the Nazis would affect them for decades to come.

As the survivors gained strength during mid 1945 the Allied moved most of them into Displaced Persons (DP) camps created to house tens of thousands of former prisoners who could not or would not be repatriated. A few thousand survivors moved into "kibbutzim", collective training farms where they prepared for immigration to Palestine. My father was one of the lucky survivors who moved to a kibbutz soon after his liberation from Buchenwald. To be more precise, he was a founder of the first *hachshara* (pioneering) kibbutz created in liberated Germany. "How did you have the strength, only days after your own liberation, to think about such an undertaking?" I once asked him. "When you need to, you find the strength", he answered laconically, belying the toll that the enterprise took on his physical health, of which I only learned years later when writing a book about the kibbutz he founded.

While some chapters of this book describe decades of my father's life, this one covers less than five months, beginning with his liberation in April 1945 and ending with his immigration to Palestine in early September. He often referred to these five months as "the dream", an intermediate period of his life separating his pre-war and wartime existence, from the years during which he rebuilt his life, fortune and family. During those five months he was instrumental in transferring hundreds of orphaned Jewish teenagers, liberated in Buchenwald, to Switzerland and France, forging documents and circumventing Red Cross regulations in order to ensure the group's safe passage. These were also the months where he used every possible contact to trace the fate of his own children, hoping that they indeed were in America. When planning his future he never dreamed that it would include a twenty-three year sojourn in the USA during which he would remarry and raise a second family. After years of just surviving from day to day, these were months during which he could dream, and plan, and hope – proving against all odds that the human spirit is at times stronger than anything which tried to destroy it.

Forty years after liberating Buchenwald, Rabbi Herschel Schacter, then a young American army chaplain, recalled his entry into the camp. "The prisoners looked like walking corpses in striped clothing", he said. Seeing the still-smoking chimneys that contained the remnants of the last camp victims, Schacter approached an American soldier and asked whether there were any live Jews in the camp. Answering in the affirmative he led Schacter to one of the blocks. "I saw pallets with people lying on the lice-infested straw mattresses, people from another planet who stared at me wide-eyed. I shouted excitedly, '*sholem aleykhem yidn: Ihr send frei. Ikh bin a Amerikaner ruv'* ('Greetings Jews: You are free. I am an American Rabbi') and they stared back at me blankly, barely breathing, barely moving. All I could think was why aren't they moving, why aren't they answering me? This was my first encounter with the survivors".

My father's recollections of that evening were somewhat different. When he talked about that day his eyes would light up and his voice would increase in timbre. "It was a *nes*, a miracle. The excitement, the emotions were indescribable." How different than Schacter's description of "walking zombies". Hours after the liberation Chaskel met Schacter and another American army chaplain who would be instrumental in his future, Rabbi Robert Marcus. Each chaplain was surrounded by

105

survivors asking how to get in touch with their relatives or receive messages from them. The chaplains had no answer and could only repeat again and again: "Now you are alive, you don't have to fear any more. For the rest you just have to be patient."

Although most survivors registered that the Nazis had been defeated, in many ways their lives did not abruptly change. If the reality of Buchenwald had being located within the triangle of "sleep", "work" and "food", not all of these parameters changed drastically upon liberation. In most liberated camps inmates continued sleeping in their blocks on the same lice-infected mattresses. For days or even weeks they continued wearing their filthy striped prisoners' uniforms as they had no other clothing. Forced labor had ended but in Buchenwald, for example, there had actually been no forced labor since late January when the transports from the east had arrived.

Food was a problem unto itself. In liberated camps throughout Germany and Austria kindhearted American and British soldiers offered unlimited K rations to former inmates whose shrunken digestive system could hardly cope with more than a slice of bread. My father remembered the incident quite graphically: "The liberators brought us all kinds of delicacies from the army kitchen which had negative results. We had been starving and people did not know limits, many of us got sicker from overeating than we had been before through undernourishment. I tried to get my friends to only eat a bit at a time but many just couldn't stop eating."

Boruch Merzel, liberated in Bergen Belsen, also noted how his survivor comrades devoured the food that the British soldiers gave them, and suffered from terrible stomach pains as a result. He had a different solution. "I remembered learning as a boy that charcoal absorbed gas and so I burned little sticks of wood and ate the charred parts, telling my friends to do the same to prevent the horrible sticky pains that we got each time we ate normal food." Most liberated inmates were not as lucky. In Buchenwald and other camps, hundreds of inmates died of overeating shortly after liberation, having tasted the flavor of freedom for only a day or even less.

One of the first questions my father asked Rabbis Marcus and Schacter was whether there was any way to obtain kosher food for the religious survivors. The only kosher food available was in the American chaplains' personal K rations which they willingly shared with the few Orthodox survivors who asked, but what they did have in quantities was leftover matzo as it was only a week after Passover. My father recalled: "They brought us boxes and boxes of matzo, that was all they could give us and

they gave us everything they had." Some of the matzo was used immediately, the rest was kept for *Pesach sheni* (the "Second Passover",
commemorated a month after Passover), when one could eat both leaven
and matzo. For most of the survivors, who had not been able to eat matzo
on Passover that year, the ceremonial eating of matzo on *Pesach sheni* was
a symbol of their freedom and redemption.

Apart from kosher food there were souls that had to be nourished. A
week after liberation, aided by religious camp inmates, Rabbi Schacter
organized a festive Friday evening service. While liberated prisoners from
various countries had prepared flags, sung national anthems, and initiated
international gatherings, the Jews of Buchenwald had no opportunity to
express any ethnic or national identity. Now they had a chance to do so.
The prayer service, held in the "exercise hall" (formerly a large punishment hut) which could hold more than a thousand people, quickly turned
into a huge demonstration of Jewish identity.

My father recalled the festive atmosphere, the hut packed with Jewish
survivors and the improvised platform from which Schacter led the
prayers: "It is impossible to describe the excitement of both the observant and the nonobservant survivors who, for the first time since the war,
were able to openly and fully identify as Jews. This was my first public
Shabbos prayer in almost six years. Everyone shed a lot of tears; it was
almost like a Yom Kippur service. Many of us felt that this marked the
beginning of a new life for us. Where would this new life take us? It was
too soon to know." We have no visual record of that event but a month
later, on May 18, when Schacter held Shavuot services in Buchenwald,
a US army photographer captured the scene. My father appears in the
fourth row on the right side of the picture wearing a dark beret and a
black jacket, his face partially hidden by the man in front of him, his large
dark eyes visible in what is still a very thin face. At the time he was recovering from a severe bout of typhus sweeping the liberated camp that had
almost claimed his life.

Before that, however, my father would organize two operations
which had a long lasting impact on hundreds of young survivors. When
Buchenwald was liberated the American troops found approximately
1000 Jewish children hidden in the camp. Chaskel, along with a small
group of survivors, helped care for them after liberation. Turning to the
two American chaplains, he and Leo Margulies emphasized that the children should be removed from the camp as soon as possible to recover in
more normal surroundings. Marcus and Schacter contacted the Geneva
office of the OSE (Oeuvre de Secours aux Enfants), a European Jewish
relief organization, and arranged for the children to be moved to

Switzerland and France. The group going to France accompanied by Rabbi Marcus left without great bureaucratic difficulty; among its members was the sixteen year-old Elie Wiesel who had lost his father in Buchenwald shortly before the liberation.

When it came to the Swiss group the situation was more complicated. Sometime in May representatives of the Swiss Red Cross arrived in Buchenwald and announced that they would temporarily transfer 500 youngsters up to age sixteen to Switzerland to be educated for a profession. Chaskel and Leo Margulies knew that they did not have that many Jewish children in Buchenwald and therefore planned to include as many older teenagers as possible and even a few men in their early twenties who needed urgent medical care. The Swiss, however, had planned for every eventuality. Chaskel recalled ironically: "Just as the Swiss were not particularly hospitable to Jewish refugees during the war, now they decided to use all of their Swiss precision and love of order and regulations to make it difficult for the young survivors to find refuge there after the war."

The Swiss representatives decided upon a selection process to ensure that no survivors over sixteen would be included in the group. All children were to undergo a medical exam by a French Red Cross doctor and a Swiss Red Cross nurse. After they would be approved as being under sixteen and in decent health ("And how exactly could anyone be in decent health in Buchenwald in May 1945?!" my father heatedly interjected), each child would receive a card signed by the doctor and assigned a number. Only children with signed cards and numbers would be allowed to board the train to Switzerland. If there would not be enough Jewish children, the Swiss nurse stated, she would make up the missing numbers with Ukrainian children from a nearby camp.

Chaskel and Rabbi Schacter found a solution to the problem. "A number of these registry cards 'disappeared' from the Red Cross office courtesy of the good offices of the Rabbi's driver Haim Schulman and myself after the Rabbi had made sure to find the key to the office. I knew what the cards looked like and found some in the room. The Rabbi had obtained a red pen because the doctor had signed the cards with a red pen, and I practiced his signature until I had it perfect. All night long we sat in the office and made out Red Cross cards which I signed with the doctor's name until we filled the quota of 500. We put in names of young men far beyond sixteen and even those over twenty who looked youngish and we decided to take a chance. It was a good night's work", he concluded with mirth.

In spite of the three's ingenuity, they did not take into account the lengths to which the Swiss Red Cross nurse ("an anti-Semite in her own way", in my father's words) would go in order to assure that not a single survivor over sixteen would join the transport. He recalled: "The nurse was furious when she saw that we had the full quota. She said that it was impossible and she wanted to check the boys out one by one. They examined each boy's card as he entered the train and couldn't find anything wrong with the cards, but as we were afraid that some of the older 'boys' would be too tall or look too old, they entered the train through the back way."

There was still more to come. "When the train was full the nurse gave an order to hold up the train while she and the doctor re-examined the boys. We gave a warning shout to the older boys and as the nurse and doctor moved from car to car they jumped out of the windows, running ahead to the cars that had already been examined so that she wouldn't find them." Finally, after checking and re-checking the transport's papers, the nurse informed Rabbi Schacter that she knew that something was afoot, but as she was unable to prove it, she reluctantly signed the necessary documents. Only then was the group, accompanied by Schacter, allowed to leave for Switzerland.

Nevertheless, as Chaskel later learned, the nurse had her revenge. When they reached border control she informed the Swiss guards to closely examine each member in the group and reject anyone even slightly suspected of being sixteen or older. Rabbi Schacter recalled: "Here they could no longer escape and 91 of the group were not admitted into Switzerland. I contacted the Jewish Agency office in Paris, told them about what happened, and within hours they had permission from the French government to be admitted to France."

I used to joke with my father that he had missed a great career as a forger. "It was only the first time that summer that we did such things, but not the last", he answered. "Reb Herschel would regularly forge documents for survivors during those months, stating that they were either older or younger than they really were in order to include them in various transports leaving Germany." From the way the two men would laugh about these incidents one could almost forget the seriousness of the matter, but one sentence from Rabbi Schacter put it all into proportion. "We were saving lives", he said "pure and simple. The conditions in the liberated camp at the time were such that it was *pikuach nefesh* ('a religious question of life or death') to get anyone who could out of Germany to somewhere with decent food and living conditions."

Before his short-lived trip to Switzerland, Rabbi Schacter was busy with another, more personal request from Chaskel, helping him find out whether his children had indeed been rescued to the United States. At Chaskel's suggestion the chaplain wrote to Rabbi Leo Jung, a German Jewish Orthodox rabbi who was now the spiritual leader of The Jewish Center on Manhattan's upper west side. Jung placed a note in the German language American-Jewish newspaper, the *Aufbau*, asking Manfred and Camilla to get in touch with him in order to receive news of their father but he received no reply. Schacter refused to give up. Penning an insistent reply, he wrote about Chaskel: "He is an unusually fine man and devoted Jew who has suffered under the cruel heel of the oppressor for over six years and I certainly hope and pray that you will be successful in locating his children for him. I am trying to do all I can for all the tragic remnants of our people, but I do have a special interest in this man." Schacter also suggested that Jung contact Rabbi Joseph Breuer, to whom he had also written, who might know something about the children's whereabouts.

Everything in life depends on timing. On the morning Schacter's letter arrived, Rabbi Breuer had received a letter from Yosef Greiver, Chaskel's brother-in-law in Palestine, giving him the children's address and asking him to care for them. Rabbi Breuer included the information in his response to Schacter, asking him to send his best regards to Chaskel of whom he wrote "I know [him] very well and estimate [esteem] very highly", and to also give him Greiver's address in Jerusalem. At the same time, Rabbi Jung's note in the Aufbau was answered by Chaskel's first cousin, Ida (Tennenbaum) Theilheimer, in America since 1940, who had been in constant contact with Camilla and Manfred after their arrival in late 1941. Ida immediately penned a message to Chaskel and enclosed notes from Camilla and Manfred who had visited her over the weekend. Almost delirious with joy to learn that his children were alive, Chaskel wrote Ida and Paul his first post-war letter: "The world has become so empty and shrunken around me . . . the children ask about their 'Mutti'! I can only console them. Where do I get my courage from?" Writing about the fate of his family in Poland and his hope to travel to America, he ended with a request to send mail to him through Rabbi Schacter. "The Rabbi is the most noble person that I have ever gotten to know with a warm Jewish heart, every moment ready with advice and help to give. He has restored my soul."

Chaskel's words to his cousins were somewhat misleading. He indeed wished to "travel to America", as he wrote, but only to collect his children and bring them to his true destination, Palestine. This was connected to Chaskel's second post-war endeavor, the creation of "Kibbutz Buchenwald". During the days following the camp's liberation younger

110

survivors would often roam the countryside or cadge a lift to nearby Weimar, returning to the camp towards evening. Although it was perfectly normal for them to desire physical freedom after years of captivity, things were not that simple. Chaskel explained: "Among many of the young people this new freedom has been used for all kinds of questionable purposes. People would take revenge on the Germans by going into stores and houses and emptying out whatever they could take. Whoever was materially interested used the goods to start black market businesses. Then there were those who lost emotional control and did all sorts of things which I don't even want to mention." In his delicate way my father was referring not only to the visits to nearby villages to secure food, but to the revenge-seekers who looted German stores, harassed Germans in general and even violated young German women in their desire to wreck havoc on the local population.

This behavior bothered him greatly as it did a number of the older survivors with whom he had gone through the latter part of the war, and particularly those who had protected young people in Buchenwald. Whether originally Zionist or not, by the end of the war many saw their future in only one place, the Jewish homeland. Noting the behavior of many of the survivors and the development of the black market in Buchenwald, Chaskel and the others feared their destructive effect upon the camp youth and approached Rabbi Schacter with a plan. We have a two-pronged problem, they stated. "We want to remove our young people from the camp so that they won't become morally influenced by what is going on. At the same time, many of them want to go to Palestine as fast as possible. Is there a way to start a training farm for them outside of Buchenwald to remove them from these bad influences and where, at the same time, they could prepare themselves for immigration to Palestine?"

The decision to approach Rabbi Schacter was not an arbitrary one. Ever since Buchenwald's liberation, the young, single, and extremely caring rabbi had become a problem solver for the liberated Jews of Buchenwald. Schacter took every query to heart which earned him a reputation as a savior among hundreds of homeless, indigent survivors. At one point, his immediate superior, an anti-Semitic Irish Catholic priest, even tried to remove him from the camp in order to halt his helpful activity among the Jews. Schacter knew that the key to the future of the young Zionist survivors was in the hands of the G-5 division commander who oversaw the civil administration of the occupied territories and he made it his business to speak to him about it in early May. He recalled: "One evening I cornered him outside of headquarters and began a heart rendering appeal to him about moving some of the young people into a more wholesome environment." Unfamiliar with the ins and outs of the Jewish DP problem the colonel replied that he didn't see why the Jews of Buchenwald were causing so much trouble and could not be repatriated to Germany and Eastern Europe. "At that moment I lost the last of my military naïvéte, and I exploded", Schacter recalled. "I remember shouting at him with tears in my eyes: 'How in the world can you expect these concentration camp survivors who went through all the Hells of Hitler, to now return to Poland, a land saturated with Jewish blood?'"

Both the appeal itself and the sudden breach in Schacter's military discipline touched a responsive chord in the colonel who began searching for a practical solution to the problem so abruptly thrown in his lap. Having investigated farms in the Weimar region, he concluded that the most suitable venue was a large estate in Eggendorf bei Blenkenheim, which had been in Nazi hands during the war. All that remained was to inform the Zionist group in Buchenwald of his decision and hand the estate over to their care. That was done in a meeting that Rabbi Schacter orchestrated in the middle of May, when the colonel informed the astonished survivors that the estate would be ready for their group by the end of that month.

I often wonder what enabled my father and his friends to consider such an undertaking. How did they differ from the majority of survivors who required a long period of recuperation after years of deprivation and suffering? All were still suffering from malnutrition, trying to overcome illnesses contracted during their years of forced labor, and all were on the emotional roller-coaster of hope and despair as they waited to hear if any family members had survived the war. Their post-war activities were not necessarily the result of their naturally activist or dynamic personalities – in fact, my father was the quietest of the group – but appear to be a continuation of the care that they had shown for young Jewish prisoners in Buchenwald during the war. That care, combined with a burning desire to reach Palestine as soon as possible, were channeled into a unique enterprise – the creation of a *hachshara* kibbutz, the first to be established in Germany during the years after the war.

On Sunday June 3, 1945 a group of eleven pioneers from Buchenwald moved to the Eggendorf farm, their new home until leaving for Palestine, or so at least they thought at the time. A brief tour apprised the group that they had "inherited" some cows, horses, oxen, pigs, wagons, fields, a garden, fruit trees, a two-storey house, a broken tractor and an inoperable car. The transportation problem was settled by "borrowing" a tractor from the camp, but the shortage of food and workers was not as easily solved. Ultimately the kibbutz at Eggendorf, which did not yet have a name, would be supported by organizations involved in feeding the survivors: the American army and later UNRRA – the United Nations Relief and Rehabilitation Administration.

Chaskel was not part of this group, nor did he reach Eggendorf until much later that month, shortly before the pioneers would be forced to move. By the time he joined his friends at Eggendorf the *hachshara* was fully functioning and had close to 80 members. Some were from Buchenwald, others came from Bergen Belsen; a number of women had come from a women's camp near Leipzig and some from camps as far as Hamburg. While the *hachshara* grew on an almost daily basis, Chaskel lay in the hospital in Buchenwald burning with fever, victim of the typhus epidemic that swept the camp during the weeks before and after the liberation. For days on end as Chaskel hovered between life and death, Leo Margulies did not leave his side, reciting psalms to help his friend. Rabbi Schacter, too, played a significant role in Chaskel's recovery. Margulies had begged him for large doses of vitamin C which would hasten Chaskel's healing process and Schacter "borrowed" oranges – a practically unobtainable luxury – from the army PX in order to supply the semi-conscious survivor with the necessary vitamins. My father recalled: "When I awoke from my sickness I saw two things, Leo Margulies sitting at the end of my bed saying *tehilim* and an orange on the small table next to me, something I hadn't seen in years." Only later did he learn the story of the orange and what his friends had done to keep him alive.

Although Chaskel's recovery was surprisingly rapid he nevertheless was forced to remain in the Buchenwald hospital for several weeks during which the group moved to Eggendorf and began setting up the *hachshara*. To pass the time during his forced bed-rest my father began writing down notes from the war period regarding his experiences. "But I no longer have them", he remarked to me when I expressed a desire to see his writings. "After the liberation I asked Reb Herschel for a pencil and paper and began writing down my thoughts, but when I became ill they must have gotten lost. While I was recovering, and later in the kibbutz I tried to continue. I wrote down all sorts of notes and thought, some of the things that I had discussed on the occasional Shabbat afternoon walks in Buchenwald, *divrei* Torah (words of Torah) and the like, but I didn't find them worthwhile to retain, maybe it was a mistake."

Sometime in June Chaskel was finally well enough to join the group at Eggendorf. The survivors there were a mixed batch, some religious, others secular, and they lived in the two buildings, three or four in a room. People came and went. There was no official membership, little organized activity, and apart from the personal level, no collective discipline with regard to any public observance of Shabbat or kashrus. Chaskel recalled: "There was not much work done because the majority of the people there had the attitude of 'What? Are we going to work on this cursed German soil ("*verfluchte deutsche Erde*")?' There were actually very few tasks, there has been a small stock of cattle to take care of, cows to milk, and then there were about 300 pigs and no one had any idea what to do with them."

It appears that my father had only a partial picture of the kibbutz tasks, possibly because he was more of a liaison with the authorities – the American army, the Jewish Brigade from Palestine, UNRRA – and dealt little with the daily running of the kibbutz. From entries written in the collective kibbutz diary it appears that there were a number of agricultural tasks that had to be carried out in Eggendorf. The problem was the survivors' lack of agricultural experience. As most of the young men and women had spent little time on a pre-war or wartime *hachshara*, they had an abstract collectivist concept of Jewish labor but lacked practical agricultural training. In view of the necessity of milking the cows, pruning the trees and preparing for the late summer harvest, the *chalutzim* were forced to overcome their repugnance for their German neighbors and employed local workers to operate the farm.

The group decided to adopt the name "Kibbutz Buchenwald", recalling their origins and delineating the collectivist-Zionist nature of their undertaking. Speaking at the Kibbutz's founding party, Rabbi Schacter stated that although the kibbutz was composed of both secular and religious members, he hoped that they would not fall into the trap of factionalism and let ideology divide them. Writing in his personal diary, one of the secular kibbutz members, Avraham Gottleib, marveled at the fact that Schacter, a Rabbi, was not forcing all of them to be religious, and noted the kibbutz's leitmotif of cooperation and unity transcending pre-war political and religious particularism. "Each person is free to imagine the way of life that best suits him and the ideological viewpoint he sees as most correct. And at the same time, he says that we should organize our life together in a democratic fashion with . . . secular Jews showing tolerance for religious Jews and the converse."

At the same party Rabbi Schacter informed the *halutzim* that according to the Potsdam Agreement, Thuringia – the area where the kibbutz was located – was to be turned over to the Russians in a few weeks' time and it was therefore vital that they move west in order to remain in the American zone. This announcement radically altered daily routines at Eggendorf and the group shelved all future plans in order to find a rapid solution to the problem. Chaskel remembered the moment that even the most skeptical members realized that they had to move fast. One day towards the end of June a German-speaking Russian General arrived at Eggendorf from the direction of Buchenwald. The General was surprised to see a group of young Jews operating an agricultural farm and greeted them with the words "Comrades, aren't you glad that we are arriving soon?!" Luckily he didn't expect a reply.

Chaskel was a man of action. That evening, he and two of the other kibbutz founders made plans to head for Frankfurt, Chaskel's hometown, to seek a solution. There were a number of former Nazi camps in that area and Chaskel had heard they contained a sizeable number of survivors who might be interested in going to Palestine. The three were fully aware of the difficulty to obtain transportation and appealed to Rabbi Schacter to accompany them to the regional commander in Frankfurt in order to explain the urgent need to move the kibbutz. Unable at that time to get away, Schacter placed both his army jeep and his driver, the indefatigable Haim Shulman, at their disposal.

The evening before their departure Chaskel, Moshe Zauderer and Victor Hirshkowitz, prepared a list of possible alternatives to Eggendorf. The potential sites included a former training farm belonging to the Bachad (*Brith Chalutzim Datiyim*, League of Religious Pioneers) movement at Geringshof. No one knew whether the farm was accessible and they decided to proceed directly to the American military government in Frankfurt in order to tender a formal request. The three set out, accompanied by "our friend Haim", as they called Schacter's driver, choosing a route that took them through the Fulda district north of Frankfurt, where the Geringshof farm was located.

"It was as if something was drawing me there", my father recalled. "Suddenly I said to the other men 'let's stop and see what happened to the Bachad camp before going on to Frankfurt', and so we did". With a sense of daring expectation, the trio entered the offices of the major of Hattenhof, the closest village to Geringshof, asking him to accompany them to the farm. Dismayed at the request, the mayor hemmed, hawed and refused to accompany them to the farm, claiming that Geringshof was not under his jurisdiction and that it belonged to a *volksdeutsche* family, ethnic Germans.

My father refused to give up and the three set out for the offices of the American military commander in Fulda, Lieutenant Finkelstein, a Jew and former Chicago lawyer. Chaskel had a letter of introduction to Finkelstein from the military governor in Weimar and a letter from Rabbi Schacter explaining about the group and asking the governor to give them every support possible. At their request, Finkelstein checked the records concerning Geringshof and following a brief telephone conversation, confirmed that it was indeed owned by a German family that had fled the Russians. Warming to the occasion, the governor immediately dictated a letter to the village major, designating the farm as henceforth the exclusive property of the Jewish community of Hattenhof. He concluded his missive with a clause to the effect that the bearers of this letter were this Jewish community's official representatives.

Haim now chauffered the "representatives of the Hattenhof Jewish community" group back to Hattenhof where they presented the mayor with the letter. Left with no alternative the village mayor reluctantly accompanied them to the farm to oversee the meeting with the German tenants. From this moment on, matters progressed rapidly, far exceeding their wildest dreams. Chaskel recalled their exceptional reception at Geringshof: "You can just imagine it, a *volksdeutsche* with his whole family. At first he wouldn't let us in but when he saw the order he had no choice. We went in and looked around, not far from the main building there was a woodshed, I can't even remember what caused me to be interested to go towards it but when we opened it we noticed *gvilim*, Torah parchments between the wood. The *volksdeutsche*, I can still remember the look on his face, shook his head as if to say, 'What are you looking for here'? I myself could not even find the words to talk to him. We threw out all the wood, collected the parchments, brought them together and held them together and left the wood for him to clear up. When it was cleared out we noticed on one rear wall of this woodshed written in German script with white crayon *'wir werden wiederkehren'* – 'we shall return', which apparently was the last will and testament left by the remaining members of the farm before their expulsion. We continued our survey of the estate and decided that we must 'redeem it' by putting down our temporary roots here until our *aliyah* to Eretz Yisrael."

Throughout my youth I heard many tales about Kibbutz Buchenwald, but when my father would tell this story his eyes would shine with a special light, which I could only imagine was a reflection of what his eyes must have looked like when he saw the parchment and then the words written on the back of the woodshed in Geringshof. A sense of closing a circle which had been left abruptly and painfully open in the middle of the war; a hope of continuing the tasks that had been begun by that last group at Geringshof, desperately preparing for a life in Palestine in the middle of the war and hoping against all hope that they would eventually make it there. Who knows what happened to that last group of *halutzim*, how many of them survived the war after their deportation?

But my father and his group from Kibbutz Buchenwald who had managed to survive would take up that challenge. They would eventually make it to the shores of the Holy Land, not only for themselves but for all of those who had preceded them at Geringshof and did not have the chance to fulfill their dream.

The *halutzim's* transfer to Geringshof was a story in itself. The move began on Saturday afternoon, June 23, when UNRRA placed vehicles at their disposal. Chaskel and thirteen other members, mostly Orthodox, remained at Eggendorf and planned to join the group the following day. At dawn, the group took a last tour of the farm and then someone came up with an idea: Buses are good for transporting people, but not a farm. Instead of leaving all the livestock for the incoming Russians, why not at least take the horses with them? "So we hitched four horses to two wagons and took a splendid journey through Germany – through Erfurt, Gotha, Eisenach", one of the adventurers recalled. "I remember the castles we passed; I even purchased picture postcards on the way. The roads were filled with wandering DPs, Germany was bombed out, people wandered – Germans, Russians – and we, we traveled by wagon for four days."

Upon their arrival the travelers immediately notice the poor conditions at Geringshof, particularly the lack of beds and food. The first group had taken blankets and equipment from Eggendorf but they had little food. For the newcomers in the second wave of arrivals, this contrasted sharply with their experiences during the journey. While on the road, they had reported each evening to the local village mayor who had provided for all their needs, from a place to sleep to a shoeshine. Here, even basic necessities were lacking.

That same day, two of the more adventurous remounted their steeds in order to secure supplies for their friends. One was Avraham Gottlieb who later wrote in his diary: "We must have suffered from wanderlust. We suddenly remembered that before the move we had brought two sacks of flour to the mill and decided to go and fetch them." Things were not so simple for the team of *halutzim* who dared to venture back to the Soviet occupied area. Gottlieb continued: "From the time we reached the mill and until we managed to rent a car the Russians appeared. They showed no interest in us, and we preceded westward until we were stopped by American soldiers. We returned to the nearby village in order to cross the border there. A chase began with the Americans only a few meters behind us. But they didn't send us back and we managed to bring a carload of flour back to Geringshof".

Hearing these stories from my father it was hard to realize that he was

117

talking about concentration camp survivors who had still been almost *musselmen*, slaves under the Nazis, just seventy-five days earlier. "Where did they get the courage to do this?" I would ask. "How could they pick up and travel two days back to Eggendorf after they had just arrived, and all to pick up a few sacks of flour?" "Everything was surrealistic", my father answered. "People had this great need to move around after years of having been confined in camps. Not only our people, all the survivors. Actually it was unnecessary, the military governor of the area eventually provided us with everything we needed. But some of the young people had to move, to feel that they were free, to get something out of their system. And of course, no one stopped them."

The desire for freedom notwithstanding, in order to run a *hachshara* kibbutz which numbered close to 80 young men and women, the group had to put together some sort of schedule and administration. At a first meeting the *halutzim* decided that the kibbutz would be administrated by a six-member council which would represent the broad spectrum of views on the kibbutz and that they would elect Chaskel as the *Rosh Hakibbutz*, the kibbutz leader. Initially, Chaskel refused to accept the position as he had learned that his two children were living in Rochester, New York and he intended to travel to them as soon as possible. However the kibbutz members insisted, stating that he would bring the members to Palestine and could then continue on to his children.

"I agreed under two conditions", my father recalled, "that one could do what one wanted in one's own room, but there would be no public Sabbath desecration, and that everyone would respect the other's background and our only ideology would be to live together in peace." The group agreed. Kosher food was a different problem. Since the liberation the army had occasionally provided the survivors with ham, the only form of meat available at the time and the secular survivors were loath to give up this treat. As in practice there were only twenty or so orthodox members on the kibbutz, and the other members were unwilling to give up their meat, the small group decided to limit themselves to dairy as it was impossible to obtain kosher food or keep a fully kosher kitchen.

At first glance, Chaskel's altruistic step – his willingness to delay his reunion with his children in order to see the kibbutz to Palestine – seems incomprehensible. "How could you postpone seeing your children by even one day?" I asked him. His answer was a practical one. "The truth is that postwar restrictions on travel from Europe to the United States were delaying the reunion as much as my sense of obligation to the kibbutz. And as it was my ultimate intention to bring the children to Eretz Yisrael, I figured it best to first have a foothold there and prepare their future home."

Chaskel's longings for his children found a vicarious outlet in a relationship that developed with a young survivor, Yehudit (Itka) Harash. The thirteen year-old Itka who had come to Geringshof with a group of girls from Bergen Belsen was the sole surviving member of her family from Lodz. Her resemblance to Camilla brought Chaskel and Itka together and a close relationship developed between the two. Chaskel unofficially adopted her as his daughter while she saw him as an authority and a paternal figure combined. Itka recalled, "I remember how difficult it was for me to call him 'Yechezkel' at first, as that was also my father's first name. I used to address him respectfully as 'Herr Tydor' until I became accustomed to the idea that using his first name was acceptable."

As the group's first week at Geringshof drew to a close, Chaskel decided that it was important to hold a festive and proper Shabbat dinner for the whole group to set the tone for the future. He recalled: "Of course it had to be a dairy Shabbat. We got rolls from town brought in from Fulda and in a world which speaks about *cholov yisrael* (milk under religious supervision) and *pat akum* (bread of non-Jewish origin) our activities seem ridiculous. For us it was enough to find a bakery which didn't use lard. Anything more at that time was impossible to demand. We sang *zemiroth* and told stories, and our Friday night *Oneg Shabbat* became well known to all. People would come from all over the area to participate, members of the Jewish Brigade, American soldiers, everyone."

In his capacity as *Rosh Kibbutz* Chaskel served once again as liaison with all visitors and with the local military administration. Lieutenant Finkelstein in Fulda was extremely helpful to the group as was Rabbi Schacter who would visit them on a regular basis, bringing supplies and information. Other visitors included officers from the Jewish Brigade who admired the group's Zionist spirit and organization and attempted to assist them in every way possible.

Like almost all survivors, when Chaskel was liberated his only possession was the concentration camp uniform that he wore. Even after he was given some basic clothing he had almost no personal possessions as he refused to join the looting expeditions from Buchenwald after liberation. He recalled. "I had no watch of my own and always had to ask what time it was, until one of the Jewish Brigade asked 'Where is your watch'. When I said 'I don't have one' he took off a sort of steel watch and gave it to me. I was not used to such behavior and I took it with great hesitation." The entire group was taken to Fulda where they were given basic personal possessions: clothing, hairbrushes and combs, toothbrushes and toothpaste. "That was the first time I had a taste of a German war product", my father told me. "It tasted awful, like chloroform. Nu, I didn't have much pity on the Germans who had to use it", he concluded. Eventually he also was given a black briefcase, some writing pads, pens and colored pencils.

In addition Chaskel and the other Orthodox kibbutz members managed to obtain a number of religious objects from members of the Jewish Brigade who visited Geringshof. "We got a few pair of *tefilin* which we shared among us. I had *tzitzit* (a ritual fringed undergarment) but no *yarmulkeh*. We all used caps, and I had a *tanach* (Bible). Later we even had a daily *minyan* although we didn't have a *sefer Torah*." After my father's group had left for Palestine the second group of survivor-pioneers who took over the farm at Geringshof indeed found a *sefer Torah* in one of the attics, a last remnant which the final wartime group of *halutzim* had hidden before being taken away by the Nazis in 1943.

Apart from the agricultural tasks, daily life in Geringshof was fluid. Everyone got up when they wished. There were study groups on both secular and religious topics but also a lot of free time when people would talk, reminisce and try to help each other work through their wartime experiences, or obliterate their memory. Although there was factionalism among the kibbutz members, it was more obvious between the groups of German origin as opposed to those of Polish origin than between religious versus secular. Being a German-speaking Jew of Polish origin, Chaskel managed to smooth over many of the difficulties and there was no parallel to the partisanship between Zionist versus non-Zionist or secular versus ultra-Orthodox that led to fistfights in some of the DP camps at that time.

My father's lack of partisanship was a major factor in his being chosen as the kibbutz's representative with the authorities. He took the task quite seriously and was proud to serve as Kibbutz Buchenwald's representative at the first Jewish survivor's conference which took place in Munich in July 1945. The conference opened on July 25, 1945 at St. Ottilien, a former Benedictine monastery not far from Munich which was an assembly center for Jews from the surrounding areas. Convening at eight p.m., discussions continued without interruption for eleven consecutive hours, until the following morning. Among the ninety-four exhausted delegates were five from Kibbutz Buchenwald led by Chaskel.

As kibbutz leader Chaskel addressed the plenum. "Each group spoke of its problems and maladies," he recalled. "Then it was my turn to represent a group that had taken the initiative to leave the camp, to live in a healthy environment in preparation for *aliyah*." Chaskel spoke of the fact that many people in the camps had resolved when they were liberated not to work anymore, feeling that the world owed them compensation for all they went through. "Our outlook has been a different one. What the world owes us they can never pay. But in order to become constructive human beings we realized that we had to build our own society, not to let others build it for us. In light of our success I suggested that others take advantage of the fluid situation to 'appropriate' confiscated estates while it was still feasible."

Despite the successful precedent of Kibbutz Buchenwald, Chaskel's words fell on deaf ears. Representatives of the London-based orthodox Va'ad Hatzalah (Rescue Committee) opposed this idea most vociferously, contending that if large numbers of Jews were removed from the camps, it would create the misleading impression among the Allied governments that they no longer needed to deal with the DP question. Nor were the Zionist organizations anxious to implement Chaskel's suggestion at the time. Fearing that by founding additional kibbutz training farms the survivors would take root in Germany, the Zionist organizations preferred to see their sense of dislocation as a useful tool for shaping world opinion in favor of a Jewish state. In other words, in the minds of the leaders of the Zionist movement, the survivors' immediate needs had to be sacrificed for the common good.

"I was a fool to think that someone would actually listen", my father once remarked. "Everyone was out for their own interests and no one was really thinking about us, the survivors. We were just tools for everyone. For the ultra-Orthodox, for the Zionists. They were all the same. Sometimes they seemed to forget what we had gone through and that first and foremost they should try to solve our immediate problems. I tried to explain and I wasn't the only one, but no one listened."

Meanwhile, Chaskel and the members of Kibbutz Buchenwald were interested in promoting their own greater good, which they saw in one direction only: making all efforts in order to reach Palestine as soon as possible. At one point, the group's members even considered leaving Germany to present themselves to the Palestine Office of the Jewish Agency in Paris and demand immigration certificates. Hearing the group's plan when he visited the kibbutz, Rabbi Marcus, who together with Schacter had been a staunch supporter of the *hachshara*, asked the group to wait two weeks until he would hand deliver a letter that they would write to this effect to the Paris office.

Historical circumstances favored the *halutzim*. The week that Rabbi

Marcus was in Paris the Jewish Agency office received a visitor from Palestine, Eliyahu Dobkin who was the assistant head of the Jewish Agency's immigration department. Succumbing to pressure from Marcus, Dobkin agreed to grant the kibbutz seventy immigration certificates remaining from the prewar reserves. Ultimately the kibbutz received eighty certificates at which point it faced a dilemma. As Avraham Gottlieb wrote in his diary, "We have eighty immigration certificates but our kibbutz does not have eighty members." In order to both fill the number and ensure that the *hachshara* would have a continuation it was time to turn to various Zionist groups among the DPs and encourage them to join the kibbutz. Two kibbutz members, Arthur Poznansky and Simcha Dimant, were dispatched to the newly established Hechalutz pioneering Zionist center in Bergen Belsen. Poznansky had been connected to the pre-war Zionist movement and soon after his return to Geringshof, a group of *halutzim* from Bergen Belsen, mostly members of his former wartime *hachshara*, joined the kibbutz. The group not only augmented the numbers of Kibbutz Buchenwald members; it also sowed discord among them. Claiming that they were veteran *halutzim* as opposed to most of the Kibbutz Buchenwald members who had not been connected to the Zionist movement before the war, they and not the original kibbutz founding group deserved to use the immigration certificates.

"Those poor certificates", my father recalled ironically chronicling the never ending saga of the immigration passes. "It appears that we were never intended to use them. First there was a scene with Dobkin who gave us the certificates but suggested that it would better serve the Zionist cause if we would remain in Germany. Then there was the demand from the Bergen Belsen Hechalutz office that we return them in protest, and finally, the request that we grant them only to Zionist movement members." How did the group react to the attack on their only venue for leaving Germany? "Some of us paid no attention, some laughed, others got angry." "And you?" I asked. "I became worried."

The increased politization of the newly appended group indeed alarmed Chaskel who decided to attract additional members from elsewhere. For that purpose he traveled to Frankfurt while another member made overtures to a group of young women from the ultra-Orthodox Poalei Agudath Israel movement who wished to go to Palestine. The young survivors, aged eighteen to thirty, were hesitant to join the *hachshara* and finally delegated two of their members to investigate and report on life at the kibbutz.

"The girls arrived at Geringshof during the second week of August and I met with them immediately", Chaskel recalled. "One of them, Rochel Shantzer, poured out her heart about the difficult situation which they were going through and how the group of girls, all former teachers and students of the Bais Yaakov movement in Galicia, had managed to keep together during the war. I invited them to come to us for a Shabbos." Shantzer and another young survivor, Rivka England, came to visit the kibbutz over a weekend. "You could see that they had a very good Jewish background and it was hard to calm them down, they spent much of the day in tears. As it was summer we learned a chapter of *Pirkei Avoth* and spoke about Jewish ethics, morals, mutual assistance and solidarity. The girls listened, participated and finally asked us to make space for their group in our kibbutz."

The girls returned to Bergen Belsen and brought a large contingent of Orthodox young women back with them to Geringshof. But in spite of Chaskel's good intentions, religious clashes with the secular majority ultimately caused many of the ultra-Orthodox to leave the group and found their own ultra-Orthodox *hachshara*, Kibbutz Chofetz Chaim near Zeilsheim, the second *hachshara* kibbutz to be established in liberated Germany.

Chaskel now began preparing the veteran group for immigration. On short notice the outgoing group packed its belongings and on the evening of Sunday August 26 Chaskel turned over the farm to the incoming group. After hours of speeches and dancing the farewell party reached its climax at midnight when the entire group stood in a circle watching a swastika burn in a symbolic act of spiritual revenge.

Meanwhile, Chaskel was still deliberating how to get 112 veteran kibbutz members into Palestine on only 80 certificates. The group had managed to board the train on a false headcount as a Jewish Agency representative had been responsible for the transport, but this would not help them board the boat in Marseilles. When they reached Marseilles they were in for another surprise, the group was only allotted 78 certificates and not 80. The morning after arrival the group was to board the S.S. *Mataroa*, an aging British ship. After consulting with Jewish Agency functionaries from Paris, Chaskel and the others decided on a strategy. "I was one of those who only had two suitcases but others had big bundles of things that they had 'liberated' from Germany, 'the spoils of Egypt' and they needed porters to carry it on to the ship. So those who would have been under suspicion have been appointed luggage carriers to bring the loads on board and they disappeared on the ship and thus the surplus has been absorbed and boarding went without problem."

The *Mataroa* was transporting more than a thousand Jews who had come from Switzerland, Belgium, France and Germany. Among them were David Frankfurter, who had assassinated the Swiss Nazi leader Wilhelm Gustloff in 1936 and Rabbi Robert Marcus traveling in his capacity as the World Jewish Congress representative. Chaskel remembered the ship as "a big transporter" and the conditions as very crowded. "There were a sizeable number of British soldiers on board and only a few rooms were available which were given to the girls. Most of us got hammocks swinging on the deck and inside. I slept on deck which wasn't bad as the weather was very warm." When I pressed my father for more details about the actual journey he added: "One ate what one had and what one could eat. We had a sporadic *minyan* which was hard to put together." Not recalling for a moment that I was speaking to a man who four months before had been a concentration camp inmate, I asked whether the physical conditions on the trip had been problematic, for example whether mosquitoes had bothered him. He laughed out loud at the thought and answered me with very uncharacteristic humor which gently poked fun at what he thought was a ridiculous question. "I don't remember any mosquitoes," he answered, "but if they existed then, believe me, they are no longer alive."

The trip from Marseilles to Haifa lasted from Monday to Saturday during which the behavior of many passengers disgusted both the Jewish Agency and World Jewish Congress functionaries. The young men repeatedly attempted to gain entry to the women's cabins while the young girls, according to one account "went only with the sailors, sponging off them". Both functionaries spent most of their time policing the ship in an attempt to instill order. In the midst of the general atmosphere of licentiousness, the Kibbutz Buchenwald group was a notable exception, eliciting praise from all.

The last two days on the ship were Rosh Hashanah, the first ones in six years that Chaskel had spent as a free man. He recalled: "We had two, maybe three *machzorim* so we *davened* with a *minyan*." On the morning of the second day the passengers saw the Carmel mountain range rising from the mist. Tears of happiness welled up in many passengers' eyes and the group began to sing "Hatikvah" as the boat docked at the Haifa port in the early afternoon. Despite the fact that it was both Shabbat and Rosh Hashanah when one must remain on board ship if one has been in transit beforehand, the Orthodox passengers were forced to disembark because the *Mataroa*, being a military transport, was about to leave immediately for Alexandria. Chaskel continued: "The Rabbinate in Haifa sent someone to say that we were permitted to leave the ship and those who don't want to leave the port can remain on the pier in Haifa until the end of the day." There was also no longer a problem regarding the fact that the Kibbutz members numbered more than their allotted certificates. He continued: "The British wanted to get rid of us. They had no interest to count those coming off the ship and relied on the fact that we had already been examined in Marseilles. As for those British on land, as there were Jewish employees at the pier, no one gave us problems with the certificates."

"How could you just sit there at the pier for half a day as if nothing had happened?" I asked my father, "after all, you had been waiting for this moment for so long." He answered with a small sigh, as if it were impossible to explain that after rushing to get to Eretz Yisrael for so long, once his feet touched its soil, he was no longer in a hurry. "If we had already waited for so long, we could certainly wait a bit longer. So we waited for the holiday to end. We sat there, entertaining each other, and finally it was time to *daven maariv*. We were surprised that the stars came out at seven in the evening and not at eight or nine p.m. as in Europe. Then we boarded the buses and traveled to Atlit to join the other members. That night a single emotion dominated our thoughts, that we had finally reached the end of our wanderings. Now we found ourselves at the end of a road that also marked the beginning of a new life."

Of all the incidents that my father spoke of to me regarding the immediate post-war months, one seemingly innocuous one stands out in my mind. At a certain point in Geringshof the American military commander had presented him with writing pads and pencils and just as he had done immediately after liberation; my father once again wrote down some of his experiences from the war years which for reasons he could never fully explain to me, he again decided not to save.

From incidents such as this I began to realize how complex my father's relationship with his wartime past really was. He obviously wanted to remember and note things down for future generations, and yet when the time came for him to do it, he would always stop in the middle and even backtrack, as one can see from his constantly making and then discarding his postwar notes. Was it that he feared seeing his experiences and thoughts written down in black and white? Could it be that as he did not know his children's fate at the time, he feared that he would have no one to leave these memoirs for? But if this was true, it didn't explain why he was equally reluctant to have me interview him about the subject thirty years later, when he had both children and grandchildren who would want to know about his past. Even then I didn't realize that this behavior was an important clue to understanding his psyche. Children, even adult children, remain children and often have difficulty trying to conceptualize their parents' ways of reasoning and behavior into a mirror of their psyche, fears and coping mechanisms.

It was only years later, when I began writing the story of his life, that I realized how this behavior was all part of a pattern that went much deeper than my father's wanting or not wanting to detail his wartime experiences. On the one hand, his bonds with his *chaverim* from camp or even with the members of Kibbutz Buchenwald were forged in steel. An example was Chaim Tyson, seven years older than my father, who he met in Buchenwald at the beginning of the war. The two men were transferred to Buna together in 1942 and ultimately returned to Buchenwald where they were liberated. Tyson's wife Gretel was a Gentile who had converted to Judaism to marry her husband and after his imprisonment in Buchenwald she publicly renounced her Judaism to the Nazis, ostensibly reverting back to her Christian origins during the war. In practice, however, she was only doing it as a cover for her real activities, which was saving as many Jews as she could. Throughout the war years she hid all the *Sifrei Torah* of their Schwabian town in her attic and was personally responsible for them being returned to the Jewish community after the war. Following the liberation Tyson returned to his wife in Germany while my father immigrated to Palestine and later to the United States, but the two stayed in touch across the ocean. Years after my family moved to Israel in the 1970s and long after Chaim's death, Gretel Tyson continued to visit my parents on her frequent trips from Germany. My mother once joked with my father that the only reason he became friendly with Tyson was because their names were alphabetical. But he would always tell her that this was "nonsense" and reminded her that she could never truly understand the kind of bonds that were formed "there".

Yet with rare exceptions, when my father moved into a different stage in life, people from his past were usually the ones to seek him out and not vice versa. When he would meet them, there would always be laughter and tears but many of these later meetings were chance ones, and my father would rarely initiate such reunions. In certain cases where he found himself in close proximity to people from his past, such as his sister's fiancé who survived the war, instead of looking to connect with him, he attempted to avoid the meeting.

"But why?" I asked my mother when I heard this story from her long

1 The house at 10 Biala street in Bochnia, 2007.

2 The garden in Bochnia, 2007.

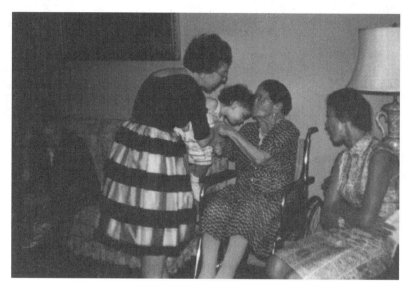

3 *Tante* Chatsha's 90th birthday, July 30, 1961; the author, Judith (Judy), is baby being held for her to kiss.

4 First cousins Ida Tennenbaum-Teilheimer (left) and Ida (Yehudis) Tydor (right).

5 Menachem Mendel Tydor.

6 Yehuda Leib Tydor.

7 Trees in the Bochnia house garden, 1988.

8 Mecha Scharf Tydor.

Israelitische Realschule in Fürth.

Schlußzeugnis.

Tieder Chaskel,

Sohn des _Kaufmanns Löb Tieder_ in _Frankfurt a/M._

R. Bezirksamts _____ geboren am _8. Okt. 1903_ zu _Bochnia, Galiz._

israelitischer Religion, der seit _Sept. 1916_ die Israelitische Realschule in Fürth besucht, hat sich als Schüler der VI. Klasse am Schlusse des Schuljahres 19_20/21_ der Schlußprüfung unterzogen und diese Prüfung bestanden.

Seine Leistungen waren [...]
[...] in der schriftlichen Prüfung in allen Fächern
vorzüglich. [...]
_[...]_
_[...]_
_[...]_
_[...]_

Im einzelnen lassen sich seine Kenntnisse nach den bei der Prüfung und während des Schuljahres gegebenen Proben folgendermaßen bezeichnen:

in der Religionslehre . . . . _sehr gut_

in der deutschen Sprache . . . . . _sehr gut_

in der französischen Sprache . . . . _sehr gut_

in der englischen Sprache . . . . . _sehr gut_

in der Mathematik . . . . _sehr gut_

in der Physik . . . . _sehr gut_

in der Chemie mit Naturkunde . . . _sehr gut_

in der Geschichte und Geographie . . _sehr gut_

in der Handelskunde . . . . _sehr gut_

im Turnen war er . . . _[...]_

Fürth, den _18. April 1921._

Der Kgl. Ministerialkommissär: Der Direktor:

[signature]   _Prof. Dr. Feuchtwangler_

9 Chaskel's matriculation certificate from the Israelitische Realschule in Fuerth, 1921.

10 Chaskel (second on left, seated with arms crossed) with classmates and teacher in Fuerth; probably taken in 1917.

11 Chaskel and Bertha's engagement picture, Bochnia, 1927.

12 Bertha and Camilla in Frankfurt.

13 The building where Yehuda Leib, Esther and Ida Tydor lived in Sienkiewicza Street, Lodz.

14 Yosef and Yaffa Greiver and their two older sons, Meir (right) and Gad (left).

15 Moshe (Moni) and Rosi (Roni) Wexler outside their Jerusalem home in 1973.

16 Camilla (back row left holding a white and black torch) in the Breuer Kindergarten.

17 Bertha, Camilla and Manfred in Frankfurt.

18 Chaskel Tider, 1939.

19 Leo and Ruth Margulies in New York with their sons Simcha, Dovid and Eli.

20 Boruch Merzel with his son Alain and daughter Lillian after the war.

21 Rabbi Herschel Schacter holding Shavuot services in liberated Buchenwald, May 18, 1945. Picture from the National Archives courtesy of the United States Holocaust Memorial Museum.

22 Chaskel with Rabbi Herschel and Penina Schacter in Israel.

23 Kibbutz Buchenwald founders. Chaskel is in the back row standing, third from the left.

24 Kibbutz Buchenwald main building at Geringshof.

25 Kibbutz Buchenwald members. Chaskel is in the back row standing, fourth from the right.

26 Gretel Tyson and Chaskel on one of her visits to Israel.

27 Chaskel and Yaffa Greiver.

28 Camilla and Manfred in Rochester, 1945.

29 Manfred's Bar Mitzvah, 1945.

30 Chaskel with Camilla and Manfred, 1946.

31 Chaskel's *Mishmar Ha'am* booklet.

32 Chaskel and Camilla in Israel, 1949.

33 Shirley Kraus.

34 Camilla Maas's wedding photo. From left: Manfred, Leonard, Camilla, Chaskel and Rabbi Herschel Schacter.

35 The Maas children: Brian, Curtis, Kenneth and Lisa.

36 Itka Charash's wedding to Yisrael Berkowitz. Bertha Kraus stands second from left; to her right is Yaffa Greiver; Yosef Greiver stands third from the right.

37 Chaskel, Manfred and Frances, August 1956.

38 The Tidor grandchildren: Bruce, Laurie, Chaskel and Janice; Judy is in the right back row.

39 Chaskel and Shirley Tydor wedding portrait.

40 Chaskel and Shirley family wedding portrait: Standing from left: Max Kraus, Bernie Easton, Bertha Kraus, Tanta Chatsha, Ida Theilheimer, Jacob Theilheimer, Paul Theilheimer. First row from left: Camilla, Shirley, Chaskel, Manfred.

41 Chaskel and Shirley leaving for their honeymoon, Nov. 14, 1957.

42 Chaskel and the Hammer family in Jerusalem. From left: Aura, Rina, Reuven, Chaskel, Rachel and Aliza Hammer.

43 Chaskel in South Dakota, Autumn 1958.

44 Chaskel Tydor in Rapid City, South Dakota.

45 Shirley in South Dakota wearing the "wink".

46 Shirley Tydor and Alex Harris.

47 Chaskel, Shirley and Judy making *Havdalah* at the close of the Sabbath.

48 Chaskel (far left) and Buna Survivors with President Dwight D. Eisenhower.

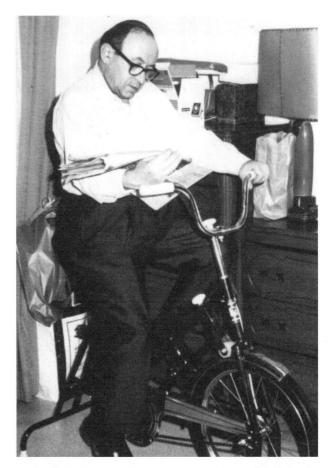

49 Chaskel reading the paper on his stationary bicycle.

50 Left to right: Camilla, Chaskel and Judy in Israel.

51 Chaskel and Manfred in Florida in the late 1980s.

52 Chaskel and one of his Israeli granddaughters.

53 Chaskel and Shirley on ther 35th wedding anniversary.

54 Chaskel Tydor and Israeli granddaughters (summer 1992).

55 Chaskel Tydor tombstone, back view.

פ"נ

ר'יחזקאל שרגא
בן ר' יהודה לייב הלוי
תידור

ומצא חן ושכל טוב
בעיני אלוקים ואדם

א' מרחשון תרס"ד
ז' אדר תשנ"ב
ת נ צ ב"ה

לזכר בני משפחתו
אביו יהודה לייב הלוי
אמו אסתר
אחותו יהודית
אשתו הראשונה ברטה גרייבר
שנספו בשואה

56 Chaskel Tydor tombstone, front view. On the bottom is an inscription stating "In memory of his family, his father Yehuda Leib Halevi, his mother Esther, his sister Yehudis, his first wife Bertha Greiver who were killed in the Holocaust."

after his death. "I can't tell you", she answered. "Maybe it had to do with the fact that he had survived while your father's sister hadn't. All I know is that he didn't want to meet him and when I asked him why at the time, he never gave me a straight answer and after a while I learned not to ask."

My first clue to understanding the workings of his mind on the complex issue of his pre-war and wartime past came from an incident which occurred in mid July 1945. On one of his trips to Fulda he met a friend from pre-war Frankfurt who said: "I saw part of your library the other day". Startled, my father asked him what he meant. After Bertha had left Frankfurt their vast library was confiscated by the Nazis and was slated to be sent to the Museum of the Jewish Past which the Nazis planned to create in Prague after their victory. Meanwhile, they were stored with other confiscated personal Jewish libraries in a warehouse in Frankfurt where they remained at the war's end.

"I had to be in Frankfurt later that week, and went to the warehouse", my father recalled. "In it I found boxes and boxes of books, I didn't know where to even begin looking for those which might have been mine. I walked around for ten minutes and was about to leave when I stumbled over some half open boxes which contained books from my library, the library which had once been so precious to me. I wandered between boxes of my books in the dusty warehouse and opened a box at random. As we had no *seforim* in the kibbutz I decided to bring back a few *siddurim*, *Chumash* with *Rashi* and a *Midrash Tanchuma*, for the kibbutz. At the last minute I decided to take three more volumes, *Meginei Eretz*, and those, together with the *Midrash Tanchuma* were all that I kept for myself. With that, I left the warehouse, closed the door, and I never went back."

The words "and I never went back" were the underlying leitmotif of the rest of my father's life, at least that over which he could have control. After having lost much of his family and all of his fortune and possessions, at age forty-two he began life almost from scratch. It was somewhat similar to what his family had gone through when they fled Bochnia at the beginning of the First World War, however they could take some money with them and the family remained together. In addition, they had family in Germany who helped them acclimatize during the early period. My father, however, had to overcome his own physical and emotional devastation and forge ahead without any such cushions, at least during the early period after the war. In order to do so, he made a conscious decision to look forward and not backward and indeed that decision had an impact not only on his choices but on his personal identity.

This decision may have been intensified by the fact that during the immediate post-war period, my father indeed felt himself totally alone. He had no idea whether any European friends or relatives had survived the war and he did not yet have contact with those who he knew had escaped before the war such as his brother-in-law in Palestine, his cousins who had found refuge there and in England, or friends such as Moni Wexler and the Breuer family. My father's solitary feeling at the time was epitomized by his answers to a de-Nazification questionnaire of the Allied Military Government of Germany that all concentration camp survivors had to fill out before a military tribunal in order to prove their identity.

After questions asking for personal information, place of arrest, and charges made, he was asked to provide the names and addresses of three reliable persons living in the locality where he intended to go (in my father's case, Frankfurt a/M) who could vouch for him. To this last question he replied laconically "all friends in Frankfurt evacuated or killed". Seven words which contained half a lifetime of personal pre-war connections, all gone up in smoke. Literally.

And so my father decided to go forward and not live in the past. He visited Germany several times after the war, but only for restitution claims or family matters. He never visited Poland, claiming that he would do so only when the last Pole would be ashes. Although he was involved with various charitable endeavors of survivor organizations, he never joined the Bochnia *landsmanschaft* in Palestine, rarely made efforts to seek out people from his past unless they played some kind of a role in his present day activities, and always looked to build and do, to learn new things and create a better future. He realized that he could not be like the two-faced statue of Janus, the Roman god of gates and doorways, beginning and endings, looking both forwards and backwards at the same time. In order to survive and prosper he would have to choose whether he would turn his life into a commemoration of the past or an adventure into the future, and without doubt he chose the latter.

While he would often speak to me about the past it was usually in connection with his parents or schooling and until I came to interview him I heard more about his Holocaust-related activities from my mother than I had ever heard directly from him. His arm bore an Auschwitz number, but I never thought of him first and foremost as a survivor but as an adventurer, a kibbutz founder, a courageous Jew with an inquisitive mind who delighted in learning new things, even in his late eighties. For that reason, it never occurred to me to engrave his Auschwitz number on his tombstone as did many children of survivors and it was only at my husband's suggestion that I added it to the title of this book. To me, he did not choose the identity of a "survivor" but rather that of a builder.

He had built a kibbutz, he re-built a family, he built a new business, and he built a new life in Eretz Yisrael.

Only in his dreams over which he had no control did he live in the past. As a child I remember my mother telling me early in the morning to be quiet as "Daddy had a bad night". When I would ask her what a "bad night" meant, she would say something like, "he had nightmares, he dreamed that he was there, you know, during the war again". I assume it was "there" that he exorcised his demons, that he met up with everyone that he had lost and that he made his accountings. His nights may have been devoted to the past but without a doubt, almost all his waking hours were devoted to the present and the future, to building and creating a new life. This was the life that he would now begin to build after arriving in Eretz Yisrael.

6

Jerusalem — Tel Aviv, 1945 – 1951

How does one feel when a dream comes true? Like many survivors, one of the things that kept my father alive during his years in camp war was his dream of building a home in Palestine when the war would be over. He was indeed one of the luckier ones, being able to fulfill this dream less than five months after his liberation from Buchenwald. If the months that he spent in Geringshof were "the dream", then his arrival in Mandatory Palestine in early September 1945 was certainly the beginning of his new reality.

While still in Germany Chaskel had announced to the members of Kibbutz Buchenwald that he could not remain with them after bringing them to Palestine as he wished to travel to his children in America and convince them to join him in his new homeland. But in order to do so, he first had to find employment and build a financial basis for his family. And he would have to begin entirely from scratch.

Unlike those survivors who made fortunes on the postwar black market after liberation and who left Europe with cash and possessions, Chaskel possessed almost nothing. His two small valises contained a few changes of underwear, three shirts, an extra pair of pants, a *siddur, chumash* and the four *sforim* which he had taken from the boxes of his own library in the Frankfurt warehouse, his briefcase and writing utensils, and a *tallis* and *tfillin* which he had gotten from a member of the Jewish Brigade. The sum total of his possessions was, as he told me, a hundredfold more than what he had possessed five months earlier on the day of his liberation. And this from a man who seven years earlier, before he was deported from Germany to Poland, had practically been a millionaire by today's standards.

At that time, he had been the owner of a successful factory, a car, a spacious apartment, beautiful antique furniture, rare editions of *sforim* and books, electrical equipment, state of the art cameras and a telescope. Attempting to take part of his fortune out of Germany he had converted cash into gold and jewelry which he had tried to send out of the country with emigrating friends. Almost everything had been impounded by the Nazis and only one small pouch of jewelry, sent to Eli Hackenbruch in London, was saved. But he would only learn that much later. "I had nothing in terms of possessions", he told me. "But I had my life, and I had my children. Compared to most European Jews, I was lucky. I was a rich man."

Those riches, however, could not be measured nor would they help him earn a living. Now he was an indigent new immigrant sent with a group of immigrants to a transit camp. Along with the other members of Kibbutz Buchenwald, Chaskel boarded a truck outside the Haifa port which drove southward towards the British detention camp of Atlit. Alighting from the truck all he could see was sand, mud, and rows of shacks surrounded by barbed wire. Atlit had been established in 1938 as a British detention camp for illegal immigrants which in wartime served as a quarantine center for persons from enemy states. Lacking streets, roads, blankets and a central office, it was now the initial collection and distribution point for immigrants from liberated Europe.

The first step in leaving Atlit was to decide on a destination for Kibbutz Buchenwald. As Kibbutz leader Chaskel provided the necessary documents for young and old. He recalled: "Everyone got his 'birth certificate' signed by me, stamped, but then each group member was interviewed by the representatives of three political settlement movements in Palestine: Hashomer Hatzair, the Mizrachi and Poalei Agudath Israel." Hearing what these representatives were asking the teenagers who were to be sent to various boarding schools, he accompanied the youngsters to the interviews to keep them from becoming "political cattle fodder" for the various political parties, secular, Orthodox and ultra-Orthodox alike.

"They wanted to know if the children had been religious so they asked them whether their father had a beard and made *Kiddush* on Friday night and what Friday night was like in their home. I protested these questions as most of the children remembered next to nothing about life before the war. But each of the political movements was looking to make these children their own." After intervening in a number of interviews Chaskel ensured that the children were evenly distributed between the schools depending on their background and personal inclination, some secular and some religious. Itka Charash, who had come from a religious family in Lodz, was sent to Kfar Hanoar Hadati, a religious boarding school in northern Palestine.

Now it was time to find a kibbutz where the older members of Kibbutz Buchenwald could continue their agricultural training before founding their own settlement. After examining a few possibilities Chaskel and Moshe Zauderer decided upon Kibbutz Afikim in the Jordan valley. Functioning autonomously within the Hakibbutz Hameuchad movement, Afikim was ideologically open-minded and willing to accept a mixed group of secular and religious pioneers as they already maintained a kosher kitchen for observant parents of secular kibbutz members.

"It was a very unsettling period", Chaskel recalled. "Every day relatives of various members visited Atlit and one by one kibbutz members decided to join them in Tel Aviv or Haifa and not continue on with the group. But we expected that. I also met for the first time with my family and reminded the group that after I would bring them to Afikim I would leave them there and join my relatives in Jerusalem."

The ten short words – "I also met for the first time with my family" – encapsulated one of the more emotional stories in Chaskel's postwar saga. Although he received his brother-in-law Yosef Greiver's address while still in Buchenwald, Chaskel had fallen ill with typhus and did not write him immediately. Meanwhile, like most Jews in Palestine during the spring of 1945, Greiver anxiously poured over lists of survivors' names being published weekly in the Hebrew press. One time he spied Chaskel's name in the list of Buchenwald survivors. "Yosef began shouting 'Chaskel is alive! Chaskel is alive!'", recalled Yaffa Greiver, remembering how excited they were to learn that someone from the family had survived the war. As soon as he heard that Kibbutz Buchenwald had arrived at Atlit, Yosef traveled to meet Chaskel, initially able to see him only through the camp fence. Soon after they met and made plans for Chaskel to join the Greiver household in Jerusalem as soon as he would complete his task with the kibbutz.

The survivors spent Yom Kippur in Atlit and on September 21, Chaskel accompanied them to Afikim. "We spent a very beautiful Sukkot together and after the holiday we had our first meeting in which I announced that I kept my promise but now it was time to elect a new *Rosh Hakibbutz*. I told everyone that I still considered myself part of the group and that I would be in touch and would visit them very often, which I later did. The entire group took me to the bus stop to say goodbye, it was very moving. Then I got on the bus, waved to everyone and started the next stage in my journey."

From being *Rosh Hakibbutz*, part of a group whose physical needs were supplied by others, for the first time since his liberation Chaskel was on his own. Although he was traveling to his brother-in-law in Jerusalem, it was his intention to become self supporting and begin preparing a home for his children who were still in America. I never asked my father what his first meeting with the Greivers of Jerusalem was like but I can imagine the tears and embraces when meeting his sister-in-law Yaffa, and reconnecting with Yosef who he remembered as a young *chalutz* about to leave Poland more than a decade earlier. As time passed he developed a special relationship with Yaffa, her brothers Zvi and Kalman and their parents, Rabbi Alter and *Rebbetzin* Fruma Meyer. But most of all, Chaskel poured his love into his two little nephews, Meir and Gad, then seven and four.

Yosef and Yaffa Greiver lived in a large apartment on Abyssinia (Ethiopia) street in the center of Jerusalem, near Yosef's travel agency, Patra (Palestine Travel Agency), located on one of the city's main thoroughfares, Jaffa–Chancellor Road. Patra would play an important role in my parents' life, but that would only begin at a later date. Meanwhile, Chaskel was still recovering physically and mentally from all he had been through during the war. At the time he was pale, thin and with sunken cheeks, still suffering the after affects of wartime malnutrition. For years he was plagued with liver problems as a result of his concentration camp experiences and these may have laid the basis for the illness that would cause his death decades later.

The first stage in Chaskel's relationship with his new relatives was putting the past to rest. From Chaskel, Yosef learned about the death of his brother, sister and parents in Bochnia. In his line of business Yosef did not fear travel and he had always been an adventurer; soon after my father's arrival Yosef returned to Poland for the first time since leaving over a decade earlier, in order to look for Greiver cousins who survived the war and bring them to Palestine; one of them, Rivka, an Auschwitz survivor, would later marry Yaffa's younger brother Zvi, becoming a member of the Greiver–Meyer family from both sides. Another young Greiver cousin, Menachem (Mundek), had escaped the Bochnia ghetto and fought with the partisans in the forest. Mundek rarely spoke of his experiences but as survivors, he and Rivka could share my father's wartime past more than any other members of the family in Palestine.

The next stage was to begin to build a life in the present. The Greivers, with whom Chaskel would live for the next five years, were a warm and welcoming family and the children in particular took to their new uncle with delight. With them he could let out his impish streak, but it worked in both ways. Meir Greiver remembered his uncle's bottomless suitcase in which they could always find everything they wanted, and how he and his friends accidentally discovered that his new uncle was ticklish. They delighted in tormenting Chaskel who would run away from them shouting *Dai Sipuki*, Talmudic Hebrew for "enough". The children, who only knew the modern Hebrew expression *maspik* and not its Talmudic equivalent, provided Chaskel with his first nickname in Palestine, *daaysi*, which stuck for years.

Now it was time to find employment to pay his way in the Greiver household and begin building a future home for his children. In late 1944, when Yosef and Yaffa first learned that Camilla and Manfred had reached America, they had wanted to bring the children to them in Palestine. Although they originally wanted at least three children, they decided to wait in expanding their own family in the thought of adopting their niece and nephew. Yosef contacted various American Jewish organizations to begin the process but was told that it would be impossible to transfer his niece and nephew to Palestine as it was in the war zone. Now they were delighted at the thought of Chaskel bringing his children to live with them.

In spite of Yosef's pleas for Chaskel to work with him in his travel agency, Chaskel claimed that he knew nothing about the travel business and that it would be better for him to work elsewhere. He even knew where "elsewhere" was. Within days of reaching Jerusalem Chaskel contacted Moni Wexler, his friend from Germany, who was now a publisher of *seforim*, religious Jewish books. For the next few years Chaskel worked with him in the publishing trade and his papers all list "book publisher" as his profession. When I asked why he made this choice he would usually sigh and change the subject. If I pressed him for an answer, the most he was willing to add was "sometimes it is better not to go into business with family".

In view of his experiences with his brother-in-law when he finally did go and work for Patra, he had little to explain. Yosef Greiver was a charming and generous man, but also a wheeler-dealer similar to his late father and brother. Business connections with a Greiver enterprise could be exciting, eventful, and always provide the unexpected. But they could often be problematic as well. For his first years in Palestine Chaskel preferred something steadier, choosing not to mix business and family. In hindsight, it appears that his choice was correct.

By late 1945 life in the apartment on Abyssinia Street settled into a routine. Chaskel worked daily with Moni Wexler, met friends and acquaintances from Germany who had escaped Hitler before the war, frequently visited Kibbutz Buchenwald members on Afikim and also checked up on Itka who was studying, rather unhappily at the time, at Kfar Hanoar Hadati. He often brought her chocolate to cheer her up, his childhood sweet tooth leading him to believe that if a true solution to a problem could not be found, chocolate, and preferably good bittersweet chocolate, was the panacea of choice. I never remember him without a chocolate bar hidden in a cabinet to be taken out at either a happy or a difficult moment; years later as small children, my daughters remember the ritual of their Zeide dividing up a chocolate bar among them, reminding them never to tell anyone about his giving them sweets between meals.

Chaskel began to build a social circle for himself both inside and outside Jerusalem. The Wexler house became a second home for him and he enjoyed his time with Roni and Moni's three children, Menachem, Ora and Uzi and later their fourth child, Benjamin Zeev, who was born after Chaskel's arrival. Moni Wexler also returned a box of *seforim* to Chaskel which he had sent him before the war, the only part of his enormous library sent out of Germany which actually reached its destination. Thus Chaskel began rebuilding at least one of the physical trappings of his pre-war life.

Other parts of his life, however, were slowly being left behind. Although he made contact with Rabbi Dr. Yitzchak Breuer, founder of Poalei Agudath Israel in Palestine, and received a warm letter greeting him stating "May the Lord grant that from now on you will begin a new period of calm and happiness and you will continue your influence and work for our [political-religious] ideal", Chaskel did not remain in constant contact with the Breuer family after the war. Nor did he have any intention of becoming involved in any political party and evinced little interest in political matters. As he used to say in jest, he had no need to deal with politics as my mother was political enough for the entire family.

Soon after settling his own professional future, Chaskel began to inquire about traveling to his children in America, requiring him to submit numerous affidavits, certificates, proof of identity and other assorted papers to various British and American authorities. The bureaucracy involved was overwhelming and an oversized brown envelope among my father's personal papers is testimony to the hours he spent in various government offices, the dozens of forms that he filled out to receive a temporary travel form to leave the country and enter the United States, the pictures which had to be affixed to a myriad of documents, each filled out in triplicate in the era when office copy machines still belonged to the realm of science fiction.

As a stateless Jewish refugee in Palestine the only documents in his possession when he began his odyssey were his provisional identification card as a civilian internee at Buchenwald signed by the Allied

Expeditionary Force Military Government in Weimar and the entry papers granted by His Majesty's Mandatory Government in Palestine upon his arrival in Haifa. In order to travel abroad he needed a Palestinian Certificate of Identity of which he received two, the first in January 1946 and a second one which replaced it in June of that year. By that time my father had somehow acquired an English name, Haskel – he never told me who had coined it for him – which he added to the German "Heinrich" that he eventually dropped. This was in addition to the paperwork which he submitted to the United States Government to enable to him enter on a visitor's visa. To receive a permanent passport instead of the temporary British ones issued for each trip he eventually applied for Palestinian citizenship which was finally granted in April 1948. Seventeen days before the end of the British mandate and after eight and a half years of statelessness, Yechezkel-Chaskel-Heinrich-Haskel Tydor became a citizen of Palestine and the proud bearer of a British–Palestine passport in which he was listed as a Jerusalem book publisher. Three weeks later, at the end of the British mandate, he and 600,000 other Jews living in the country at the time, became citizens of the State of Israel.

Glancing through my father's earliest passports they appear to be not only personal travel documents but also a reminder of the military and diplomatic history of an era. His first British passport has a stamp stating "Not valid for travel to countries for which a military or Control Commission or other permit is required unless such a permit has first been obtained", alluding to the years during which Germany and Austria were divided among Allied control necessitating special documentation for those wishing to visit. His first Israeli passport still bears the stamp "Good for all countries except Germany", which appeared in Israeli passports until after Israel signed the reparations agreement with Germany in 1952. Even after the war my father was living through a very eventful era, but like many people who were still going through personal upheaval, his stories of that time often did not reflect the events of the period as much as they did his own personal odyssey.

Some during the spring of 1946 Chaskel began making final steps for his first trip to Rochester, New York. Although he was grateful beyond words that his children were alive, the placement policies of the refugee children's organization which had found an American foster home for Camilla and Manfred compelled him to face a difficult situation regarding his children's religious upbringing. While Jewish refugee children in the USA were only sent to Jewish foster families, the means test requiring foster families to meet certain economic and physical conditions excluded most Orthodox families from offering potential hospitality. Few could guarantee no more than two children in a bedroom and even fewer possessed the fifty dollar bond required for each refugee child. At one point during the 1930s the New York office had even informed the immigration department in the central organization of Jews in Germany not to send any more unaccompanied Orthodox children to America as there were almost no orthodox homes in which to place them.

Another difficulty stemmed from the personal prejudices of the organization's chief placement officer, Lotte Marcuse. A former student of political history, philosophy and economics at the Universities of Berlin and Heidelberg, Marcuse had a commendable devotion to duty but was also known for her prejudice against Orthodox Jewish children. When they reached New York Camilla and Manfred's files had been sent to Marcuse for placement. Although Camilla insisted that she and her brother were Orthodox, Marcuse refused to accept that a nine year-old girl who had already been a refugee for two years could remember her family's religious affiliation. She therefore insisted upon sending the children to a family affiliated with the Conservative movement instead of to an Orthodox Jewish family. This was doubly ironic in view of the fact that Rochester, the city to which they were sent, was the only city on the organization's list to which the notation "there are many Orthodox Jewish families willing to take refugee children" had been added. Camilla and Manfred were placed with Sol (Chubby) and Shirley Lapides, a Jewish couple with one daughter, Marjorie (Margie) who was eight at the time. The Lapides family were a wonderful caring family who did all they could for the children. Nevertheless, Marcuse's insistence of not sending them to an Orthodox Jewish family would have repercussions on Chaskel's relationship with his children for the rest of his life.

Religious incongruity notwithstanding, both children rapidly learned English, forgetting the German and French in which they had previously communicated. Camilla remembered much about her childhood and Manfred less; both, however, refused to speak about their experiences with social workers or their foster parents. Manfred found it harder than Camilla to adjust to the Lapides household and he spent a year on a Jewish farm in Spencerport near Rochester, returning to the Lapides family only towards his Bar Mitzvah celebration in the spring of 1945.

It was not easy for the children to reconnect with their father. He was an Orthodox Polish-German-Jewish survivor who had gone through years of horror; by 1946 they were two American Jewish middle class children brought up in the Conservative movement, who only spoke English. The religious overtones of the upcoming meeting frightened them greatly as did the fear that Chaskel would want to take them away from the life they had gotten to know and love in America. A well-meaning Jewish Social Services worker in Rochester with whom Chaskel had corresponded before his visit had only made things worse. Informing the children that their very Orthodox father would be extremely upset with how they were being raised, they should expect "an explosion" when he arrives. She concluded by stating that they would certainly be facing a battle as his only intent was to take them away to Palestine – "that country full of sand, flies and Arabs" – and should prepare for that eventuality.

"I never understood why she told them that", my father would say, his dark eyes uncharacteristically overflowing with tears, showing the depth of his emotions about this sensitive subject. "I was just so grateful to the *Ribono Shel Olom* (Master of the Universe) that they were alive, that they had survived the war. Why did she have to make them afraid of me, of what she thought I would do?!"

Chaskel and his children had time to contemplate the upcoming reunion as he made his way to the United States by boat. The trip took almost three weeks during which the passengers leaving Haifa had time to become acquainted with each other until they reached New York. Chaskel, however, found himself in a unique situation during the voyage which changed his life in many ways. My father never talked much about the logistics of his first trip to America except to mention that the trip had been a long one, unlike the twelve-hour plane flights of today. I finally learned more about his journey by chance, over a discussion we were having about Satmar Chassidim and their attitude towards the State of Israel. When I expressed myself vehemently against the outspoken anti-Zionist attitude of the Satmar *Rebbe*, the late Rabbi Yoel Teitelbaum, my father stopped me with a look. "Do not talk about people about whom you know very little. Although I may not agree with his path, the Satmar *Rebbe* was a Zaddik in various ways." I looked at my father quizzically, not understanding why he would defend the promi-nent Hungarian Chassidic Rebbe who was saved in the famous Kasztner train from Hungary, lived in Palestine for a short time and ultimately re-established the Satmar dynasty in America. In response, my father told me the following story.

"When it became known that I was going to America I was approached by someone in Jerusalem who asked whether I could take upon myself a very important task. The Satmar *Rebbe*, Rabbi Yoel Teitelbaum, would be traveling on the ship and a number of Satmar survivors asked whether I would be willing to act as a *shamus* (assistant) to him during the journey and care for his needs. At first I was afraid to take on the task, but they pressed me to do so and I agreed. For almost three weeks I spent many hours each day with the *Rebbe*, speaking with him, learning with him, seeing him act. He was a *lamdan* (a learned man) and had a great knowledge of Kabbalah although he usually hid it from people. He was a great man. Although we disagreed greatly about the Zionist movement I realized how much of a Zaddik he was. You may not agree with his path nor did I, but never speak of him in the tone you did", he rebuked me. From my father's story I learned yet another lesson in *derekh eretz* (respect); how one should always be careful in referring to great Jewish rabbis even if one disagrees with their ideology.

Just as the children had last seen their mother at a railway station in Frankfurt in February 1939, so they first saw their father at a railway station in Rochester in September 1946. For Chaskel, just reaching Rochester was an event in itself. "The train trip from New York took several hours, and each time we stopped at a town on the way and the conductor would call out to the passengers 'watch your step', it sounded to me as if he were saying 'Rochester' and I would jump up, worried that I had missed my stop". Both children were equally nervous. "I was excited, frightened and apprehensive at the same time", Camilla wrote in her memoirs. Both Manfred and Camilla remembered a short thin man in a grey suit carrying a small suitcase who walked towards them across the platform, enveloping them in a strong embrace. At least one of the children's fears had been put to rest. At first they didn't know how they would communicate with Chaskel as they remembered no German, but he was fluent in English, albeit heavily accented.

Once they reached the Lapides household a small but constant stream of presents emerged from what appeared to be a seemingly bottomless valise. Albums and books about Palestine for the house, more personal items for its occupants and particularly for the children and finally, a beautiful silver bracelet for Camilla, just right for an almost sixteen year-old girl. Yet not a word about religion, observance or lack thereof, of disappointment, plans or dreams. No word of what he or they had been through since their last meeting almost eight years earlier, of the bureaucracy that he had to untangle as a stateless refugee in order to reach America, or any desire to take them back to Palestine. All that would have to wait for the next day, week, month.

"Of course I wanted to take them back with me immediately", my father recalled "But I knew it was impossible. First, because of the paperwork involved. But even before that, we had to get to know each other again after so many years of separation. I knew that to live with me in

Palestine they had to learn more about the religious content of Yiddishkeit which they had forgotten as well as knowledge of Hebrew." In his letter to the Jewish social services worker in Rochester he had stated outright: "Most of my fellow sufferers who survived with me have lost their concept of this world and their faith in the chaos of the last years. This is not the case with me . . . I wish to influence them [Camilla and Manfred] in a positive way to balance the Jewish ideals in contrast to their American ideals."

Chaskel spent part of his visit in New York with friends and relatives, including his cousins, Ida and Paul Theilheimer, and the rest of the time in Rochester with Camilla and Manfred. At a certain point he broached the subject of their coming to Palestine for a visit and eventually the possibility of their returning "home" with him. While Manfred who was less attached to the Lapides household did not veto the possibility outright, Camilla's anxieties over the suggestion grew from day to day and she was not afraid to express them. "I was a teenager and had settled into a life in which I felt comfortable", she wrote in her memoirs. "I did not want to start all over in a new country . . . I had a sense of stability in my life and did not want to make a change." Manfred, although more reticent, was equally concerned. He recalled: "It must have been very difficult for Dad, since he must have sensed that I was afraid that he would take me away from a life I had just adjusted to and cause me to have to adjust all over again. Initially, Rochester and America were a difficult adjustment. I spoke French and German, and no one we were with in Rochester spoke either. I had difficulty adjusting to school. And then Dad comes back into my life with the prospect that I would have to go through the whole experience again in another place."

At some point Camilla stated her fears outright. "Dad, I don't want to go. I want to finish school here." Chaskel accepted her decision with much pain and sorrow, knowing that Manfred would be unwilling to part from her. Manfred on his part was relieved. "I was in familiar surroundings in Rochester and while I had family in Israel, I didn't know them. And my own father was a stranger. While I remembered him, I had been without him for almost eight years."

Chaskel was unwilling to admit defeat. He knew that his plans would have to change but still hoped that he would ultimately convince Camilla and Manfred to join him in Jerusalem. Soon after that first trip he began to plan another visit and obtained a business visa allowing him to remain in America for three months at a time. His next trip was in 1947 when he stayed mainly in New York City, first with relatives and later in a midtown apartment hotel. One of his most poignant reunions was with

Tante Chatsha, his only remaining aunt, from whom he received pictures of his paternal grandparents, father and sister. No pictures of his mother were to be found anywhere.

Camilla and Manfred remembered a few highlights of their visits to New York City, one of which was a visit with their father to the Hayden Planetarium. "Dad was always so knowledgeable about astronomy", Camilla recalled, "it was a high point of our visit with him." Chaskel enjoyed the closeness with his children and used these visits to teach them about both Palestine and Yiddishkeit. But at the same time he felt torn between his love for his children and his love for the Land of Israel. After much torment he decided to return to Palestine in the fall of 1947 but began corresponding with David Crystal, the executive director of the Jewish Social Services Bureau in Rochester, about applying to become a permanent resident in the United States.

"Did you really want to become a permanent American resident?" I asked my father in surprise. He looked at me with a steady gaze. "Do you think that is what I wanted?" he answered, "I wanted to bring my children to me, but I knew that I had to spend time with them in America to convince them that they would have a wonderful future in Jerusalem. And for that I would have to stay for more than three months at a time."

But a war was about to interrupt everyone's plans, the Israeli War of Independence. Soon after Chaskel returned to Jerusalem on November 29, 1947 the United Nations voted to partition Palestine and the countdown leading to the end of the British mandate began. Jerusalem soon found itself under siege and convoys to and from the city were attacked by bands of Arab fighters. Like many middle-aged men past the stage of active military participation, Chaskel joined *mishmar ha'am* (The People's Guarding Force) and was called up for local guard duty. Life in the apartment on Abyssinia street was tense. Yaffa was expecting a third child, Yosef went back and forth to the coast with convoys bringing foodstuffs to Jerusalem and Chaskel was often away guarding the city outskirts. On Friday May 14, 1948, Chaskel did not hear Ben-Gurion's historic proclamation of Israel's independence because he was busy patrolling the city border at the outskirts of Bayit Vegan where the Wexler's lived, an hour's walk from the city center.

Apart from guard duty and visiting the Wexlers, Chaskel had an additional reason for visiting that area during those months. Another friend from Germany, also a former industrialist, lived there and owned a cow. "During the siege of Jerusalem I would often walk to Bayit Vegan and back fresh milk for Yaffa to drink which she needed in her condition and which could not be obtained in the stores because of the siege."

The siege of Jerusalem was not only being felt in the lack of fresh milk. As all foodstuffs were brought from outside the city and the roads were practically cut off, food and even water was rationed. Like the other Jerusalem residents, Chaskel learned that water would be re-used for five things in a particular order. Drinking, washing people, washing dishes, cleaning floors and finally to flush the toilets. Because of Yaffa's impending delivery Yosef moved the family to Tel Aviv but with his various connections, he and Chaskel continued going back and forth to the beleaguered city with food as consular representatives of the Czechoslovak consulate, presenting documents that stated that Chaskel Tydor and Yosef Greiver were bringing presents of food for the inhabitants of Jerusalem from the Czechoslovak people and should be allowed to pass. This state of events continued throughout the summer of 1948 with Chaskel traveling to Jerusalem to bring food and other goods as a representative of the Israeli Air Force. In view of my father's non-existent military participation in the Israeli Air Force, I can only presume that these documents were obtained in some way through various Greiver travel connections.

Meanwhile, in Rochester, Camilla and Manfred anxiously followed the news in Palestine, waiting for word of their father's safety. "There was a short time where we heard nothing from him and had no idea what was happening in Palestine and later in Israel", Camilla said. But by the end of 1948 there was regular correspondence between Rochester and the apartment on Spinoza Street in Tel Aviv where the Greivers now lived. In mid August a third Greiver son – Zviki – was born and Yosef opened up a branch of Patra in Tel Aviv. Chaskel remained in the publishing trade but also began assisting in the new Patra office, thus learning the travel business. This situation continued until he left for his next visit to America two and a half years later.

The move to Tel Aviv began a different chapter in Chaskel's life. With the birth of a new baby life in the Greiver household was livelier but also more crowded than before. The move to Tel-Aviv meant a change not only in geography but in social orientation. Chaskel became closer to Yaffa's parents, aunts and brothers who lived in Tel Aviv and it was her father, Rabbi Meyer, who would write a newspaper article celebrating Chaskel's fiftieth birthday a few years later.

Meanwhile Chaskel had not given hope of bringing his children to the newly founded State of Israel, a hope shared by the entire family in Tel-Aviv. During the summer of 1949 Yosef traveled to the United States to lay the groundwork for setting up a New York branch of Patra and convinced Camilla to visit Israel and see her father. Although she had planned to attend the State University at Brockport and begin a degree in physical education, she agreed to postpone her studies and come for a six-week visit in the autumn of that year.

Chaskel was ecstatic. He finally had an opportunity to show one of his children the beauty of his new country and hoped that the love she would experience from her father, uncle, aunt and cousins would convince her to remain. For six weeks Camilla stayed with them in the apartment on Spinoza street, touring the country with her father and uncle. "It was a memorable trip", she recalled "And both Dad and Uncle Joe did what they could to convince me to stay but I wanted to go to college and become a United States citizen."

With a heavy heart Chaskel accepted her decision and she returned to America. However instead of registering for college, Camilla insisted to her father that she wanted to study secretarial skills and enrolled in a Rochester business school. "I had really wanted to become a physical education teacher but when I realized Dad's financial situation I didn't want to ask him for tuition fees", she said. "What a terribly sad mistake", my father replied when he learned of her true consideration only years later. "I would have done whatever was necessary for her to go to school and pay for college, but she never mentioned it to me . . . how could I have known?" Another set of crossed wires that would change the rest of my sister's life.

As the months passed Chaskel became more and more involved in the travel business, initially against his will. "I knew that Yosef needed help in the business and having been a businessman I did what I could to assist him." But Yosef the adventurer needed more than assistance; he needed a partner in his various undertakings of the time. Through what was ostensibly called the "travel business" Chaskel found himself involved in several adventures involving air travel and connected to the mass immigration to Israel, the largest of which was Operation Magic Carpet in which brought 49,000 Yemenite Jews to the State of Israel between June 1949 and September 1950. One of those involved in providing the transport planes for this operation was another adventurer, a non-Jewish supporter of Israel named James Wooten who became a friend of both Yosef and Chaskel, and would later play a major role in my father's wanderings. One of the best known stories about Wooten involved one of the small airlines that he ran and a deal that he was brokering in South America. In response to the other partner's accusation that the hard-negotiating Wooten was a Jew, Wooten stood up and dropped his pants, showing his negotiating partner physical proof of his being a Gentile. Wooten's non-Jewish background notwithstanding, he was a longtime friend of the Jewish state and a good friend to both my father and Yosef Greiver for many years.

It was during this time that Chaskel was approached by Benjamin Mintz, one of the leaders of Poalei Agudath Israel, asking whether he would be willing to be listed on the party's Knesset list in 1949. Having learned much about Yishuv partisanship during his years in the country, Chaskel feared anything having to do with political strife. He answered Mintz that although he still felt close to the movement he would only run for Knesset if all the religious political parties in Israel would promise to unite on a permanent basis. Mintz could of course not guarantee such a step and thus my father declined the chance to be a member of the first Knesset. I often wonder what our family history would have been like had he agreed to Mintz's request.

Around the same time as Mintz turned to my father regarding his future, another piece of his past fell into place. While he knew the precise date of his father's murder, he had only general information about the approximate dates when his sister was deported and when his wife was taken away by the Gestapo and only knew the season when his mother had died. In late 1948 the Chief Rabbinate of Israel decided to designate the fast of the 10th of Tevet as a memorial day for all those who had lost first degree family members during the Holocaust and did not know their *yarhzeit*. From that time onward until his death my father would observe the 10th of Tevet as a memorial day for his mother, wife and sister and would say Kaddish for them on that date.

Nineteen fifty-one was a watershed year for Chaskel and the beginning of another series of wanderings. Camilla had turned twenty, Manfred was about to finish high school, and Chaskel hoped to convince his son to come to Israel. To do so he would have to spend time with his children. How could he do this and at the same time support both himself and them? The solution came when his brother-in-law asked him to take over the New York branch of Patra which had been managed during its first few months by Lotte Fuld, mother of Palmach heroine Bracha Fuld who had been killed in 1946 during a military operation against the British. Until then Chaskel had been adamant about not working full time with Yosef. As much as he admired and was grateful to his brother-in-law, he knew the dangers of entering into a business arrangement with him. However managing Patra's New York branch would solve his financial problem. In order to provide added incentive Yosef promised Chaskel that after he built up the overseas branch he would not only receive a salary but a portion of the profits; if the branch would prosper Yosef would eventually be willing to sell it to Chaskel who would then have capital of his own. Chaskel gave in and prepared to move overseas for a year or two – no longer – in order to be near his children. It was his fervent hope that he would still be able to convince them, or at least Manfred, to return with him to Israel after that time. Finally applying for the permanent visa to the United States of which he had spoken years earlier, in 1951 Chaskel moved to New York – temporarily in his mind – to begin the next stage in his adventures.

My father's first years in Palestine were punctuated by constant illegal immigration of survivors from Europe, bloody battles between the British and the Jewish underground movements and even between the various underground movements themselves. But his stories of these years never mentioned any of this. Like many survivors and particularly the older ones, he was busy with his own struggles at the time: the battle to rebuild his life after the war, and in his case, the desire to reunite with his children and convince them to join him in Palestine. For much of that period he was traveling back and forth to the United States and even when in Palestine his efforts were focused on maneuvering through the bureaucracy involved in his next trip, earning the funds to cover its cost, and calculating the best ways to convince his children that the Middle East was not the sandy hellhole they feared.

My father belonged to two categories and his stories of that period were a mixture of the experiences of both. On the one hand, he was a survivor trying to piece together a new life. But on the other hand, he was also in his mid forties, a unique generational category among survivors. His age group in Palestine included the small number of older survivors who left Europe right after the war and veteran Israelis encompassing native born and pre-war immigrants. While younger survivors, pre-war immigrants and natives were often intimately involved with defense issues or underground movements, the over-forty generation, to which my father belonged, was usually busy with their daily existence, making a living, raising a family. That could also explain the lack of military tales in his repertoire, other than his reminiscences of *Mishmar Ha'am* guard duty, particularly on the day that the State was established.

Unlike survivors who later spoke of having been silenced when they wanted to talk about their wartime experiences, I never heard such stories from my father regarding his years in Palestine. He was never told by anyone "not to dwell on the horrors". He shared stories from the Hitler era with his relatives, told Yosef and Yaffa about the fate of the Greivers in Bochnia and spoke openly with friends who had gone through the war such as those from Kibbutz Buchenwald.

He was only silenced when speaking about his experiences in Rochester when the head of a Jewish organization said that it was too depressing to hear these stories and he should "better try to forget". As he was a man who looked forward and not backward, he certainly did not usually dwell on the past and put his energies into building a future for himself and his family. But he also learned an important lesson. While in Palestine there was a certain amount of understanding regarding life under the Nazis in general and during the war in particular, in America there was not. By that well meaning but wounding remark he learned that among the American-born everything had to be whitewashed; Americans preferred their stories free of horrors. At least in Israel he never had to hide the fact that he was a survivor, as more than one person suggested to him to do in America during the early 1950s.

When it came to life in Palestine his stories were very down to earth. Although he would always refer to the establishment of the State of Israel as a miracle, his tales were never about the miraculous nature of that event but about the daily nitty-gritty involved in living in Jerusalem under siege. And while he was constantly surrounded by family during that time in his mind he was often alone, working through his own experiences and figuring out his future. The six years between leaving Europe in 1945 and moving to the United States in 1951 were a period of limbo during which he could paraphrase the medieval Jewish poet Yehuda Halevi who had stated that his heart was in the east while he was at the very end of the west. For my father, during the months that he was in America with his children, his heart was certainly in the east. But during the time that he was in Israel a certain part of his heart always remained in the west, with his children.

7

New York, 1951–1957

There is a popular belief in many cultures that events occur in threes. Births, deaths, windfalls, losses, celebrations, tragedies. Karl Marx reportedly stated that the original event is history, the first repetition is a tragedy and the third is a farce. My father would have said that it depends upon your viewpoint. A tragedy is rarely positive but one person's farce is another person's opportunity. Everything depends on your perspective.

So it was when my father moved to New York in 1951 for what he hoped would be a temporary sojourn outside of Israel. This was his third physical upheaval excluding Nazi deportations. As a child he had left Poland overnight to find refuge in Germany. After the Second World War he moved to Palestine with two small suitcases holding all his personal possessions. Now he was starting a new life for a third time, moving to a third continent, once again packing his possessions into two suitcases, albeit larger than the previous two that he had brought to Palestine six years earlier. For him, this second repetition of history was certainly not a farce but an opportunity. An opportunity for *hakoras hatov* (acknowledging kindness), repaying his brother-in-law by managing his New York office for a while. An opportunity to convince his children to move back to Israel with him, or so he hoped.

Patra's New York office was actually a storefront in midtown Manhattan and Chaskel's first step was to put it into working order as Lotte Fuld had left it in shambles. Although he rented a two-room apartment on Manhattan's west side, he actually spent most days and evenings at the office where together with another travel agent and a secretary, he began building up the travel business. Patra's specialty was travel to Israel, and with New York's large Jewish population Chaskel hoped there would be no lack of potential customers for the service he wished to provide. But to do so with his meager staff it meant spending long hours at the office, dealing not only with customers but also with the bureau-

cracy involved in becoming a bona fide member of the travel organizations of at that time.

Despite his hesitation in becoming involved in the family business,
Chaskel's brief encounter with the Orthodox business world during his
previous visit to New York had convinced him that he was better off in
a more general line of work. At the time he had agreed to act as a sales
representative for Moni Wexler's religious publishing firm, and his first
foray into the American-Jewish Orthodox business scene ended in
disaster. At one point he was even involved in a *Din Torah* (religious court
case) regarding the sale of *seforim*. "That was probably why he was willing
to work for Patra and not continue in the book publishing business", my
mother once mentioned.

In his spare time Chaskel reacquainted himself with friends and family
who were living in the United States. The Theilheimer house in Queens
became a second home to him, and he had a special place in his heart for
Ida's children, Bernie and Rochelle. Rochelle was then a young teenager
and Bernie was already in his early thirties, far from being the child who
had visited Chaskel in Frankfurt. Rochelle adored her older cousin and
remembered how Chaskel had bought her an etiquette book for her
sixteenth birthday. Like many immigrants from Germany the
Theilheimers continued to speak German at home and when Chaskel
visited them it was as if time stood still. Language, manners, and even
furniture were all of a different world, something that surprised Chaskel
in view of the fact that his own children were totally Americanized.

Chaskel also renewed his friendship with a number of wartime
chaverim who had moved to New York after the war such as Leo
Margulies, Leo Zeigel, Norbert Wollheim and Ernst Michel. He was
especially close with Jacob Reiss who had been married to his cousin
Freida Klausner. Shortly before the war Reiss left Germany on a visa to
Cuba but was unable to secure one for his wife who was deported and
murdered by the Nazis. Reiss and his second wife Fanny remained
Chaskel's good friends for the rest of their lives. It was in Fanny Reiss's
store that Chaskel had stored the remains of the *seforim* from his short-
lived publishing sales representative venture during the late 1940s until a
fire swept the storeroom and the books became unusable.

Another person who re-entered Chaskel's life was the newly married
Rabbi Herschel Schacter who had recently completed his long military
service. Herschel and Penina Schacter were among his closest friends and
he celebrated the birth of their two children just as he rejoiced when his
wartime friends married and started families of their own. This was my
father's social circle in America, consisting of his few relatives who had

escaped Germany before the war and his *chaverim* who found a post-war haven in the United States. With few exceptions such as the Schacters, the adults in this group communicated in German. Many were Orthodox, most were traditional.

For Chaskel, watching his friends marry and start their own young families was a reminder of his life almost two decades earlier, when he was newly married and beginning his life as a father in Weimar Germany. Now his children were almost grown. Camilla was about to finish business school and Manfred was starting his second year of college, having been encouraged to continue his studies by both Shirley Lapides and his high school teachers. "I was always curious about how things worked so I applied to engineering schools." Manfred was ultimately granted a two-year tuition scholarship from MIT with a contingency for an additional two years.

Similar to what he had done for Camilla a year earlier, during the summer of 1950 Yosef Greiver offered Manfred a free agent's ticket to Israel as a high school graduation present in the hope that he could convince him to stay in Israel with his father. But Manfred asked him to postpone the generous offer as he had a summer job in preparation for college. In the autumn of 1950 he began studying at MIT in Boston, joining a fraternity that offered room and board in exchange for kitchen services. Although he was sorry that he had not yet visited Israel, Chaskel was proud of his son's successes and hoped that he would be able to use the ticket at a later date.

Meanwhile, Chaskel was slowly growing closer to Camilla. Having completed her business studies, to Chaskel's delight she decided to join him in his rented apartment for the first few months of her working life. "I wanted to establish a closer relationship with my father and this was the only way I could think of to do it", Camilla recalled. For close to six months the two lived in the small apartment, getting to know each other as adults. Camilla had no problem with the laws of *Kashrus* as the Lapides family had kept a kosher home and she soon adapted herself to her father's Orthodox way of life while not becoming Orthodox herself. For Chaskel, such a situation must have required a large degree of religious tolerance but he had long learned when to turn a blind eye in order to remain close to his children.

That tolerance was soon to be put to an additional test. Shortly after reaching New York Camilla met a girlfriend from Rochester who had come to the city to study art and had no place to stay. Chaskel and Camilla offered her a home and for several months the two girls shared Chaskel's tiny apartment while the art student showed Camilla and her father a different side of New York. "She introduced us to all sorts of bohemian types that I didn't even know existed", Camilla recalled, "Dad took it all in his stride." Chaskel was content to see his daughter happy; for him it was enough to be able to live with her under one room for the first time in thirteen years.

Just when Camilla was about to return to Rochester to marry her high school sweetheart, another young woman entered Chaskel's life. In early January 1952 Shirley Kraus began working in Patra, first as a secretary and later as a travel agent. The slim, energetic twenty-three year-old redhead had studied languages at college and the travel business was a perfect outlet for her knowledge of Yiddish, Russian, Spanish, French and German. Newly divorced after a brief marriage, she had the time to match Chaskel's never-ending work schedule, and seemed to enjoy the excitement of the travel business.

Although her early job performance must have left something to be desired, causing Chaskel to consider hiring a more experienced secretary, Shirley asked for a second chance and threw herself into the job, making herself indispensable and becoming one of the few people who was capable of deciphering Chaskel's cursive Gothic-German style hand-writing. She recalled how difficult it was to sell people trips to Israel as they were afraid to travel to what they still perceived as a war zone. "I remember telling people 'go to Israel now, you never know how long the country will be around for' and their saying 'well maybe we should see it before it disappears'". It soon became normal for the office to stay open until late and night, and to keep their new secretary happy Chaskel learned of her weakness for éclairs and would bring a few back to the office many an evening to provide fuel for their long working hours.

In June 1952 Chaskel traveled to Rochester to celebrate Camilla's marriage to Leonard Maas, her beau who had now completed law school. Rabbi Schacter came in from New York to perform the ceremony. Camilla and Leonard settled in Rochester where Leonard opened a law practice and Camilla gave birth to their four children, Brian (Zvi) who was followed at three-year intervals by Curtis (Menachem), Kenneth (Nachum) and Lisa (Yaffa), named for Camilla's mother, Bertha. The birth of his grandchildren gave Chaskel tremendous joy, reminding him that in spite of all that the Tydor family had gone through during the war, there was a new generation to continue the line. Busy with work, Chaskel did not travel to Rochester as much as he wanted to but Camilla and Leonard would occasionally bring the children to New York to see their "Grandpa" who would spoil them with love and treats.

Chaskel was equally proud of his son's activities. When he was a sophomore at MIT Manfred was introduced to Frances Fishman, a petite and charming high school senior who was about to begin studying at the nearby Simmons College. Between his fraternity work, lab jobs and summer job at Kodak in Rochester Manfred found time to date Frances throughout their college years and continued to do so while he finished his MS in Engineering at the Carnegie Institute of Technology from which he graduated in 1955.

During the summer of 1954 between his undergraduate and graduate studies, Manfred finally got to use the ticket that his uncle had given him as a high school graduation present and traveled to Israel to meet the rest of his family. Chaskel was no longer there but the Greiver family stepped in and hosted him for several weeks. Now he had an opportunity to spend time with Yosef, Yaffa and his first cousins Meir, Gad, and Zviki, then sixteen, thirteen and six. Manfred recalled a wonderful three-week visit with his family. "They were delightful. I could write a tome about being with them." Yosef in particular still hoped that Manfred would be smitten by the country and would want to stay. "Joe [Yosef] did not want me to leave and kept putting off my departure. I explained that I had a college project which I had to begin for my graduate studies, so he finally made the arrangements for me to go back to America."

Throughout his college years in Boston, Manfred, who retained the more Germanized spelling of the name, Tidor, visited his father in New York, and like his sister before him, he spent time at Patra and got to know the staff including Shirley. Chaskel, who was delighted with his son's scientific bent, enjoyed talking mechanics and astronomy with the young student. Shirley enjoyed her employer's children's visits to New York as they were close to her age, and she would send Manfred packages to college as he had no family to do so. She recalled how they began to correspond: "He used to write me about Franny, saying how much he loved her and how happy he was with her, and I would write back to him and tell him that he was a lucky young man."

As time passed Shirley grew close not only with Chaskel and his children but with the entire Greiver–Meyer clan in Israel. In 1953 Shirley's mother traveled to Israel, joining Yosef and Yaffa Greiver to celebrate Itka Charash's wedding. Chaskel had remained in constant contact with Itka and continued to help support her just as he did his own children. When it came time for her to marry he was unable to leave the United States because of his visa status but asked the Greiver family and Shirley's mother to represent him at the wedding. Even Yaffa's parents, Rabbi Alter and *Rebbetzin* Fruma Meyer, traveled to Haifa in order to bring joy and a family feeling to the young orphan bride.

Later that year Shirley made her first trip to Israel, staying at the Greiver apartment on Spinoza Street. During much of her vacation she helped out in the Patra office in Tel-Aviv. From then on all of her "vacations" to Israel became working trips and she spent most of her free time there socializing with the Greiver–Meyer family.

Shirley's mother grew closer to Chaskel as well. Bertha Kraus would often visit her daughter at the office, noting that Chaskel wore only long-sleeved shirts, presumably to cover his Auschwitz number. One day she came to the office with a short sleeved shirt, and told him to wear it as it was summer and very warm. Although she was only seven years older than he she began caring for him in a motherly way. On Passover, when it was difficult to find kosher food in midtown Manhattan, Bertha would bring home cooked meals to the office and Chaskel enjoyed her Eastern-European Jewish cooking which reminded him of home.

While Chaskel's relationship with Bertha Kraus was relatively uncomplicated, the same could not be said for his relationship with her daughter. Shirley was twenty-five years younger than Chaskel. He was a middle-aged European survivor; she was an American-born woman in her mid twenties. He was an Orthodox Jew, she was a former communist like her father and although her mother ran a traditional home, her parents were cultural Jews and could by no means be called religious. And yet the sparks between them began to fly. Although Chaskel never overstepped the bounds of propriety, he was intrigued by a young woman who was only twenty-five months older than his daughter.

Shirley knew that a chasm of years, experiences, and knowledge separated Chaskel's lifestyle from hers, but she also realized he was her true match. How could she get him to realize that? Slowly she began learning more about *yiddishkeit*, about the various aspects of religious Judaism, and about Jewish history. Chaskel saw the changes in his young secretary and was not blind to the reasons for her behavior and sudden interest in various subjects. But he was not interested in beginning a relationship. For years he had been approached by friends and acquaintances trying to interest him in meeting appropriate women for him to marry; after all Judaism posited that it was not good for a man to be alone and it was long enough after the war for the middle-aged widower to finish mourning and find a wife. Most of the women to which people wanted to introduce him were of his own age, in their late forties or early fifties. Among them was the Bobover *Rebbe*'s sister, who had also lost her husband in the war. Time and again Chaskel gently pushed off meeting these women, and as the calls were often routed through his secretary, many blamed Shirley for his response. She recalled: "People were sure that I wasn't giving him messages when in truth he just didn't respond in the hope that they would give up."

But Shirley wasn't willing to give up. Eventually she let her feelings be known to Chaskel and after great personal deliberation he began to secretly court her, making sure that no one in the office or in his family would find out. Was it only because he was lonely and she was persistent? "Perhaps at first", Shirley answered, "but afterwards it was more than that. He wanted a new life, not a continuation of the one he had in Europe."

In his usual understated way Chaskel communicated the seriousness of his intentions to Shirley. She recalled: "Once we sat in a coffee shop, and he ordered a piece of cake for us saying 'We love *mohnstrudel* (poppy-seed cake) don't we?' Only then did I realize that he felt the way I did. Actually I hated *mohnstrudel* but it was years until I would tell him!" In spite of what the two felt for each other they could not yet make their relationship public. Once when they were leaving a show Chaskel saw friends standing at the theatre entrance. Stopping to speak to them, he let Shirley walk ahead and out of the theatre, acting as if he didn't know her. Seeing that he had not followed her on to the street, she ended up going home alone. "How could you stand it?!" I asked her. "I had no choice", she answered. "He was afraid to let anyone know that we were together until we were officially engaged."

While Chaskel had grown to deeply love Shirley, he would not marry before both of his children were settled with families of their own. In August 1956 Manfred married Frances Fishman in Boston and for the occasion, Chaskel once again donned a top hat, the second one he had worn in his life. As happy as he was about Manfred's wedding for its own sake, he was doubly happy now that both his children were married and he could finally plan his own future.

Before doing so, however, he had several tasks at hand. Having lived in the United States for five years, in the spring of 1956 he made his first business trip out of the country to Britain, Belgium, France and Italy. In late October he traveled to Israel to see his family and to take care of Patra related issues. Several days after he arrived, Israel invaded the Sinai Peninsula and the Sinai Campaign began. Alone in the office New York and with no way of communicating with Chaskel, Shirley was beyond herself with worry. "We had no idea what was going on in Israel, all I knew is that he was there and there was a war going on." But the war was short lived and Chaskel returned safely to New York in early December.

During these trips he also made his first visit to Germany since leaving in August 1945, in order to deal with restitution claims for his property and possessions. It was not easy for him to return to a rebuilt Frankfurt and to experience Germany's booming economy in the late 1950s. How could each step not bring back memories of his past life? And yet, he had to put that life to rest, relegating it to the past before he could truly begin to build a new future.

After Chaskel's return Shirley began pressing him to make their relationship official. "I would leave him notes all over the office with the letters 'MM', standing for 'marry me'", she once told me. "I would put it on everything. Correspondence, memos, lunch notes, you name it." Although Shirley did not care how the world would relate to them, Chaskel was aware of what people might say. Even though his own brother-in-law was impressed by Shirley's capabilities, Chaskel knew that Yosef would not be happy at the thought of them marrying. He was correct. For several years after the marriage Yosef's relationship with Chaskel and Shirley cooled somewhat and it was only after I was born that he reverted back to his usual closeness with us.

"He may have been in love, but your father also knew exactly what he was doing", my mother once said. "He wanted a second family and for that he needed a young wife, not a middle-aged survivor like those being suggested to him. He wanted an American woman to whom his children could relate, who could be a bridge between him and them." Equally important, she made him laugh, she introduced him to parts of New York which he had never been to, and they never grew tired of each other. "She always keeps me on my toes", my father would say, his eyes twinkling with the memories of those first years in New York City.

In the late summer of 1957 Chaskel decided to officially approach Shirley's father, Max Kraus, and ask his permission to marry his daughter. Kraus was a far cry from the Orthodox Holocaust survivor who came to speak to him. In 1906 he had come to the United States from Czarist Russia as Mordechai Karasik, an atheist and a communist. Soon after, he married another Russian Jewish immigrant and had four sons but lost his wife to heart disease when their youngest son was almost twelve. Six months later he was introduced to Bertha Eisenberg at a friend's house and within three hours of meeting the two decided to marry. Bertha was thirty-one, traditional and single, an almost unheard of situation among religious or traditional Jewish immigrant women in America. It had been love at first sight. As my grandmother recalled, "We were introduced, shook hands, and forgot to let go." Twelve days later they were married and eleven months after the wedding their daughter Shirley was born.

While Bertha Kraus with her close ties to Jewish tradition understood her daughter's choice it was somewhat harder for Max Kraus to accept Shirley's choice of a husband. True, he himself had fallen in love with Bertha at first sight and asked her to marry him after only a few hours' acquaintance and before he had even told her that he was a widower with four young sons. There had been a large gap in their lifestyles. He was an atheist and a cultural Jew, she was traditional. He believed that religion was the opiate of the masses; she would go to *shul* on holidays, lit candles every Friday night and insisted on keeping a kosher home although she never asked what he did outside the house when he was alone. But they were both European born, came from the same culture and the age difference between them was not that great.

Chaskel may have approached Shirley's father with trepidation but Max appears to have taken it in stride. After Chaskel asked Max for permission to marry his daughter Max answered in Hebrew with the biblical quote "Let us call the young woman and ask her" which had pertained to Rebecca's marriage to Isaac. Max's decision to answer in Hebrew, a remnant from his *cheder* education in Russia, was in itself an answer. Although Chaskel's lifestyle was far from his, and he was only fifteen years older than the middle-aged Holocaust survivor, he understood that Chaskel and Shirley were deeply in love and that they would reach their own compromises to create a life suitable to both of them.

While it was a memorable moment for Chaskel to face his future father-in-law and ask for Shirley's hand in marriage, it was also a somewhat ritualistic event, possibly tinged with *deja vu*. After dealing with Hirsch Greiver's economic machinations during his first set of *tenoyim* in Bochnia, meeting with Max Kraus, a retired housepainter, in New York was a relatively uncomplicated undertaking. Shirley, on the other hand, was ecstatic. "I was so relieved that he had finally asked my father", she recalled. "I remember that we took the bus uptown back to the office from meeting my parents and all I could think of was why do I need a bus? I felt like I had wings and could fly from happiness."

By the time I was old enough to ask Zeide Max about his feelings towards my father it was obvious that he adored his son-in-law who called him *shverleben* ("beloved father-in-law") and had come to terms with his Orthodoxy. While staying at our home he would always wear a *yarmulkeh*; when I would stay at their apartment in Brighton Beach for weekends he would make Kiddush for my grandmother and me on Friday nights, something which he certainly never did throughout my mother's childhood.

Bertha was thrilled with her daughter's choice. In spite of the small age difference between her and her son-in-law to be, she mothered him in ways that he had not experienced since long before the war. In addition to buying him shirts, she frequently made him sweet gefilte fish or carp and other delicacies which were common to both Bochnia and the Bukovina where her hometown, the Mihova, was located.

Now it was time for Chaskel to introduce Shirley to his family. Sometime during the summer he brought her to the Theilheimer home in Forest Hills for Rochelle's engagement party where she met three generations of relatives: Tante Chatshe, Ida and Paul, and Bernie and Rochelle who accepted her graciously and with open arms. On the first day of Rosh Hashanah Shirley walked from her rented apartment in Kew Gardens to Ida and Paul's home where Chaskel was staying, and they announced their engagement to the family. Chaskel presented her with a diamond engagement ring, the family drank a *lechayim* toast and their relationship was now official. "We didn't want people in the office to know yet," Shirley recalled, "so I wore a band aid over the ring at work that month."

But the issues at Patra went much deeper than the boss becoming engaged to his young secretary. Yosef Greiver was not happy with his brother-in-law's choice whether out of loyalty to his sister or dismay at what he considered to be an unsuitable May–December relationship. But there was also an economic aspect that matched the personal one. Six and a half years earlier one of the incentives which made Chaskel reconsider his original refusal to work for the family business was Yosef's promise that Patra's New York office would eventually be his. During the interim however Yosef had gone through various financial upheavals and as a result, he had recently decided to sell the New York office to his and Chaskel's old friend James (Jim) Wooten to cover various debts that he had incurred. Chaskel found it difficult to continue to manage Patra under those circumstances and after the wedding he and Shirley both planned to leave the office. Not only that, they were planning to leave New York for a while and begin their life together elsewhere, giving them a chance for a true new beginning.

I often wondered how people reacted when my parents announced their intention to marry. Only a handful of people had known about their relationship as it developed and it was obvious that to many the match would seem awkward if not outright incongruous. Chaskel was fifty-four; Shirley was not yet twenty-nine. He was a European Holocaust survivor with two grown married children, two grandchildren and a third – Manfred and Frances' first child – soon to be born. She was American born and two years younger than his daughter. He was strictly Orthodox; until recently she had been completely secular and only now was taking her first steps to live an Orthodox Jewish lifestyle. His "hobbies" outside of work were stamp collecting, astronomy, and above all, learning Torah. Hers were Russian folk dancing and reading political manifestoes, preferably communist in orientation. So many people had wanted Chaskel to remarry after the war; they must have tried to introduce him to dozens of "suitable" women, all of whom he had politely refused to date, even before he had met Shirley. And now that he had finally decided to remarry, twelve years after the war had ended, it was to a woman his daughter's age who was the diametrical opposite of any woman to whom they had tried to introduce him.

My mother's friends must have also been surprised, to say the least. They knew that she was unconventional, lively, a rebel at heart. And here she was, marrying a man who was not only old enough to be her father, but an Orthodox Holocaust survivor to boot. Upon her marriage she would not only become a stepmother, but a step-grandmother before she even had her own children. Only her best friend understood; she had virtually "held her hand" throughout the years that Shirley had waited for Chaskel to take that final step.

Although the choice may not have been what they once expected, both Camilla and Manfred were happy about their father's decision to marry. Chaskel's gamble to wait until both his children were married and settled in their own homes before he announced an engagement had paid off. There was no jealousy or resentment, only happiness that their father was finally going to have a home of his own. Camilla in particular was delighted. "It may have been quite selfish of me but with Dad settled I knew that I wouldn't have to take care of him in his old age", she once remarked to me. "Besides, it was obvious that they really had something special between them."

"And it wasn't even love at first sight", Shirley once said. "But once it happened, I knew that there would never be anyone else for me." During the next weeks they planned an extended honeymoon in Europe, combining pleasure with personal business that Chaskel had to finish in Germany. As travel agents they could avail themselves of free or reduced rate airfare and hotel rates and they planned the trip of a lifetime, over six weeks of traveling through England, France, Portugal, Italy, Switzerland, Germany and Belgium. At the same time they worked long days to finish their work at Patra before handing over the agency to the new owner.

Apart from the pre-wedding bureaucracy required by New York State, Chaskel had one additional issue to take care of. A few days before the wedding he appeared before a *Beit Din* with Jacob Reiss bringing proof that he was a widower and able to marry. As in so many cases after the war, there was no concrete proof of Bertha's death, only the stories of her having run out after her parents when they were taken away by the Gestapo in Bochnia and being taken away with them, never to return. In view of the circumstances it was enough in such cases to bring witnesses that could claim the person in question had been married and that their spouse was last seen in a situation such as deportation to a death camp or being rounded up by the Nazis, from which in almost all cases, no one returned. In view of the fate of Bochnia Jewry in general and the Greivers of Bochnia in particular, Chaskel was declared a widower in front of the *Beit Din*, allowing him to remarry.

Shirley also had an "initiation rite" to go through before the wedding. Once, when she was visiting the Theilheimer home, Tante Chatshe asked Shirley to accompany her for a walk around the block. As Chaskel no longer had a mother, she, as representative of the older generation of Tydor women, had decided to speak with the bride-to-be about various motherly matters. Knowing that Shirley had come from a traditional but not Orthodox home, she asked her delicately whether she had learned the intricacies of *taharas hamishpacha*, the laws of "family purity" that govern the intimate aspects of Orthodox marriage, and was reassured that at age 87, she at least did not have to teach her new niece about that aspect of Orthodox life.

During the days before the wedding Chaskel and Shirley worked late into the night every evening as they were leaving New York the day after the wedding and had to finish the transfer of all Patra business before that time. As it was a second wedding for both, the couple did not adhere to the Jewish tradition of the bride and groom not seeing each other for the entire week before the wedding, something that would have been extremely difficult under the circumstances as they had mountains of work to finish before leaving the business on their wedding day. On the night before the wedding, after hours of work at the office in Manhattan, Chaskel accompanied Shirley home by taxi to her apartment in Kew Gardens – after all, he said, one does not leave a bride alone on the evening before her wedding – deposited her at her door and then asked the taxi to turn around and take him back to Manhattan for the last time. She should take the morning off and rest, he said to her, to get ready for the wedding. He, on the other hand would probably still have to go into the office to finish off a few last things before they left for their honeymoon the next day.

And indeed he did. Wednesday, November 13, 1957 was a beautiful but chilly day. Shirley spent the morning at her apartment with her parents, resting and fasting as is customary for Jews on their wedding day while Chaskel, also fasting, was busy at the office taking care of last minute issues. Later in the day Shirley and her parents went over to the Theilheimer home where the wedding was to take place that evening. Waiting upstairs, she kept looking out the window to see if her fiancé had arrived. As his taxi pulled up, she uncharacteristically burst into tears. "I guess until the last minute I was afraid that he wouldn't show up", she said.

At nightfall the small party of wedding guests filed into the garden where the ceremony would take place. Four members of the extended Theilheimer family held the *chuppah* (wedding canopy) over Chaskel as he stood there in a dark suit preparing to greet his bride. This time he was married in a dark suit and *yarmulke*, eschewing the top hat that he had worn at his first wedding ceremony. Shirley appeared in the doorway wearing a blue satin suit and a hat with a short veil. To ward off the November chill Ida threw a mink stole over the bride's shoulders as she walked to the *chuppah*. "And of course by the next morning there was already talk in Forest Hills that I had gotten married in a mink stole", my mother once remarked to me, referring ironically to the speed with which stories traveled among Orthodox Jewish circles in that neighborhood. Thrilled that his friend had finally decided to marry, Rabbi Schacter, acting as witness together with Chaskel's old friend Jacob Reiss, performed the wedding ceremony. After reciting the traditional marriage formulations, Chaskel placed a simple gold ring on Shirley's finger, stepped on a glass in memory of the destruction of the Temple in Jerusalem, and they became husband and wife. For the first time in fifteen years, on the 20th of Cheshvan 5718, there was again a Mrs. Chaskel Tydor.

"I can't remember much about the wedding itself except for the fact that I was so happy", my mother remarked when I asked her about anything special that she recalled from that occasion, but when I pressed her, she recalled one funny incident. "Because we were limited in space we had only a few people to the dinner and in most cases we asked only the men to attend so that we could have a *minyan*. Two of my uncles were there but without their wives and so was a cousin of your father. But when Jacob Reiss walked in with his wife Fanny and we looked at him with surprise, he took us aside and said, 'You go tell her that she isn't invited, I was afraid to do it!'"

It is often not easy for a child to attend his or her parent's wedding as I learned when I remarried in my late forties. Both Manfred and Camilla not only attended their father's wedding but were delighted that he was remarrying and happy with his choice. Neither of their spouses could be at the wedding. Leonard had remained in Rochester to care for the children and Frances was beginning her ninth month of pregnancy and could no longer travel so far from Boston. She would soon give birth to their first child, Laurie (Bella), who would be followed during the next few years by Bruce (Yehuda) and Janice (Nechama), thus giving Chaskel a total of seven American-born grandchildren.

Because Bernie, the family photographer, was one of those holding the *chuppah* we have no pictures of the ceremony but only of the dinner and especially of my parents sitting in the Theilheimer family chairs which they would soon inherit. In the pictures you can see a jubilant bride sitting next to her exhausted groom, testimony to his last efforts that day to finish the work that had piled up at Patra without his trusty secretary, now his wife, at hand.

For their last night in New York Chaskel and Shirley stayed at a small hotel in Kew Gardens, meeting the next morning for breakfast with Camilla and Bernie before she returned to Rochester. That evening, after all the out of town guests had returned home, Chaskel and Shirley finally embarked on their honeymoon. "In those days seats on planes would lean all the way back and that way your father could sleep all the way to Europe." While Chaskel's exhaustion showed in some of his wedding pictures, the picture taken the next day shows a cheerful couple, she with her wedding corsage still pinned to her jacket, waving to the photographer in front of the plane. Now they could leave the worries of Patra behind them and for a short while forget about everything waiting for them when they would return to New York. After almost five years of waiting to be married they were finally about to begin life together as a family.

When I was a young girl, the story of my parents' courtship and wedding always seemed like a fairy tale to me. The older survivor and young American girl falling in love; his waiting for his children to be settled until he would marry; her waiting for him for almost five years until she finally became his wife. My mother always treated my father with tremendous respect. While speaking of him to others she referred to him as "my husband" or occasionally as "Haskel" but throughout all their married years when speaking to him directly she never called him by his first name, not even when alone. In private she used endearments such as "honey" or "sweetheart" but in public it was always "Mr. T.", the name she used to call him when they first began working together. Even after 35 years of marriage she could never bring herself to call him by his first name. Could it be that in her mind, "Chaskel" was the man who had belonged to a different life, one before she met him? Heinrich was long gone; Haskel was an American "made up" name, to her it wasn't real. Besides, it was so much more respectful to speak to him this way, she once said, just as I always stood up when my father entered the room.

It was only when I got older that I realized how difficult much of that situation had been for both of them. How could a religious man of fifty who had been through all that he had in Europe and Eretz Yisrael, fall in love with a secular woman half his age who knew nothing but the American life into which she had been born? How could he explain to his friends and relatives that he was marrying a woman who had been an atheist and even a communist and was basically becoming Orthodox because of her love for him? How could he tell his children that their new "stepmother" was only a year or two older than they were? How could she tell her friends that she was marrying someone her parents' age and was giving up her entire lifestyle to become an Orthodox Jew out of love? How did she have the courage to wait for him for so many years until "he got his act together" as I once put it? "It wasn't easy," she told me, "but the minute we were married I forgot everything that came before. From then on life began for us."

But in truth, each of them carried baggage from their previous life, my father much more than my mother. He had the memories of half a lifetime, and some memories which would haunt him for the rest of his life. Each had been married before, but my father's first marriage had ended quite differently than my mother's. "It wasn't that complicated", she once said to me. "He loved his first wife very much and they had a wonderful marriage; he loved me very much and we had a wonderful marriage as well." But it was not that simple. I can only imagine that for many years the loss of his first wife and family had haunted him, putting any thoughts of remarrying out of his mind until he met my mother. He must have missed Bertha terribly but put her out of his mind during the war in order to survive. Afterwards, though, it must have taken him years to work through his feelings of guilt over her death; after all, her immigration papers had arrived before his and she remained in Germany during those fateful days at the end of August and after his arrest at the beginning of September so as not to leave her husband. I never spoke to him about it; the subject was too painful. But my mother was well aware of what she was getting into. "Before I married your father I spoke to Bertha in my mind and promised her that I would take care of him for

161

her", she once said to me at an unguarded moment. For my father, marrying my mother was closing a circle. For my mother, it would at times be like opening a pandora's box whose contents she could not yet imagine.

"We gambled," she once said to me, "and we won". After my father's death my mother gave me a greeting card that she had given him for their thirty-first wedding anniversary in 1988, containing a poem by Edmund O'Neill. "You and I took a special chance\ the first time we met . . . ," the card began, "we both knew enough of love and life\ to understand that two people don't fall in love,\ they grow into it, slowly . . . you and I took a special chance\ the first time we said, 'I love you' . . . for we knew that we would share stormy as well as sunny times\, laughter and tears,\ some dreams that would come beautifully true,\ and others that would fade in our memories . . . we took that very special chance . . . and found a very special love." To which she had added four words in pen: "this says it all."

"I only made one mistake", she told me years later. "When your father married me he was fifty-four and he asked me whether I was concerned with the age difference between us. 'Promise me thirty-five years' I told him, and he did. And that's exactly what we had. Thirty-five years of marriage. I made such a mistake", she concluded. "I should have asked for more."

Looking back at my father's life it seems to have been divided up between two types of periods: those during which he "acted for the *klal* (the community)", in the sense of doing for others, and those few years in which he allowed himself to "act for himself". During his childhood he was able to act for himself, however as soon as he had to leave university and help support his family, he entered into a period where he acted for others, in this case his parents and sister. Then came the years during which he built his own family, again a period when he could act for himself but it was followed by the war, an interruption of all normalcy during which he attempted to keep himself alive yet at the same time, did so much for the *klal*. During the immediate post-war period he devoted most of his time and efforts to the *klal*, establishing Kibbutz Buchenwald and bringing its members to Palestine. This was followed by a period of several years where he once again did for himself, rebuilding his health and fortune and reconnecting with his children. The next years, those described here, were years during which my father once again acted for the *klal*, in this case for his extended family, by building up their business in New York, something to which he devoted day and night for over five years. Now he was once again about to begin a period when he would be able to "act for himself", this time in the United States, building a new family that would hopefully encompass his previous one as well, thus closing a circle that had remained painfully open for so long.

The wedding ceremony itself had been the closure of another circle. Rabbi Schacter had provided the couple with the *chuppah* under which it took place, the same small canopy which he had used when marrying couples in liberated Germany after the war. For him, this, too, was a symbolic closing of a circle, one that he had opened when helping to create new families right next to the very site where so many families had been torn asunder. This was the *chuppah* under which he had married both Camilla and Manfred. Now he had performed their father's wedding ceremony under it and the last of the Tydors had finally become a married man.

Once again, the significant world events of this era, and even those on the American or Israeli scene, appear to be mostly absent from my father's narrative. The Cold War, the Korean War, West Germany becoming a sovereign state, the McCarthy hearings, the American hydrogen bomb test, the beginning of the American national civil rights movement, just to mention a few. Only the Suez crisis – during which my father found himself on a visit to Israel – received active mention in his stories but was basically relegated to a minor role in spite of the fact that he had family members serving in the Israeli Defense Forces at the time.

In practice though, many of the other events in world history had bearing upon my father's life in various direct or indirect ways, for example the McCarthy communist "witch hunts" of the earl 1950s. At some point during this period my father was unexpectedly visited one evening by two members of the US State Department. Being a foreign citizen my father came under automatic suspicion regarding his political persuasion and he was "visited" in order to check out his past and present political affiliations, and plans to obtain future citizenship. Although he originally had no intention of staying in the United States for any length of time, this polite "discussion" actually did have somewhat of an impact on his future decision to ultimately take out American citizenship, something that he did only after I was born, nine years after he came to America. My mother's political background also made her suspect in the "witch hunting" climate of the early 1950s and she was questioned separately for having been a member of "students for Wallace" during her college days. Ultimately, neither of my parents was under serious suspicion but these visits were a reminder, at least for my father, that even in a "free" country one could find oneself in an unexpected predicament that would not necessarily end well. A reminder of the past.

German's changing status also had a certain impact on my father's life. It was after West Germany became a sovereign state that he could travel there with his Israeli passport in order to begin investigating the possibility of obtaining reparations for his factory and home. The change in Germany's status, together with the 1952 reparations agreement signed between the State of Israel and West Germany, were probably two of the most significant international events that ultimately had financial bearing on my father's life. But that would only be in the future, after I was born when he would file a last-minute claim for personal reparations. Not for his property or possessions for which he would never receive compensation, but for the years of slave labor in Nazi camps. Meanwhile, though, the only financial thoughts that my parents had were of how they were going to make a living in the near future, now that they had both left Patra and were ostensibly unemployed. But only temporarily.

As my parents flew off to Europe they knew that the next six weeks were a short hiatus during which they could catch their breath before beginning the next chapter of their adventure. Because when they got back it would not be to a comfortable and familiar existence in New York City but to parts unknown. For the first time since reading about his adventurous hero as a small boy in Galicia, Chaskel Tydor, who had once told his friends that he would one day be "Buffalo Bill from Bochnia", was indeed going to be moving with his young wife to the "Wild West". There he would spend the next eighteen months managing a uranium mine deep in Indian territory and living a life that he could have barely dreamed about as a young Chassidic boy in a Bochnia *cheder*.

8

Rapid City, South Dakota and Deer Lodge, Montana, 1958–1959

At the end of December Chaskel and Shirley returned to New York after the honeymoon of a lifetime. For six weeks they traveled through Europe, visiting friends and relatives, enjoying the attractions of Lisbon, London, Paris, Rome, Brussels and Zurich, a fringe benefit of the long hours invested in the travel business. Tel Aviv or Jerusalem were not on their travel agenda; in view of Patra's sale and Yosef's cool attitude towards the match, they figured it prudent to stay far away from Israel for the time being.

The trip gave them an opportunity to reconnect with friends and relatives. In London, Shirley met the Klausner family, Chaskel's cousins Hermann and Bertha and their children with whom he had remained close over the years in spite of geographical distance. All except the grandchildren born in Britain had been close with Bertha Tider but they accepted Shirley with open arms, delighted that Chaskel had remarried. During one of their talks Bertha Klausner imparted to Shirley family words of wisdom. "Never boast about your husband or children," she told the young bride, "because they will invariably embarrass you afterwards." "How right she was!", my mother always said.

They also met the Hackenbruchs who had tried valiantly to obtain a visa for Chaskel and Bertha before the war. Eli Hackenbruch had already returned the pouch of gold jewelry that Chaskel had sent him from Frankfurt. Some pieces had been given to Camilla; others were now presented to Shirley, his new bride. This, too, was the closing of a circle.

The few days that they spent in Germany were used for bureaucracy. In addition to claiming restitution for his property, Chaskel had pieced together documents proving him eligible for German social security.

Although it is incongruous to think of a new bridegroom dealing with old-age pensions, Chaskel was only a decade away from retirement and had a young wife to support. But documents for certain years had disappeared in the bureaucratic machinery of the *Bundesrepublik Deutschland*, the Federal Republic of Germany, and in spite of his valiant attempts Chaskel never received compensation for his twenty-four years of work for the Germans before and during the war.

As personal compensation for having to deal with such bureaucracy in Germany on their honeymoon my father bought my mother two sets of Rosenthal china – it was a Jewish firm, he told her, and he had no problems purchasing such a product. As a young girl I was the only one in the family who abhorred the thought of buying German products while my father had little difficulty doing so. He did, however, draw the line at buying a German car; that must have been too much even for him. But small items such as his electric shaver were German made. After all, as he said with what always sounded to me like a tinge of *local-patriotism*, "the best made things come from Germany, don't they"? Only when I was in my late thirties did I finally allow German-made goods in my home, at which time I inherited one of the two sets of Rosenthal china, a reminder of my parent's honeymoon that graces my dining room until today.

Once they returned to New York Chaskel and Shirley began married life in earnest, but they would soon find themselves at opposite ends of the country for several months. In view of Yosef's attitude towards the match and his sale of Patra, Chaskel and Shirley decided that it would be best not only to leave Patra but to leave New York for a while. The question was where they would go and how they would support themselves. Unexpectedly, the answer was provided by the very person to whom Yosef had just sold Patra, Jim Wooten.

Apart from his travel and airline ventures, Wooten also owned a number of uranium mines in the American northwest. For months the mines in Montana and South Dakota had been losing money and Wooten suspected that profits were being siphoned off locally. To put the mines in financial order he needed a trustworthy person with a sharp eye and a working knowledge of bookkeeping who would be willing to live in the area to put the mines in running order. Aware of Chaskel's business acumen, Wooten approached him with the proposition and after discussing it with Shirley, Chaskel agreed to go out west for a period of time in order to settle Wooten's financial difficulties in the area.

No matter how many times my parents told me this story in my youth, I still found it difficult to fathom how they could begin their married life together in the "wild west" far away from their families, far away from any organized Jewish community, and basically far away from modern civilization. Today, in the world of instant communication the world has truly become a global village but in those days the distance between Montana and New York City was not measured in miles but in light years. Although my mother's parents in New York had a phone at home, the thought of calling cross-country was not in either her or their realm of possibility. All communication took place by regular mail; telegrams were reserved for solemn occasions such as serious illness or death. Even when my mother found herself expecting, she wrote to her parents to inform them of the good news, never even once entertaining the thought of calling them to hear their delighted reaction.

More than the separation from friends and family, I could never understand how my father agreed to live so far away from an organized Jewish community, even for only a year and a half. Although these were the days when the Lubavitcher Rebbe was sending the first of his Chassidim out to *shlichus* (being an emissary), the only person "sending" my father to the "wild west" was Jim Wooten. But knowing my father, I was not surprised at how things worked out, lack of Jewish community notwithstanding.

In late January Chaskel left New York to check on Wooten's mine in Deer Lodge, Montana. The small mining town of Deer Lodge was the second town to be founded in Montana in the mid 1800s when gold was first discovered found in the area. Taking its name from the warm springs mound that provided a natural salt lick for the local deer population, the town was located in a valley where most of the local wildlife would winter when the temperatures dropped sharply in the high country. But the bucolic description belied the reality of temperatures in Deer Lodge, as my parents would discover. The word "warm" was a relative term, my mother remarked, remembering the freezing winter that she spent in the town and snow that would shut them in for days on end.

Surrounded by mountains, streams and creeks, Deer Lodge was a hub of copper, gold and uranium mines and home to the largest prison in the State. At the end of the twentieth century its population was 3,500 persons; when my parents lived there it was much less with the town boasting a main street, several side streets and numerous ranches in the vicinity. My father talked little about Deer Lodge's demographics but my mother would say: "After we got there it was a town with two Jews, five hundred white people, five thousand Indians and fifty thousand head of cattle".

Deer Lodge is also part of "Big Sky Country", made famous by movies such as the 1992 "Diggstown", with primeval forests, gleaming mountaintops and abundant wildlife. My father, who loved nature, told me stories about the mountain hiking he enjoyed during his eighteen months in the area. Although he was certainly not a hunter or fisherman, those sports, along with horseback riding and cross-country skiing were favorites of both locals and tourists. Nevertheless, his stories from that time were certainly adventurous enough for a man who I pictured either working in an office or pouring over a volume of the Talmud. To me he spoke of never ending spaces, swift flowing streams and rolling hills and valleys, hot springs and of course, his first face to face contact with American Indians.

For someone whose last experience with a small town was early twentieth-century Bochnia, Deer Lodge may have been reminiscent in some ways of the town of his childhood. There, however, in a Galician town of 3,500 persons, Jews had made up 20 percen of the population. After my parents' arrival in Deer Lodge, the Jews of the town composed a massive 0.1 percen of the total local populace.

From Deer Lodge my father headed to check out the second uranium found outside of Rapid City, South Dakota. Unlike tiny Deer Lodge, Rapid City was indeed a city, with a population of over 30,000. Located on the eastern edge of the Black Hills, the city was founded in 1876 as the "gateway to the Black Hills" and soon became a natural hub of railroads, a regional trade center for the upper Midwest, and ultimately a tourist destination. In 1941 work was completed at the nearby Mount Rushmore where four American president's faces – Washington, Jefferson, Lincoln, and Theodore Roosevelt – were carved in rock. Soon after, the Ellsworth air force base opened, doubling the town's population. During the Cold War, missile installations proliferated in the area, adding to the population of the air force base which would play a major role in my parent's experiences.

Although there were about ten Jewish families in town, there was neither rabbi nor synagogue. There were, however, around thirty Jewish military personnel on the base, some married with children, and the deputy base commander was a Jew. From the summer of 1958 the base even had a Jewish chaplain, Rabbi Reuven Hammer, accompanied by his wife Rachel and their baby daughter Aura, who ministered to the religious needs of the Jewish military personnel, and at times, even those of the town Jews, eleven miles away. Although his home base was in Rapid City, the tall dark-haired Jewish chaplain spent much time on the road, serving air force bases in Montana, New Mexico, Texas and Nebraska and even traveling to Spain for Pesach to conduct a *seder* for American troops in Spain and North Africa.

While there was no official connection between the air force base and the town, Rabbi Hammer soon forged that connection, at least between himself and the Jews of Rapid City. In addition to caring for the Jewish airmen on Ellworth, he began classes for Jewish children and adults in Rapid City and its environs. Among his special "congregants" were the Adelsteins, the "rich Jews" of the town involved in the construction business, having built the air force base as well as much of the area. The connection was Zionist as well, as the Hammers were staunch Zionists and the senior Adelstein had been involved in smuggling arms to Palestine during 1947–1948.

During my parents' stay in Rapid City the Hammers would become their close friends, not only because of the religious connection, but because the Hammers spoke Hebrew at home with Aura and my father loved the chance to speak Hebrew with them. Another connection was biological. Rachel and my mother became pregnant around the same time, and they shared the experiences and concerns of pregnancies carried far away from family. That friendship continued after my parents returned to New York and Reuven served in pulpits in Ohio, Colorado, and Illinois. Eventually, they moved to Jerusalem with their five children in 1973, a year before we moved to Israel. There the friendship continued in close geographic proximity as it had fifteen years earlier.

But all this would be in the future. Meanwhile, Chaskel was alone out west, preparing the groundwork for his job and family. During that time he had to learn the ins and outs of the uranium mining business while preparing a home base in each town. Initially he decided to rent rooms in both places to have somewhere ready when Shirley would join him after Passover, figuring that at worst they could look for a better apartment after she arrived. What he couldn't take into account was the dearth of rentals in the "metropolis" of Deer Lodge, and so my parents ended up living in a miniscule basement apartment during their months in town, with my mother cooking on a hot plate, balanced on a bathroom shelf.

I have no idea what my father did other than work during the weeks that he was alone but he probably discovered that his dreams of what the "wild west" were not what he faced in reality. Yes, there were cowboys and even Indians but they were primarily found on reservations and were more often drunk than sober. Nevertheless, this was his chance to live the life of "Buffalo Bill of Bochnia" of which he had dreamed as a child.

William Frederick "Buffalo Bill" Cody had been an American soldier, bison hunter, showman and one of the most colorful figures of the American Old West. His nickname came from his having supplied the

Kansas Pacific Railroad workers with buffalo meat, slaughtering 4,280 buffalo in eighteen months to give them food. A scout, trapper, pony express rider, stagecoach driver and Indian fighter, he was best known for his "Wild West" show involving horseback parades, Sitting Bull and his twenty Indian braves, re-enactment of Indian attacks on wagon trains and the famous finale of Custer's Last Stand in which Cody himself portrayed General Custer.

At five foot two and 140 lbs. Chaskel was far from being cowboy material, his natural courage notwithstanding. I am not sure whether he sat on a horse at any time during his 89 years, with or without a saddle. But for someone who spent more than 85% of his life in major urban centers, he had a tremendous love for the great outdoors and enjoyed the freedom of open country, possibly a reaction to the years of incarceration in Nazi camps. And yet, living in the "wild west" had been a childhood dream, long before he had stepped foot in Germany. Now, at 54 and newly married, he could reconnect with his early dreams, before his family was destroyed and his fortune dissipated. He had the requisite western cowboy-style hat which he sometimes used instead of his cap, but he never got the cowboy boots to go along with them, preferring high shoes when traipsing through the mines he often had to visit.

After two months of traveling between Rapid City and Deer Lodge, Chaskel returned to New York to celebrate Passover with Shirley and bring her back west. Her first reaction to Montana was surprise; she had no idea that Chaskel was driving a big truck, the one he used to pick her up at the airport, running out of gas going back to town as he had forgotten to fill up the tank. Looking at him, she had a feeling that her husband was enjoying playing cowboy with his pickup truck and western hat. Her next reaction was dismay when she saw the miniscule apartment he had arranged for them in town. "Think of how much less there will be to clean", Chaskel said to her in jest when he showed her the combined bathroom/kitchen facilities.

Deer Lodge was an eye opener for my parents in many senses. For both it was the first time that they were living far away from other Jews and their first experience with rural American concepts about the "chosen people". "At some point I noticed a few ladies in town looking at me in a funny way", remarked my mother. "After we became friendly, one asked whether I wore a hat outdoors to cover my horns. After all, she said to me in all seriousness, everyone knew that Jews had horns." My mother removed her hat and showed the woman that indeed she had no horns. "They must be hiding somewhere", the woman muttered, unable to accept that unlike the famous Michelangelo statue of David, modern-day Jews appeared to either have very small, imperceptible horns, or no horns at all.

When living among Gentiles and particularly those who had never met a Jew in their lives, certain issues had to be dealt with differently than when living in an urban center with a large Jewish population. When my mother took my father's wool *tallis* (prayer shawl) to be professionally cleaned out west, she explained to the dry cleaner that the striped, fringed textile had to be treated with reverence. "I told him that it was a family heirloom, passed down from generation to generation, and used . . . as a piano cover!"

Better yet was the quest for kosher food. In Deer Lodge my parents finished the salamis they had brought from New York but in Rapid City, where the town boasted a supermarket, kosher salami was shipped in from Denver or Omaha, 400 miles away. My mother remembers striding into the local "Piggly Wiggly" supermarket, brandishing her own meat knife to make the first cut into the salami and ensure that no non-kosher utensils would touch the kosher meat, rendering it inedible for them. Otherwise, they subsisted on eggs, grains, fruits and vegetables as it was difficult to even find kosher bread without shortening.

My father's truck, initially a source of surprise for my mother, played a prominent role in their life out west. Equipped with a large cabin and winter snow chains, it was possible to drive it under all weather conditions, sometimes causing my father to miscalculate travel possibilities. When he was behind the wheel he seemed to lose track of time, looking out at the never-ending landscape of mountains and valleys, seeing the animals, small and large, moving gracefully in the distance. In the winter he and my mother would spend hours watching the deer for which Deer Lodge had been named, some of which would even come up to the back door of the basement in which they lived. Everything was blanketed with snow, outside it was freezing, but inside the house or the truck's cabin, they could watch the winter wonderland from the comfort of a heated area. One Friday when my father went out of town to check on a mine he was caught in a severe snowstorm preventing him from returning to Deer Lodge for the Sabbath. Luckily he found a small motel where he spent the next 26 hours, subsisting on the bag of apples that he had with him at the time.

Another truck story was a lesson on how safety belts could act as double-edged swords. Having learned to drive before cars were equipped with safety belts, my father was suspicious of these contraptions, never using one voluntarily. Once, when negotiating the Montana wilderness, he found himself about to go down the side of a ravine as the country road he had been navigating had no warning sign stating "road ends – cliff ahead". In a split-second decision my father wrenched the cabin door open, leaped from the descending truck as it shot into the gorge, and saved his life because he didn't have to take the time to unfasten a safety belt. That was also why he never locked the door of any car in which he was driving.

Having been saved by his split second decision Chaskel was found by the locals and taken to a nearby hospital. From there he called Shirley to tell her that he "might be a bit late coming home that day". How did my mother react to hearing that her husband had lost their truck and had almost lost his life? "It was par for the course", she remembered. "All our life out there was one big adventure and we could always count on the unexpected happening." For a city girl, seeing small fox footprints come up to their back door in the snow was a new adventure, as was experiencing a northwest winter wind, the likes of she had never felt in New York City. "I was always freezing outside", she remembered, "Nothing I had ever experienced could prepare me for the unbroken miles of snow that blanketed the countryside in winter". When she became pregnant, she did not stop smoking – "my one vice", my mother used to say until she quit at age 54 – but she could not stand the smell of cigarette smoke and kept the back door of the room open while she smoked, even in subzero weather. To keep her warm my father bought her a "wink", a fake mink coat that kept her toasty from head to toe. She wore it everywhere, pulling up its thick collar to cushion the back of her neck and protect her from the wind. With her penchant for pretty hats and curly red hair, she must have been a sight in that outfit.

One of my father's favorite sayings was "One is never sure of life, as long as one lives". But he would also add, "Life is the biggest bargain, you got it for free, but it is up to you to give it meaning". And meaning they gave it. For Chaskel and Shirley, these were definitely months of adventure, far away from family and friends. There was no Jewish community, no communal life and in fact, no other Jews in Deer Lodge. During their weeks in that town Chaskel's weekday and Sabbath prayers took place in the living room cum bedroom with the beds made up into a couch. There was no synagogue, no sisterhood or any of the other activities that would exist had there been a Jewish community.

Meanwhile, though, they were a "young" couple with a sense of adventure. As they had no friends and few acquaintances in Deer Lodge, my parents used their spare time to visit local sites of interest. My father was an avid hiker and enjoyed wandering in the mountains, exploring the many caves in the area to my mother's chagrin as she was deathly afraid of bats and mice. Packed into my father's truck they traveled to Mount Rushmore and other nearby national parks. Another favorite spot was the Mammoth site and fossil deposits in the Black Hills. The summer was the best time to travel and explore. Although it was hot dry and sunny, with temperatures in the 80s and sometimes even the 90s, it was better than traveling around the west during the winter when the average monthly snowfall in the Black Hills was fifteen inches. "We had to choose between sweating and freezing," my mother said, "but whatever we did, we had a marvelous time." For both of them it was a hiatus from life in which they could indulge themselves as newlyweds. At night they would drive fifty miles to the "local" drive-in and watch movies. "We didn't care what was playing", my mother recalled. "We would go just for the fun of it. We thought nothing of driving for miles on end to get out and see something interesting."

Most of all, they were on their own, far away from parents, children and grandchildren, thus able to begin cementing their own family unit. The motto of South Dakota – "under God the people rule" – was surprisingly apt for them at that period of their lives. While keeping as strictly as they could to the letter of Jewish law, during their time out west they were not bogged down with the issues of being someone's "children" or "parents" but could just be a newlywed couple, getting to know each other under new circumstances. When Shirley became pregnant in late 1958, their joy was boundless. After being torn apart and decimated during the war, the Tydor clan was once again expanding.

In addition to the Hammers, my parents became friendly with another Jewish family in Rapid City, the Rifkins, who were the only ones in town trying to keep a kosher home and raise their five children as Jews. Hearing of their difficulties to give their children a Jewish education and surprised to hear that there were almost twenty Jewish children in town, my father saw an opportunity to introduce the Jewish youth of Rapid City to Jewish practice.

In late summer 1958 Chaskel informed the Rifkins that on Saturday morning he would hold a short children's service followed by a Kiddush of cake and drinks. Expecting to see the five Rifkin children and possibly a few more at the service, he was astonished to find over thirty Jewish children knocking at the downstairs door that Sabbath morning. "It turned out that there were quite a number of Jews living within a fifty-mile radius of Rapid City and when they heard about the Sabbath services they wanted their children to see what it was like", my father recalled. Week after week, deep into the winter, the services expanded until mountains of snowshoes and galoshes were left by the stairs, with the adults who had brought their children to the service upstairs ultimately remaining to enjoy the warm winter Kiddush that had taken the place of the light summer fare. My father, in his usual spirit of tolerance, never asked how people from out of town had gotten there on a Sabbath morning although it was obvious they hadn't come on foot. "It was the only way these children would ever see anything of Judaism", he would tell me, "and I hoped that some of them would remember and it would help them remain Jews. I didn't ask, they didn't offer any explanations of how they got there, and everyone enjoyed the Kiddush. It was a chance for Jews to be Jews", he concluded.

My father was right. At least one of the children who attended the service in that overcrowded living room ultimately joined the Lubavitch movement; another moved to Chicago and Rabbi Hammer converted his fiancée to Judaism. Everyone seemed to be happy with the Saturday morning services, except my parents' landlord who was aghast at the noise that more than sixty adults and children made going up and down the stairs in his house. Tinged by anti-Semitic feelings regarding having a synagogue service take place under his roof, he ultimately asked my parents to move and cease the Sabbath morning services immediately. Knowing that they would soon be traveling eastward for Shirley to give birth, Chaskel transferred the services to the Rifkin house where they continued for some time. And indeed, shortly before Passover my parents bade farewell to their friends in Rapid City and returned to New York. Chaskel later travelled to South Dakota for several weeks but by late June 1959 the "wild west" period of their life had come to an end.

Back in New York, Shirley and Chaskel were about to enter a new phase of life. For Shirley, a first child; for Chaskel, another chance at parenthood and hopefully a child that he would be able to raise fully, unlike his older children who were snatched from him at age six and eight, never again to live with him during childhood. For Shirley, after working since age fourteen, becoming a stay-at-home mother; for Chaskel, the beginning of a new professional adventure. He had already been a bookkeeper, metallurgist, factory owner, religious book publisher, travel agent and uranium mine manager. Who knows what the future would hold?

Shirley gave birth on July 13, 1959 having spent much of her labor painting a bookcase and cleaning house. The evening before she and Chaskel had taken a taxi to Polyclinic Hospital in Manhattan where the examining nurse told them to go home and come back after midnight. At 1:15 a.m. after sitting outside the delivery room for an hour and saying *tehilim* for his wife's safe delivery, the nurse informed Chaskel that he was the father of a baby girl. Twenty-eight and a half years after Tzipora Camilla had been born at home in Frankfurt a/M, his second daughter, Esther Yehudit named after his mother and sister, was born in a hospital in Manhattan. He was fifty-five years old and another chapter in the incredible adventures of Buffalo Bill from Bochnia was about to begin.

My parents' life in South Dakota and Montana appears to be the epitome of unconventional behavior at that time. Going out west, starting a new life far away from friends and family, changing professions, traveling and in general, having a good time. From the few pictures my parents have from that time they look so happy, always smiling and not necessarily for the camera as is customary in such photos.

Trying to understand the source of that happiness I leaf through the components of their life out west: togetherness, adventure, travel, new friendships, new professions, new locations, new experiences. Over and over I return to the word "new" as the adjective of choice. And then I look at what wasn't there: family, organized community, and most of all, Holocaust. My father was certainly the only Holocaust survivor in Deer Lodge, Montana or Rapid City, South Dakota. He had no family or friends around to remind him of bygone days. Not only was it an opportunity for my parents to build a new life as a couple, it was an opportunity for my father to heal for the first time since the war, not surrounded by artifacts or persons from his pre-war or wartime past. For a person who believed in moving forward this was a G-d sent opportunity where he could be himself, and not Chaskel Tydor, a Holocaust survivor. There would be enough time for that later, after their hiatus from "real life" during which they created enough memories of the "wild west" to last a lifetime.

But the hiatus was over. Shortly after returning to New York, my father found himself thrown into Holocaust-related events once again. Within days of moving to Queens he joined the nearby Kehilas Adas Yeshurun, an Orthodox *shul* with many formerly German-Jewish members, once again *davening* with the melodies of his teenage years and onward. Within weeks he was involved in establishing a committee convened to mark the fifteenth anniversary of the liberation of Auschwitz-Buna. And within months he found himself in a place where even Buffalo Bill from Bochnia had never expected to be, in the White

House in Washington, standing in front of Dwight D. Eisenhower and pronouncing the blessing for Kings and national leaders as the American president bowed his head.

9

New York, 1959–1974

Even when people try to escape their destiny, it often catches up on them. After returning to New York, the four issues which my father left behind during his sojourn in the northwest came back to take over his life in spades: the travel business, family issues, community matters, and the Holocaust. In doing so, they left their mark not only on him but like ripples on the surface of a pond, on everyone and everything surrounding him for the next decade and a half.

The order in which I listed these four issues mirrors their reality in his life between ages fifty to seventy-five. It took an inordinate amount of time to build up the travel business, his fifth major career switch in thirty years, and his work day often lasted until close to midnight. After work-related issues came family matters. Raising a second family, he tried to remain active in the lives of his married children and grandchildren, while maintaining contact with other relatives throughout the world.

Community matters were next in the race for my father's limited leisure hours. In Kew Gardens we attended the Adath Yeshurun syna-gogue, modeled on the Breuer-Hirsch *shul* in Frankfurt. As a small child in *shul* I remember my father regaling me with stories of Buffalo Bill from Bochnia, the little Galician cowboy who had conquered the "wild west", while his seat neighbor, the well-known educator, Rabbi Abraham Besdin, told me stories from the Chassidic repertoire of R. Shmelke of Nikolsburg. As a child I was certain that "Buffalo Bill of Bochnia" was an alias of the courageous R. Shmelke and was surprised to learn the truth as I grew older. Later, when we moved to Woodside, Queens, my father became president of the Woodside Jewish Center and found himself spending long hours dealing with a topic he abhorred – *shul* politics.

In last place vying for his time were Holocaust matters, particularly the establishment of the Auschwitz-Buna memorial scholarship fund. In addition, once a year, on the anniversary of his liberation from Buchenwald, our family would get together with some of his *chaverim* and particularly the Margulies family from Washington Heights, and have a festive meal commemorating the miracle of their liberation from Nazi slavery and their survival. Most of the talk at these meals dealt with the present and the future. Only later, after retirement, would my father and his friends recall their past lives, reviving memories and re-facing ghosts from another lifetime.

All other issues – learning Torah, staying in touch with friends, or just resting, had to take place on Shabbos afternoons, late at night, or on the one work-vacation a year when my parents would rest in between looking at hotels and meeting with local tour agents. Only after retiring – "and never looking back", as my father would remind me – was he able to find a healthy balance in his life in which family, friends, and learning Torah came first, followed by Holocaust-related matters, as the dwindling community of Holocaust survivors became his "community of reference".

Chaskel returned to New York in June 1959 with no job or concrete plans for the future other than managing the investments that he and Shirley had made during their time out west. Apparently untroubled by the future, he was certain that something would turn up within a short time. Today I realize how much of this seemingly cavalier attitude was born from his financially secure childhood in which all one needed to succeed was ability, connections and seed money. And he appeared to have all three, or at least the first two in spades.

But there was no "lottery money" anymore in the Tydor family and there were now three mouths to feed. In addition, Chaskel was diagnosed with phlebitis, requiring him to rest with his leg elevated for several weeks. Nevertheless, as my father used to say, in order to succeed one needs ninety percent *siata dishmaya* ("help from heaven") and ten percent "good luck". Shortly before giving birth, Shirley visited a friend in General Tours, a travel agency which often worked in cooperation with Patra, and the friend mentioned to her boss that Chaskel was looking for a job. For the owner of General Tours, a Polish Jew from Lodz who had gone through half the war in a Soviet Gulag and the rest as a soldier in the Russian army, this was a heaven-sent opportunity. Having inherited the travel agency from an uncle, Alex Harris built it up into a well-known firm but desperately needed a manager due to his own personal difficulties. Asking Chaskel to meet him at General Tours, Harris made him an offer that he could not refuse. As he wrote in his autobiography:

"I invited Haskel to my office, offered him 30 percent of my company, and asked him to manage it in order to give me time to regain control of myself. He looked at me benignly with his warm, brown eyes and said, 'My dear Alex, I'm honored by your proposal, but I have no resources to buy into your agency, as much as I would like to do it.' 'Give me one dollar, please', I said, extending my hand to receive the bill. Puzzled, he reached into his pocket and came up with a dollar. I took it, stood up, and said, 'Welcome, partner, you just bought thirty percent of General Tours. Here are the papers confirming your ownership.' The contract I had asked my attorney to prepare changed the company's hands and changed the course of our lives."

Soon after becoming the general manager of General Tours, Alex Harris asked Chaskel to serve as Executive Vice President of the firm which he did until his retirement fourteen years later. Realizing that with Chaskel's long work hours she would never see him at home, Shirley went to work in General Tours two years later, first as Chaskel's secretary and later as a full-fledged travel agent.

As a child I took it for granted that both my parents worked in the travel business, just as I considered it normal in my Jewish school to think that everyone's father had a number on his arm as did mine and many of my classmate's fathers. Only later did I learn that there was a concept known as a "stay-at-home-mother", who was available to bake cookies and cakes for school events. "Did you ever bake a cake?" I asked my mother when I was writing this chapter. "Of course I did, once", she responded, "I followed the directions on the back of the package." "But that was from a cake mix mother", I told her, "I mean a 'real' cake". "You mean like from scratch?!" she looked at me in dismay, "you must be kidding!" Chaskel did not mind his wife's disinterest in the domestic aspect of life and was happy to purchase prepared food for Shabbos if it made life easier for her once she was working full time. Eventually, when Shirley's parents moved in with them, his mother-in-law took over running the kitchen and taking care of all domestic matters, leaving them free to work long hours together at the office, seeing each other in the present while building up their financial future.

General Tours acted as a pivot for the Tydor family, similar to what Patra had been a decade earlier. Meanwhile, the relationship between Alex Harris and Chaskel grew, particularly as Alex began confiding to his older partner and friend about his guilt feelings of having been the only member of his immediate family to have survived the war. "I shared my feelings with Haskel", Harris wrote in his memoirs. "He became my soul-searcher and confessor. His small physical stature would not match his towering character, his wealth of moral fiber, and his reverence of G-d. He never advertised his deep religious beliefs, never tried to impose them on others, and was extremely tolerant of those who did not share them. He never looked down upon them."

General Tours also had an added advantage. Specializing in tourism to the Eastern Bloc, an idea which Alex Harris had developed through his connections with Russia and Poland, it was also possible to use some of those connections to reach Jews in those areas during the years that the Iron Curtain had shut them off from Judaism. Those activities had to be carried out in secret using some of the professional connections in the Eastern Bloc that had been made being on the job. Others, whose sympathy with the issue was in doubt, would be tacitly sidestepped for such tasks.

Although Chaskel invested long hours in General Tours, he had great satisfaction from his work. Not only was he a partner, unlike in Patra, but he and Shirley received agents' tickets and subsidized hotels allowing them to travel the world. Throughout the 1960s and early 70s they visited England, Scotland, Portugal, Spain, France, Belgium, Holland, Luxembourg, Switzerland, Germany, Italy, Yugoslavia, Greece, Mexico, the Bahamas, Morocco, Japan, Hong Kong, and Polynesia. In a Jewish world which was not yet into luxury kosher cruises, my parents never carried the ubiquitous tuna fish cans abroad but managed to tour the globe subsisting on whatever permitted foods could be found locally.

Now it was time to care for family matters. In the late summer of 1962 my parents and I took an extended visit to Israel. There was no tension as Yosef Greiver had returned to his usual cordial relationship with my father soon after I was born. The Greiver family was delighted to have some of the Tydors back in Israel and while the adults would enjoy the Tel-Aviv evening sea breeze at a café on Dizengoff street, I would be left sleeping on their terrace two blocks away, babysat by their enormous gentle dog, Bobush.

For almost two months Chaskel enjoyed his family and friends in Tel Aviv and Jerusalem, rekindling relationships with members of Kibbutz Buchenwald, now on their own settlement, Netzer Sereni. As in Chaskel's previous trip to Israel in October 1956, this trip too was over-shadowed by military developments. These were the days of the Cuban missile crisis and both the Wexler and Greiver families tried to convince him to remain in Israel. After all, they said, if America was about to engage in a nuclear war, what safer place was there than in the Middle East! The crisis, however, passed and by the end of October he returned to New York, making four more trips to Israel that decade.

Other family issues gave him both joy and concern. In addition to trips abroad that allowed Chaskel to remain on close terms with relatives outside the USA, his family in America continued to play a major role in his life. First and foremost were his children and grandchildren. After many years of having a somewhat distant relationship with his two older children, he tried to develop closeness with his grandchildren in Rochester and Boston, inviting the families to New York for Chanukah and Pesach vacations. But as the years progressed, the gap between his grandchildren's secular upbringing and his religious beliefs grew, causing him great sorrow in spite of the fact that he never commented to them about their irreligious lifestyle. "This was what Hitler *yemach shemo* (may his name be erased) succeeded in doing", he would occasionally mutter when faced with a spiritual distance between himself and his grandchildren that was becoming harder than ever to bridge. Nevertheless, at every opportunity he gently tried to teach them a bit about Judaism and was thrilled when his oldest grandson Brian chose to go to Israel with his mother Camilla for his Bar Mitzvah trip in the mid 1960s.

In addition to his older children, he now had a young daughter who changed his existence. "If the *Ribono Shel Olam* ("Master of the Universe") will give me life," was one of his favorite sayings regarding his future plans, always aware of the uncertainty of seeing me grow to adulthood, particularly as I was born when he was already fifty-five. But he finally had an opportunity to heal past wounds and raise me as he would have wished to have raised my older brother and sister had Hitler not intervened. "Know where you come from and to where you are going", *Avoth*, 3,1), was a favorite quote which he would write on my birthday cards. On other years he would inscribe them with "Know him in all your paths" (Proverbs 3,6), or "The beginning of wisdom is to obtain wisdom" (Proverbs, 15, 32), giving me a continuous but subtle push towards the path I was expected to take.

Although my father had little time to spend with me during the week, he made up for it on *Shabbos* afternoons. When I was a small child he would take me for walks in the neighborhood, telling me about Jewish or family history. A favorite destination was a nearby park with its huge statue of Atlas. When we would reach the park my father would tell me about the hero who bore the world on his back, whom he called *koyach* ("strength," in Yiddish). I often confused that Greek hero with "Buffalo Bill of Bochnia", although I figured that the latter was probably better dressed than the loosely draped muscular fighter towering before me.

One of my father's favorite topics was astronomy, a somewhat unusual choice to discuss with a three or four-year old. I never remember him speaking to me as one does to a small child but rather as one would talk to a young adult, increasing my vocabulary weekly with expressions drawn from the various languages into which he would effortlessly switch during the course of a normal conversation. Once, in the middle of a walk, I suddenly felt his hand gently pressing my head down to face the sidewalk. "Don't look up", he said, explaining that he had forgotten there would be an almost full solar eclipse that afternoon and it would be dangerous to look directly at the sun. I remember the growing darkness as we walked back home, his explanation of what an eclipse was, when he had first experienced one, what "our Sages of blessed memory" had written about eclipses and what they meant to modern science. It was Saturday, July 20, 1963, exactly a week after my fourth birthday and the major solar eclipse of the decade.

Another important family relationship of Chaskel's that grew throughout the years was with his in-laws. Soon after I was born and until my grandfather's death in 1970, my grandparents spent weeks on end at my parents' home, other than during the months when they wintered in Florida or California. After that time, my grandmother lived with us until we moved to Israel in August 1974, joining us three months later. Only in the early 1980s did she return to New York to live out the rest of her years in the Daughters of Jacob home for the aged in the Bronx.

Not every man is capable of living under the same roof with his in-laws, but Chaskel Tydor was certainly not every man. In many things, including age, he was closer to his European mother-in-law – *shvigger-leben* ("dearest mother-in-law") as he called her – than to his American-born wife. The only problem was a lack of space. Seeking a larger apartment in a growing Jewish community, Chaskel and Shirley's choice fell on Woodside, Queens. There, the local Orthodox Rabbi promised them that numerous Jews had already registered for apartments in the large co-op being built nearby. Apartments were indeed beautiful, spacious and relatively inexpensive but a vibrant Orthodox community never developed in the area. Chaskel and Shirley became friendly with a number of families from their new synagogue, the Woodside Jewish Center, but it was a spiritual wasteland compared to Kew Gardens. Respected for his religious knowledge, Chaskel was asked to serve as president, bridging the gap between two sets of members who belonged to the synagogue, the German-Jewish founders and the younger American families who joined when the co-op had been built. Although he would *daven* in the main sanctuary, for part of Yom Kippur my father would always go downstairs to the "Germans", a last vestige of his years in Frankfurt and an opportunity to hear the tunes of his teenage years and early adulthood.

Memories of his past received a concrete outlet for Chaskel in the early 1960s. In 1950, a *chaver* of his from Buna, Norbert Wollheim, had sued the I.G. Farben conglomerate for his salary as a slave laborer during the war and compensation for damages. Wollheim's lawsuit was the first test case of a former slave laborer against a company in Germany and in 1953 he was awarded punitive damages by a court in Frankfurt. Later on there was a global settlement awarding several thousand of the former slave laborers of I.G. Farbenindustrie AG the equivalent of $5,000 a piece. Wollheim, who had emigrated to the United States in 1951 and settled in New York, remained friends with Chaskel and a number of other survivors including Ernest Michel who was active in the United Jewish Appeal. Feeling that they could not take the money for their personal use, Chaskel, along with Wollheim and Michel, contacted a number of survivors, asking them to donate the money in order to form the Auschwitz-Buna Memorial Scholarship Fund. The Fund, created in memory of those who had died in Buna, was to be used for the living, for children of survivors who had no parents to pay for their education, or students wishing to study about the Holocaust and its aftermath.

Chaskel, Michel, and Wollheim succeeded in reaching a large number of survivors whose names appeared on the claims that were filed as part of the Farben settlement. Almost all were eager to participate in a positive action which would memorialize what they had been through. After several months of planning, an "Auschwitz Memorial Dinner" was held on Sunday, March 20, 1960 at the Concourse Plaza Hotel in the Bronx. Officially co-chaired by former Senator and Governor of New York Herbert H. Lehman and Senator Jacob K. Javitz, the organizing committee consisted of Norbert Wollheim, Ernest Michel and Chaskel Tydor. Following Michel's opening remarks, the crowd of over 500 survivors and their spouses rose to their feet to sing the American National Anthem and Hatikva. Providing the religious backdrop to the event, Rabbi Herschel Schacter and Cantor Aron Beidner performed a memorial service and recited the *El Mole Rachamim* memorial prayer before the dinner was served.

As waiters entered the hall with platters of food, middle-aged men, some with tears in their eyes left their tables to greet those whom they had not seen in over fifteen years. "It was a remarkable event", my father recalled, "and tremendously moving for all of us to see how far we had come in life since being slaves to the Nazis." The program continued with a number of remarks by survivors and dignitaries, the launching of the scholarship fund, and a presentation of a scroll addressed to the people, the Congress and the Government of the United States by the Auschwitz-Buna survivors in the name of freedom from tyranny. A second scroll was presented to a representative of the United Jewish Appeal and the evening ended with an address by Dr. Nahum Goldman, president of the World Jewish Congress.

Chaskel was among the speakers that evening. In a speech beginning with the words "Dear *Chaverim* and Friends", he spoke, mostly in English but interspersed with Hebrew quotes, about the day that they left Buna, marching for hours in deep snow to an unknown destination. "The 18th of January 1945 was not the day of our liberation. Consequently this anniversary of ours today is not a celebration", he continued. Describing the comrades they had left behind who died *al kiddush Hashem* – as martyrs for the Holy Name – he stated how they all grappled with the question of why they, and not the others, survived. Whatever their personal conclusion was, he continued, they all have a legacy to carry on with their lives, to give that life a purpose.

Having described the establishment of the scholarship fund he alluded to the debate among the founders as to which university should administer it. Should they choose one in Israel or in the United States, and if in Israel, should it be a religious or a secular institution? Publicly presenting his opinion on the matter he stated: "It is however self understood that we who have have been privileged to live so see *atchalta degeula* – the beginning of the redemption – with the establishment of the State of Israel shall reserve for Israel a place of honor in the scholarship program." Eventually his opinion won out and the entire scholarship fund was given to Bar-Ilan University in Israel. For the three decades until his death Chaskel would receive lists of potential applicants for the scholarship from the university, and he administered a committee that decided on the worthiest recipients.

The dinner had a continuation. Ten days later, on March 30, 1960, a delegation of six Buna survivors including Chaskel, travelled to Washington to meet with president Dwight D. Eisenhower and present him with a memorial scroll. After the delegation members were ushered into the oval office, the President shook their hands and asked them about their personal experiences. Ernest Michel, who summarized that day in a *Reader's Digest* article entitled "My Long Journey to Eisenhower", spoke about what he had gone through and the President responded by recalling his own shock at the horrors of the death camps that he liberated and expressed pride that so many survivors had come to America.

The delegation then presented the scroll to the President who read it carefully and thanked them for the honor. As they were about to leave the room, Chaskel turned to the President and began to speak. The rest of the delegation froze in surprise, knowing and fearing what was about to happen. When they had prepared for the meeting, Chaskel had expressed his desire to pronounce a Jewish blessing on the President but the other members had asked him not to do so, telling him that they preferred to appear before the American President as American citizens and not as Jews and that as a non-Jew, the President might even be offended by a Jewish prayer. Ernest Michel described that moment in his article.

"Tydor spoke up. 'Mr. President, we Jews have an ancient prayer that calls G-d's blessing on the heads of our government. I would like to call that blessing upon you.' Haskel Tydor kept his eyes on the President and said, 'Do I have your permission?' 'Indeed you have', the President said. He had been leaning against his desk but now he stood erect and bowed his head in reverence.' Haskel Tydor put on a skullcap and opened a prayer book. He recited the ancient prayer in Hebrew and the President listened to the alien words. Then Tydor repeated the prayer in English and this time the President could understand. He heard the words 'Blessed art Thou, Lord our G-d, King of the Universe, Who has given of Thy glory to mortal man.' Ernest saw tears in Tydor's eyes. Then he looked at the President and saw that he, too, was deeply moved. The President said in a low, emotion-filled voice 'Thank you very much'."

As Michel wrote, at that moment the delegation members realized how wrong they had been and how right Chaskel had been to bless the American President. "It was wrong to think that they should leave part of themselves in the old world. Here at last they could be whole men, Jews and Americans at the same moment."

The foundation of the Auschwitz-Buna Memorial Scholarship Fund and his participation in the delegation to the President were two milestones which shaped Chaskel's future. After the restitution claim for his factory had been turned down, Chaskel had refused to file a claim for German restitution for his years in concentration camp. Like many survivors he wanted nothing from the Germans for his years in camp, and abhorred any bureaucratic dealings with them. Only at the last moment before it would no longer be possible to file a claim did he agree to Shirley's pressure to do so, partly because of the Wollheim case that led to the founding of the scholarship fund and partly because he understood that he now had to provide for a young wife and child.

In addition, after years of being an Israeli living in the United States, the day after meeting with President Eisenhower Chaskel became an

American citizen. Although he always planned to return to Israel, his changing family status emphasized to him that his temporary American sojourn no longer had an end date. While never officially relinquishing his Israeli citizenship, the activity surrounding the commemorative scroll and the upcoming visit to Washington propelled him towards taking the bureaucratic steps to become an American. On March 31, 1960, after almost nine years in the country, petition number 600230 for naturalization was granted and Chaskel Tydor official became a citizen of the United States.

For the next few years it looked as if the Tydor family would remain in New York, living a typical Orthodox American-Jewish life. Other than their work-related trips, they spent time with family and friends such as Chaskel's wartime *chaverim* and their families and made weekly visits on Sunday afternoons to Tante Chatshe at the senior citizens home where she resided until her death at age 96.

As the years passed, and the Tydors continued to visit Israel on a yearly basis, Shirley began to understand her husband's love of that country. On these trips Chaskel often met friends from the past, wartime *chaverim* or those from Kibbutz Buchenwald. Walking down Ben Yehuda Street in Jerusalem one summer, she noticed a young man standing on a first floor balcony staring at them. "*Ze Tydor, ze Tydor*" ("It's Tydor, it's Tydor), he shouted to the man next to him, gesturing towards my father. Suddenly, without warning, he appeared in front of us, taking my father in his arms. Not wanting to miss him while taking the stairs, he had jumped off the balcony and onto the sidewalk in order to embrace my father. I must have shown my fright because I remember my mother saying "Don't worry, that must be one of Daddy's 'boys' from camp or kibbutz". And indeed it was. This was my first exposure to stories about Kibbutz Buchenwald, which had somewhat disappeared in between the Auschwitz-Buna and Buchenwald stories that were more common in our household.

Another turning point was Chaskel's reconnecting with Boruch Merzel. After the war Merzel had settled in Lyon where he married and had two children. When his daughter Lillian showed an aptitude for art, her principal called Merzel in for a meeting to discuss sending her to Paris for further schooling. "He told me about the advantages of study in Paris for such a girl and emphasized that although these were the days of 'Danny the Red', the 'student revolutions' of the late 1960s, he was sure she would spend her time in study and not in demonstrations. I thanked him profusely for his suggestion, left the building, and said to my wife that no daughter of ours would study art in Paris. We put Lillian on the first plane to Israel and enrolled her in the Hebrew University in Jerusalem." To cement the fact that he intended for her to stay in Israel, Merzel came to Israel to buy Lillian an apartment. But to do so, he needed to exchange foreign currency to give the construction company a down-payment. Just that afternoon the banks were closed and as he was returning to Lyon the next day, he remembered that his old friend Tydor had a brother-in-law who owned Patra who might be willing to cash his check, at least temporarily.

Merzel walked into the Patra office on Nahalat Benjamin Street in Tel Aviv, turning to Yosef Greiver and explaining who he was. Greiver in turn informed him that his friend Tydor just happened to be in Jerusalem and called Chaskel, who told him to hold Merzel in the office until he arrived. Taking a taxi directly to the office, Chaskel and Merzel fell into each other's arms. Although they had corresponded sporadically throughout the years, their friendship was re-cemented at that moment, particularly as Yosef provided Merzel with a cheque in local currency to cover the apartment's downpayment. Merzel told Chaskel that he, his wife, and son Alain were moving to Israel the next year when the boy finished school and would be living in Tel Aviv where Merzel would work in the diamond bourse. He urged Chaskel and Shirley to plan to move as well and already buy an apartment which would be ready for them when they made *aliyah*.

Just a few weeks later a series of incidents highlighted how correct Merzel was. In early September 1970 Chaskel slipped and fell down a flight of stairs, tearing muscles and ligaments in his right leg. After a lengthy operation his leg was put into a cast and he remained in the house for three months, sitting in a wheelchair with his leg extended. For months afterwards he did physical therapy on an exercise bicycle, giving him time to realize that at age 67 he was lucky to regain full moment of his leg but it might be time to begin thinking about retirement.

Soon after Chaskel's return from the hospital, the sudden death of his father-in-law, Max Kraus, emphasized to him how tenuous life was. Unable to attend the funeral due to his own immobile state, Chaskel had time to reflect on what he wanted to do with the rest of his life. Even more than Chaskel, Shirley began to realize that if she wanted to spend quality time with her husband, the only way to do it would be for them to both leave General Tours and retire. The thought was not so strange. Chaskel was nearing seventy and Shirley's early retirement would enable them to spend the next years together. Writing to the Wexlers about their tentative plans they received a joyous letter in response with information about apartment prices in Israel. "It will be simply wonderful, don't you think so?!" wrote Roni exuberantly. "At long last!"

Shirley had been the main reason for Chaskel's not returning to Israel after his children's marriage, and now she pushed him in the other direction. Turning to him as he left for the airport in early 1971 to celebrate a Greiver wedding in Israel, her parting words were "Don't come back without an apartment". He took her seriously. Ten days later Chaskel came home and informed her that he had signed a contract for an apartment in Ramat Gan which would be completed in two years' time. Yaffa and Yosef Greiver were delighted, making plans for the future when the extended Tydor–Greiver clan would once again be together in the same country.

But it was not to be. One Sunday morning in March 1973 the phone rang in the Woodside apartment. Yaffa Greiver was on the line, informing Chaskel that his brother-in-law had suffered a heart attack the previous day and had been buried that morning. Chaskel moved slowly towards the liquor cabinet, taking out a bottle of Scotch which he almost never drank. Reaching for a small tumbler, he filled it to the brim, made a *brocho*, and drained it in one swift movement. "Yosef is no more", he said, tears pouring from his eyes as he turned to Shirley who was looking at him in shock. For Chaskel, it was more than the end of an era. Yosef's untimely death at age sixty-three was a wake-up call, another reminder of how tenuous life was and how at close to seventy it was time for him to think what he wanted to do with the rest of his.

The loss of his father-in-law, his brother-in-law and his own miraculous recovery from a crippling accident were all stepping stones towards his future. Knowing that Chaskel would never leave to retire to Florida, Shirley hoped that the idea of moving to Israel would be a better incentive for him to stop working. Not only would such a move be a *mitzvah*, she reminded him, that of settling the Holy Land, but it would remove them from a secular American environment which could become spiritually dangerous to their daughter as she grew older. Chaskel had been torn from his two older children and wanted to ensure that he would raise his third, not only physically, but spiritually. That was the deciding factor which compelled him to retire, knowing that it would enable him to spend time with his youngest daughter during her youth and provide her with the personal example his two older children had missed.

In late August 1973 Chaskel and Shirley announced that they would be making *aliyah* a year later. Neither the Yom Kippur War nor the terrorist attacks in the spring of 1974 deterred them from their decision. On Friday May 31, 1974, as Israel signed a cease-fire agreement with

Syria, Shirley purchased appliances and furniture to be shipped to Ramat Gan. Soon they began packing books, dishes and clothing, and moved into Shirley's mother's tiny apartment for the weeks before they left.

Just as Shirley and Chaskel had worked late into the night at Patra on the eve of their marriage, so they ended up working late at General Tours the night before leaving for Israel. Hoping to give them a good send off, Shirley's mother had bought them rib-steaks – the first and last time she bought such pieces of meat in her life – but watched them become charred and inedible in the broiler as she waited for them to come home. When they eventually walked in at close to two o'clock in the morning, Shirley turned to Chaskel and exclaimed exhaustedly "Thank G-d, it's finally over!" Looking at her and thinking of what was ahead he just smiled and answered, "No, now it just begins."

A few hours later the Tydor family took a taxi to the airport where they were met by friends and relatives who came to say goodbye. More than one must have thought them crazy to be moving to Israel at that time, only months after the end of the Yom Kippur War, instead of retiring to a comfortable condominium in Florida. Those thoughts would soon be echoed by my Israeli classmates who would gently ask: "Did your father lose his job?", trying to understand why anyone would move to Israel while the country was still licking its wounds from the terrible war.

After tearful goodbyes, my family boarded the El Al flight that was to take us to our new home. Sitting next to my father as the plane began to taxi down the runway, he asked me what I was thinking. "Three things", I answered with the determination that only a fifteen year-old could have. "That I may never see America again. That if I am lucky, I will never see snow again. And as I hate flying, that after getting off this plane, I will never have to get on a plane again for the rest of my life!"

"Never say 'never'", he answered, amused at my vehement response. "By the time you are my age, you will be very surprised at how many of these 'nevers' you will have experienced again throughout your life." "Oh, Daddy", I think, as I write this, remembering my numerous trips back to America, my "adventures" in the snows of Jerusalem, and the hundreds of thousands of airplane miles which I have logged since moving to Israel, "you were so right".

My father's years in the United States fall into two categories, "before" and "after". Before moving out west, and after returning to New York. Although he worked in the travel business both "before" and "after", "before" he was working for someone else, and "after" he was working to build up his own business. "Before", he had been on his own, living in a small apartment-hotel and trying to become close to his two older children. "After" he was married with a second family and was as close to the trappings of normal life as he could be since the beginning of the Second World War. "Before" he had no real community and spent Shabbos attending one of the west side synagogues or visiting relatives. "After" he was once again a *balabus*, an upstanding lay member of a permanent religious community.

I often picture my father's life in America as a ongoing line of work, family, and community, while imagining the months that passed as a spiral surrounding that line, punctuated by festivals, important events and other milestones. A single helix progressing along the sands of time. Some of those milestones were tugs of the past. The time he took me to meet the elderly Rabbi Joseph Breuer who commented how much I resembled my grandfather Yehuda Leib. The days before the Six Day War when he called Itka in Israel, offering to care for her children if she wanted to send them to New York, recalling how his own children's lives were saved almost three decades earlier. The fear of what could happen to America, the country whose nationality he now bore, when tragic events such as the assassinations of President John F. Kennedy, and later those of Robert Kennedy and Martin Luther King, shocked the nation. He had seen such assassinations in another lifetime, that of Republican Premier of Bavaria Kurt Eisner in 1919 and of the Jewish Foreign Minister of Weimar Germany, Walter Rathenau in 1922, and knew what could happen in their aftermath.

Others were glimpses of the future. Sitting in front of the television watching Neil Armstrong take his first steps on the moon in July 1969, he laughed when the commentator on television said that there are those who think we will find G-d on the moon. "Why only on the moon?" my father chuckled, "one day they will go from planet to planet only to learn that the whole universe is filled with his presence."

Looking back, it appears that the cultural revolution of the late 1960s and early 1970s bypassed the Tydor household. Although I owned both a hula hoop and a frizbee, the "youth culture" of miniskirts, free love and drugs did not even enter into our realm of thought. Neither the music of the Beatles nor that of the Rolling Stones was ever played in our house. And although my mother was an active consumer of interesting innovations such as inflatable chairs and paper dresses, we were the only modern Orthodox family I knew in the mid 1970s without a color television set.

But even though the general beat of the household at that time was definitely not that of the students protesting at Columbia or taking over the administration building at Harvard, there were certain moments of interface between the two. In the autumn of 1969 Camilla's oldest son Brian began his studies at Harvard College and Chaskel worried about his involvement in non-academic issues. The anti-war protest movement and indeed the entire Vietnam War was little more than a muted backdrop on the evening news until there was talk of drafting college students, of which we had several in our extended family.

Although we looked like a typical middle-class New York family, we certainly moved to a different drummer than did most. Our frame of reference was always Jewish, primarily Orthodox, and heavily weighted towards Israeli issues because of my father's background. While most people put on the news at 8 p.m., we would tune into *Kol Yisrael Lagolah*, Israel's overseas broadcasts from Jerusalem summarizing the Israeli news of the day. As we were constantly traveling abroad because of my parent's work, long before it was fashionable for most people in our social and cultural groups to do so, my Purim costumes were always genuine national costumes of countries throughout the world and my international doll collection as a child was the envy of my peers. Stamp collecting was too easy to be interesting. Within a week of culling the General Tours mailroom I would have stamps from fifty countries in the world go through my fingers. Looking at their grandfather's stamp collection recently my daughters could not believe my nonchalance as I explained to them the speed with which he had put together the contemporary stamps. Only the pre-war ones were actually interesting, I told them, and he had received those from friends who still had envelopes he had sent them in the 1920s and 30s.

Despite his desire to finally raise one of his children as he wished, in America my father spent little time with me, being tied up with work matters all year long. Most of my memories of him were from our trips abroad. Bargaining in Spanish at the Acapulco open market to buy me silver earrings; testing me on medieval Italian architecture at the Piazza in Venice and not letting us continue our tour until I could identify the various forms in seconds; walking together through the old town of Dubrovnik; touring the Acropolis in Athens and hearing him speak about the Greek empire and the Jews, climbing with him on the Swiss Jungfrau and hearing about his mountain climbing as a boy. As I got older my father and I spent little time with each other apart from Shabbos when he would fall asleep at the table, exhausted from a 72-hour work week. I missed the time we used to have together and assume that he did as well. Could it be that another reason for his finally agreeing to retire at

70 and move to Israel was the hope that there we could once again recapture the experiences we used to have as a family when I was younger? Was it a last chance to enjoy being the father of a teenage daughter before she would grow up and he would have to face the fact that "Buffalo Bill of Bochnia" was reaching the winter of his life?

10

Ramat Gan–Givatayim, 1974–1993

It is amazing how much can happen during an eleven and a half hour flight from one continent to another. When Chaskel boarded the El Al plane to Israel on August 7, 1974 Richard Nixon was President of the United States of America. By the time he disembarked Nixon had announced his resignation in the wake of the Watergate scandal. During those hours in flight the English singer Brian Harvey was born, the former leader of the Hitler Jugend Baldur von Schirach had died, and French acrobat Philippe Petit walked across a high wire slung between the twin towers of the World Trade Center in New York, showing how the fate of one tower was imperceptibly yet firmly connected to that of the other as the world would learn some twenty-seven years later.

The first time that Chaskel Tydor made *aliyah* in 1945 he came by boat to Haifa as the head of a "family" of over 100 kibbutz members. This time he came by plane to Ben-Gurion airport as the head of a family of three. The first time he went with his kibbutz members to a detention camp in Atlit where he stayed for two weeks. This time he went with his wife and daughter to an absorption ministry airport office where he stayed for two hours to deal with *aliyah* bureaucracy. The first time it had taken Yosef Greiver several days before he learned that Chaskel was in the country and went to meet him at Atlit. This time Yosef's son Gad met him practically at the plane and went upstairs to assist in filling out the forms. It was a warm August afternoon, the office had no air conditioner, and they were offered orange juice by the Jewish Agency representatives to combat the heat. "Remember this moment", Gad said to his uncle in jest. "It is the last time that you will get anything for free in this country."

Gad's presence at the Jewish Agency office also had a more long-term impact on Chaskel's life. Hearing him call his uncle "Chaskel" and not by his full Hebrew name "Yechezkel", the clerk automatically listed him as "Hezkel" in his identity booklet without asking questions. In the future that would cause a great deal of confusion every time Chaskel had to fill out a form. As government offices were not yet computerized there was no way to know that the new immigrant "Hezkel Tydor" was in fact one and the same as veteran Israeli citizen Yechezkel Tydor and so he was given a new identity number. Several years later the numerical bureaucratic mishap was fixed and Chaskel was given back his old five-digit identity card number, but his official name, both on his new identity card and on mine, continued to remain "Hezkel". The ways of the Almighty may be unfathomable, but so, it seems, are the wonders of Israeli bureaucracy.

If this was to be the winter of the life of "Buffalo Bill of Bochnia", its beginning appeared to be relatively mild and a welcome rest from the hectic years which had preceeded it. With General Tours rapidly receding into the distance Chaskel's priorities became family, friends, learning Torah, and dealing once again with Holocaust-related issues. Although he lived in a religious community in Ramat Gan, it never became "his community" in the sense that it had in Frankfurt, Kew Gardens or Woodside. He had a permanent synagogue seat, but never again felt that sense of belonging, partly because Shirley never learned Hebrew and their social circle was composed of new immigrants, extended family, and friends from Chaskel's past.

During their first months in Israel Chaskel and Shirley spent most of their time dealing with immigration bureaucracy. Their savior was Baruch Merzel who would arrive every morning to drive them to whatever government office they needed to be in that day. "It was my first chance to do something for Chaskel", Merzel wrote in his memoirs, and indeed for the next nineteen years, except for when one of them was out of the country, there was not a day that the two did not speak on the phone, nor a week when they did not get together several times to learn Torah. A raconteur par excellence, Merzel would keep everyone enthralled with his stories, told in a combination of at least six languages – English, Hebrew, French, Flemish, Yiddish and German – with the occasional Russian or Polish phrase thrown in. "If you are not a polyglot when I begin talking to you, you certainly have to become one by the time I am finished with you", he used to say in jest.

Life is like a continuous filmstrip, someone once wrote, but the human mind is incapable of remembering each and every frame. Instead, there are usually a number of stills – individual pictures – that we recall, either because of their absolute uniqueness or deep personal meaning. Looking back, our family's first years in Israel appear as a kaleidescope of jumbled events with a number of them standing out and having special significance: Celebrating Itka's daughter's wedding shortly after we made *aliyah*. The housewarming at the Hammer's new home in Talpiot Mizrach overlooking the Judean desert. Watching Israel Independence Day fireworks every year from Yaffa Greiver's home in Tel Aviv. My parents being bumped off the El Al flight that was hijacked to Entebbe in June 1976, taking a later flight to Paris that day without informing anyone, causing confusion, panic and ultimately, relief. My marriage to a fellow American immigrant, Shimon Baumel in 1978 who I met as a student at Bar-Ilan University. Camilla and our father breaking the emotional ice of their past after they attended a Yad Vashem conference together in 1980. My grandmother's return to New York in 1981. Asking the amublance doctor taking my father to the hospital with a serious bout of pneumonia in 1982 whether he will live, and receiving the reassuring answer "for many years yet, *halevai* ("may it hopefully be")". He was correct.

Although Chaskel was supremely satisfied with having made *aliyah* Shirley was not. Just as she had once thought of Israel as a land of sand and camels, Shirley had come with a number of illusions which were shattered during her first years in the country. That, together with her mother's ill health triggered a bout of depression over having moved to Israel.

Shirley began pressing for the family to return permanently to America, which Chaskel had no intention of doing. But for their twenty-fifth wedding anniversary he surprised Shirley with an extended visit to America where they rented an apartment in Florida for several weeks. Shirley was eccstatic and Chaskel had an opportunity to spend time with his American children and grandchildren. When they returned to Israel, not only did they leave their apartment, moving two blocks away in nearby Givatayim but from then on they became "commuters", spending winters in Florida. The rest of the year they lived in Israel, down the block from their two Israeli-born granddaughters, Rivka Michal, named for Chaskel's grandmother Mecha and Rina Hannah named for Shirley's mother who passed away in 1984.

An additional family issue did not have such a simple solution. Brought up as secular Jews, Chaskel's American-born grandchildren were following the accepted social patterns of that time, including intermarriage. Chaskel was distraught when Camilla's oldest son Brian announced that he was about to marry a non-Jewish woman. "For this the Master of the Universe saved me from the Nazis," he cried, "so that my great grandchildren would be *goyim*?" Chaskel tried to interest Brian's fiancée Carol in converting to Judaism but the wedding date was set before any move was made in that direction. He and Shirley refused to attend the wedding and gave Camilla a warning. "If you go, you are sending a message to your other children that you condone the choice to marry 'out' and will accept their making a similar choice in the future."

His fears were correct. Soon after, Brian's younger brother Curtis announced that he, too, was about to marry a non-Jew. This time the story had a different ending. Chaskel found out that Curtis's fiancée's mother had originally been Jewish, and had converted to marry her non-Jewish husband. As Judaism does not accept that a Jew can "leave" Judaism, by Jewish law, her daughter was Jewish. Cathy accepted her Jewish heritage and she and Curtis agreed that their children would be brought up as Jews. This time Chaskel and Shirley attended the wedding ceremony.

The process continued. Now it was Manfred's son Bruce expressing his intentions to marry his non-Jewish girlfriend who had no intention of converting to Judaism. By this time Chaskel was in a deep despair regarding the spiritual future of his American family. Over and over when facing the issue he would mutter "This is what that murderer Hitler *yemach shemo* (may his name be erased) did to my family, not only killing us then but now as well". He often thought of what his two older children would have become had they not been child refugees, growing up first among Gentiles in Europe and then in an American Jewish but secular foster home.

And yet he never gave up hope, remaining in contact with his grandchildren and trying to "keep the door open" in order to eventually bringing at least their children back to Judaism. "And a fourth generation shall return" (Genesis 15:16), he would often quote with a deep sigh, adding to me that he prayed that it would take less then four generations before all his descendants would once again be Jewish. "*Betach ba'Hashem veAseh tov*" ("Trust in the Lord and do the right thing", Psalms 37: 3) he would often add, preparing another package of children's books about Judaism to give to his great-grandchildren in America on his next visit, hoping to keep those who were Jewish interested in Judaism and to slowly move those who were not Jewish towards more interest in their grandfather's faith.

Having reached what most people would term "old age" Chaskel found solace in two things, learning Torah and spending time with his Israeli granddaughters. I would often come into my parents house and find my octagenarian father in his study, bent low behind his large desk chair. "We are playing hide and seek", he would whisper to me in his pronounced European accent, waiting for my daughters to "find" him so that he would have to redeem himself with yet another piece of chocolate in order for them to let him go "free".

A third solace for him during his twilight years were his dealings with Holocaust-related issues. In America his days had been taken up with work. In Israel he finally had time to reflect on his past surrounded by friends and family, almost all of whom had a direct connection to the Holocaust. The atmosphere in Israel was conducive to such reflection as the Holocaust was part of its collective history. Although Chaskel did not find himself drawn back into the past, his personal experiences acted as a bridge between past and present, particularly with regard to his daughters.

The ice between Chaskel and Camilla had been broken after they attended a session together at a Yad Vashem International Conference in 1980 and met Prof. Shamai Davidson, a psychiatrist and psychoanalyst who spent over thirty years dealing with Holocaust survivors and their families. Entranced with his talk, Camilla approached Davidson after the session and he offered to meet with her the next day to discuss her own experiences. The meeting was a turning point in her relationship with her father. For the first time she began to internalize the depth of her experiences and their impact on everything that followed including her attitude towards Chaskel throughout the years. As the barriers between father and daughter slowly dissolved, the two were able to discuss issues that had long been buried. In her memoirs entitled "For the Next Generation" written fifteen years later, Camilla voiced her feelings about her relationship with her father after the war. "The most painful experience of my life was the rejection of moving to Palestine with my father", she wrote. "Of course, I did not fully realize how deep the pain and sorrow must have been for him until after I became a parent. I cry when I think about this. Then, I marvel at the strength of this man, my father, survivor of more than six years of concentration camps, enduring things I can not begin to imagine."

The Holocaust also acted as a bridge between me and my father. Always drawn to history, I decided to take my graduate degree in Holocaust studies, giving me an opportunity to spend more time with my father, learning about his experiences. Each of my first academic books was connected to my family's experiences: the rescue of Jewish refugee children to America during the Nazi era, Prayer and the Holocaust, the history of Kibbutz Buchenwald, and the "Double Jeopardy" of being Jewish women under the Nazis. My father lived to see the first two of my books published and was involved in the third, about Kibbutz Buchenwald. Although he never refused to answer my questions, I could sense his reticence in discussing incidents concerning positions he had held during the war or shortly after. "You can't be modest Daddy, this isn't for me, it's for History, with a capital "H", I would say to him in jest when confronting him with stories I had heard from his *chaverim* about the same incidents. "So better you should hear it from other people", he would answer me with a smile. "Remember, *'Meod meod heve shefal ruakh!'* ("One should be exceedingly modest", *Avoth* 4,4).

As I began writing the first chapter of "Kibbutz Buchenwald: Survivors and Pioneers", my father began complaining of weakness, curtailing his usual schedule and spending more time at home learning and resting. When he suddenly turned yellow in May 1992 we thought that he was suffering from jaundice but at the hospital he was diagnosed with a malignancy in his bile ducts. He was eighty-eight at the time and was given about six weeks to live. Only close family was told the truth. Manfred visited Israel twice that month to see his father. Curtis and Cathy came to Israel for a weekend. When he was finally sent home from the hospital and the six weeks became six months Manfred came for a third visit followed by Curtis and then Camilla. It was only during his visits with Manfred that I saw another side of my father and learned that he had a crazy sense of humor. "Of course he did", my mother told me long after he died," he was just afraid to let people see it." How sad to learn that there was an entire side of my father I never knew.

By now my father was losing strength and weight from week to week and although we never discussed his illness, he realized that his time on earth was rapidly growing shorter. Accompanying Manfred to the door at the end of his visit in November and embracing him at length, my father slowly returned to the living room, leaning heavily on the walker he was now forced to use. Sitting down in his armchair, he turned to me with tears in his eyes, "I will never see him again," he said to me poigni-antly, "I will never see my beloved son again."

The days passed. We celebrated my father's eighty-ninth birthday at home but for my parents' thirty-fifth wedding anniversary a few weeks later he suddenly had the strength to leave the house. Walking along a nearby lake in the Ramat Gan National Park with my parents that day, I told them to turn towards me so that I could take a picture to mark the occasion. My father drew himself up as tall as he could and leaned towards my mother so that they could look like a happy couple celebrating their wedding anniversary instead of a sick man leaning on his wife during what would be his last visit out of doors. Smiling for the camera, for the first time I could suddenly see the twenty-five years that separated my parents. The picture now sits in a frame in my living room, a reminder of my mother's words: "I shouldn't have asked him to promise me only thirty-five years, maybe that way we would have had longer together."

The seasons changed. For Chanukah we bought my father six pair of warm new socks as he was suffering from the cold, having lost so much weight. "Why so many?", he asked, "I won't need them all". "One for each day of the week Daddy", I responded, "so you should enjoy new things, even now." He shook his head with a sad smile in response. "If the *Ribono Shel Olam* will give me life, I will get to use all of them", he answered. All of a sudden, the phrase he had used for so many years – "If the *Ribono Shel Olam* will give me life" – took on a very different meaning.

In late February my mother left for Florida for a week in order to complete some urgent paperwork and I moved into their home to give my father round the clock care. The time we spent with each other was unforgettable. If our Sages state that a man is recognized by three matters, "*bekoso, kiso, veka'aso*" ("by his cup [intoxication], his pocket [money], and his anger", Tractate *Eruvin*, 65), one might possibly add a fourth matter, his death, or the days leading up to it.

Chaskel Tydor was a fighter. Every morning he would make his way to his study to *daven*, sometimes taking up to half an hour just to put on his *tefilin* from lack of strength. He would often fall asleep during prayers, wake up, shake his head and continue. Each morning he insisted on trying to learn, asking me to help him take out a volume of the Talmud and open it to where he had finished the previous evening. "At the end, this is what we have", he said to me. "Torah, and *mitzvos* (commandments)." Only once did he refer to his illness, after an exhausting walk from the living room to his bed. Suddenly turning to me, his big dark eyes luminescent in his gaunt pale face, he whispered "How much longer?" We both knew what he was referring to. I didn't know what to say. How does one answer such a question? "Not much longer Daddy", I answered. "*Gott sei Dank*" ("Thank G-d") was his reply. He was ready for his suffering to end.

But he waited. Although the home hospice nurse noted in his charts that his hours were numbered he hung on for several days, waiting for my mother to come home. The look on his face when she walked into their bedroom from the airport on Friday afternoon was indescribable. A combination of love, relief, and joy that I have never seen in my life. He could barely talk but the smile that crossed his face as the tears rushed to his eyes and hers said it all.

The next day was Shabbos and my father spent most of it sleeping. During the chilly morning hours he slept in bed while we tiptoed in to check on him, reassured by the rhythmic rise and fall of his chest. At lunchtime, when the winter sun had slightly warmed the room, my mother helped him out of bed and gently fastened the quilted robe around him so that he could sit at the Shabbat table with us. Leaning on her arm, he had just enough strength to walk the length of the corridor, stopping every few seconds to catch his breath.

At the entrance to the living room he could walk no further and sunk slowly into the large wooden armchair next to the sideboard, that which had come from Tante Chatshe's home. Lately it had been his favorite resting place when he didn't have the strength to make it into his study. Closing his eyes, he smiled faintly as he heard the *zmiroth* coming from the table a few feet away, a tired smile of someone who was already hovering between two worlds. Listening to the traditional melodies he was transported back to the Shabbat table of his childhood where he would sing those same tunes as a young boy. Over eighty years later he could still picture the great wooden dining table in Bochnia, his grandfather Menachem Mendel with his flowing patriarchal beard holding court at the head of the table. His father Yehuda Leib with his black beard and glowing eyes sitting beside him. At the other end of the table sat the women – his mother Esther, grandmother Mecha, and his baby sister Yehudis – waiting to hear the other three join their voices in harmony during the Shabbat meal. Now they were all gone. A different world. A different life.

But the melodies lived on. These were the melodies which my grandparents had taken with them on their flight across Europe during the First World War. These were the melodies which my father had sung with Bertha and my brother and sister in Germany after Hitler came to power. These were the melodies which he had hummed in secret with his *chaverim* in Auschwitz-Buna and Buchenwald on Shabbat afternoon, doing forced labor for the Nazis. These were the melodies which he had shared with his fellow survivors on Kibbutz Buchenwald as they rebuilt their shattered lives. These were the melodies that he had taught me as a small child in America, and these were the melodies which his little *sabra* granddaughters were singing now, standing by the great wooden armchair and holding his hands during what would be the last Shabbat of his life.

After most of the family had gone home, my father closed his eyes and dozed in the chair. Where did his dreams wander to, if he was dreaming at all? His parents? Grandparents? Children scattered throughout the world? Friends long gone? Bertha and her family, murdered by the Nazis? My mother, quietly cleaning up the house after my daughters had left for home? I will never know.

Hours later, he sat up suddenly and opened his eyes, looking around the darkened room in confusion. "*Bring mir a tallis und tfillin*", ("bring me a prayer shawl and phylacteries") he rasped to me, one of the only two sentences that he had uttered all day long. Moving quickly to his side I answered him in English. "It's Shabbos Daddy, it's nighttime, you don't need them today". He nodded and closed his eyes once again.

Those were his last words.

The next day he was gone.

Chaskel Tydor was no more.

My father died on the 7th of Adar, customarily believed to be the day of Moses's birth and death. For that reason, the 7th of Adar has become the traditional day of the *chevra kadisha*, when burial societies hold a festive meal and distribute charity to the poor. The *chevra kadisha* representative who came to transport my father's body from the house told us that it was a special honor to die on that day, something that is reserved for *zaddikim*, holy men. I do not know whether my father was a holy man but he certainly tried to live his life on earth in holiness, even during his years in the Nazi hell.

His funeral took place the next day at the Kiriyat Shaul cemetery in Tel-Aviv, where his brother-in-law Yosef Greiver had been buried twenty years earlier. Looking around at the large crowd which gathered on the sunny afternoon of March 1, 1993 I could see the various parts of my father's life converging into one. Relatives from Poland, Germany, Belgium, Switzerland, England, America and Israel. Friends from pre-war Galicia, Munich, Frankfurt and, London. *Chaverim* from Buchenwald and Auschwitz. Members of Kibbutz Buchenwald. Business acquaintances from Jerusalem, Tel-Aviv, and New York. Post-war friends from Bayit Vegan, Kew Gardens, Rapid City, Woodside, Ramat Gan and Givatayim. Rabbis, doctors, publishers, educators, professors, yeshiva students, travel agents, truck drivers, businessmen, diamond

201

dealers, storekeepers, kibbutz members, repairmen and construction workers. Charedim, Modern Orthodox, Conservative, Reform, unbelievers. An entire slice of Jewish life during the almost ninety years of his lifespan.

At the gravesite, Boruch Merzel gave the eulogy for Chaskel, recalling incidents from Buna where Chaskel had saved his life and those of so many others. The selections where he pulled people out of the death line and hid them in the infirmary. The *mishloach manos* which he had sent Merzel, reminding him that even there, in Buna, they were still Jews. As he spoke about Chaskel the *chevra kadisha* members attending the burial drew closer to listen to the stories about the elderly man whose body they had just placed in the earth of Eretz Yisrael. "They began looking at each other and whispering, not having realized who it was that they had been dealing with and hoping that they had given him enough respect", Merzel wrote in his memoirs.

During the week of *shiva* my mother and I sat together in the apartment in Givatayim, speaking daily to Manfred and Camilla. Each was sitting separately in America, not being able to make it on time for the funeral which they had asked us to hold immediately, aware of the Jewish custom to bury someone as soon as possible after their death. We decided to have the tombstone unveiling in the summer when a large number of family members and friends from abroad could attend, and asked Rabbi Herschel Schacter, who had married my parents thirty-five years earlier, to preside at the occasion.

On a warm afternoon in August 1993 my brother, sister and I entered the cemetery together with my mother, followed by family and friends, and walked towards the gravesite. As I was the only one who had been there since the funeral it was up to me to lead the group in the right direction. Having reached the correct section I looked around, blinded momentarily by the sun, when I suddenly glimpsed my father's name on a headstone in the distance. Not thinking of how it would sound, I called out to my mother who was walking behind me, "There's Daddy!" She turned to me in surprise, a look of astonishment and delight on her face. Following the direction of my outstretched hand with her eyes I could see her age twenty years in a split second as she realized that I was referring to the tombstone with his name on it. "I'm sorry", she said to me with tears in her eyes, "for a moment I thought that he was really there."

Epilogue
Bochnia, 2007

"Gezera al hames sheyishtakach min halev" ("It is decreed that the dead will be forgotten from our hearts", based on Tractate *Pesachim*, 54b), state our Sages, otherwise life could not continue. Unlike siblings, spouses and children for whom one mourns for thirty days, we mourn a parent for an entire year. During the year following my father's death I received a number of poignant reminders of his presence on various occasions. My father had been a firm believer in making Shabbos special and as a small child he had taught me to say *lichvod Shabbos kodesh* (In honor of the holy Sabbath) before beginning to eat on that day. My children also learned the ritual formulation and during the nine months of their Zeide's illness, each Shabbos they had added on the words *"vishe Zeide yihiyeh bari"* ("and may Zeide be healthy"). The first Shabbos after his death, when we began eating and said *lichvod Shabbos kodesh*, my six year-old daughter continued unthinkingly, *"vishe Zeide yihihe bari"*. Realizing her mistake she looked towards heaven and quickly added, *"biGan Eden"* ("in heaven").

Another incident occurred on what would have been my father's 90th birthday. Seeing how sad I was and remembering her grandfather's birthday party the previous year, my younger daughter turned to me and said, "Don't worry Mommy, Zeide is having a birthday party". "How can that be?" I asked her. She answered simply, "His mother will be able to make him a party this year."

Additional reminders of my father came to light over the following months. Throughout the years my father would write notes to himself while learning and leave them in his *seforim*. Leafing through his Talmud volumes I would find small pages torn out of the miniature spiral pocket notebook that he would keep on his desk with references to Maimonides and other commentaries, or verses from Psalms, Proverbs, or Ecclesiastics which he found appropriate for the topic he was learning at the time. I found additional notes in his large siddur, the *Beit Yaakov* of Rabbi Ya'akov of Emden from which he would *daven* in his later years.

However the most poignant of his notes I only found while preparing a chapter of this book.

Looking through his small daily siddur where he noted the days of birth and death of family members I found a small note I had never seen before in his handwriting, pressed between the pages of the additional prayers one adds on the various days of the week. The note contained three names – Leo Diament, Janek Grossfeld, and Nathan Weissman – his three *chaverim* from Buna who were hung by the SS in October 1944. *"Gezera al hames sheyishtakach min halev"*. It may have been decreed that the dead will be forgotten from our hearts but Chaskel Tydor obviously did all that he could so that the decree would be postponed for as long as possible and he would continue to remember his comrades almost five decades after their death.

Having shared my personal and professional life with my father for so many years it took me by surprise each time I realized that I was involved in something which I had not discussed with him. Writing a new book. Traveling to a new place. Teaching in a new university. I once asked my sister about it and she laughed, a sad laugh. You are a "new orphan", she said to me, having lost her mother as a child, "just wait, you'll get used to it". Reading through the first draft of this Epilogue, sixteen years after our father's death, she corrected herself. "You never get used to it", she said. "It only gets worse year after year."

She was correct. As the years passed there was not a day that I didn't think of my father; however, he became more of a background music to my life rather than a continuous presence. When dealing professionally with the topic of identity and linguistics I often thought about what it was like for him to live his life in so many languages and how he identified himself in his own mind. For the first eleven years of his life he had spoken Yiddish, for thirty-one years his main language of speech was German, for twenty-three years he lived in an English speaking world and for almost twenty-five years he lived in a Hebrew-speaking country. To one set of grandchildren he had been *Zeide*, just as he had called his own grandfather. To another he was Poppa and to a third group he was Grandpa. I often wondered what language he would revert to in his old age and recalled that his last two sentences to me had been spoken in Hebrew and finally in Yiddish in spite of the fact that he had always conversed with me in English. During those last few moments, at least in his mind, he had finally gone home.

How did he think of himself? What did he consider to be his essence as opposed to the trappings of his life? Although the Holocaust played a major role in his experiences Chaskel Tydor certainly did not identify himself first and foremost as a "Holocaust survivor". For that reason it never occurred to me to mention that fact on his tombstone. At various times he had dressed like a Galician chassidic boy, a German-Jewish businessman, an American travel agent, a western (cowboy) style manager, and a retired European Jew living in Israel. His experiences bridged the history of almost an entire century and encapsulated a slice of Jewish life in Europe, the United States and Israel.

Among his friends and acquaintances one could count ultra Orthodox and communists, Reform and Conservative rabbis, businessman, politicians, yeshiva directors, professors, lawyers, electricians and farmers. Among those Rabbis and *Rebbes* with whom he had various forms of interaction during his life were the Bobover *Rebbe*, R. Shlomo Halberstam (who would always ask mutual friends coming for an audience, "when is Chaskeleh going to visit me?"), the Ponivizher *Rebbe*, R. Joseph Kahanaman, Rabbi Joseph Breuer, the Satmar *Rebbe*, R. Yoel Teitelbaum, and Rabbi Joseph Ber Soloveichick whose lectures he would faithfully attend during the early 1950s at the Moriah synagogue, founded by Polish Jews from Antwerp on the upper west side in Manhattan where my father lived before marrying my mother. But he had only one *Rebbe* to whom he reverred as "my teacher and rabbi", Rabbi Shlomo Breuer, "the *alter* (elderly) Rabbi Breuer" as he used to call him.

Looking back at his almost nine decades of life Chaskel Tydor was a somewhat unusual and certainly remarkable man. But he was not a saint and he would have been the first to admit it. He was a unique human being with human failings, desires and hopes. He had a love for sweets and spent some of his later post-war years being stocky. Although he always tried to control it, at times one could see a seething temper being kept in check. But he had an unsatiable curiosity to learn new things which kept him young at heart even when he was in his late eighties. He had G-d given health and energy which allowed him to be an active father to a small child while in his sixties, and an equally active grandfather more than twenty-five years later to two young grandchildren. He came from a long-lived family; after all he remembered his great-great aunt at ninety-six gathering round the children at a wedding and cracking walnuts with her bare hands. "Tell your children and grandchildren about this, *kinderlach* (children)", she had said. No wonder that when I visited my father's first cousin Ida Theilheimer in New York after his death at eighty-nine, she, from the vantage point of her mid nineties, looked at me sadly and said, "*Ach* poor Chaskeleh, he died so young".

"For everything there is a season, and a time for every purpose under heaven" (Ecclesiasties, 3, 1) was one of the verses that my father would often quote to me as a child. As the seasons of my life changed in the years after my father's death, my children grew up, I changed jobs, suffered illness and recovered, and parted from the man I had married in my youth. In the course of time I met Joshua Jay Schwartz who became my second husband, a historian like myself and also a former American, but with no immediate family connection to the Holocaust. We married when he was fifty-four, the exact age my father had been when he married my mother, and delighted in the kind of love that I can only imagine my parents must have known. My one sorrow was that although he had heard many stories about his late *shver* (father-in-law), he would never know my father.

Finding ourselves with a merged family of five adult children and a new son-in-law soon after we married, we had litle chance to contemplate a honeymoon of any kind and certainly not the six-week European tour which my parents had enjoyed after their marriage. As we neared our first anniversary my husband suggested that the time had come for us to have a belated honeymoon. "Where do you want to go?" I asked him, thinking that he would suggest a beautiful European capital such as London, Rome or Paris. His answer could have knocked me over with a feather. "I want to go with you to Poland," he said, "to Auschwitz, to Bochnia where your father was born." If I hadn't been sure why I married him until then, at that moment I knew why I felt he was the other half of my soul.

Two months later we were in Poland, basing ourselves in Warsaw and Krakow. Not everyone gets to go to Auschwitz for their honeymoon, I thought faceciously as I showed Josh through the main camp, having been there professionally as a Holocaust historian several times in the late 1980s. Together we toured the grounds of what had once been Buna, a site which I had never seen during my past visits to the general area. Showing us the entrances to the underground shelters that had been part of the camp, our driver explained that unlike Auschwitz I and II which had been restored by the Polish government as a memorial site and tourist attraction, Buna-Monowitz was left to decay and was eventually built over with one family houses and gardens.

The next morning was chilly and overcast and more like a winter day than one in early July. At 9 a.m. our driver picked us up and drove in the direction of Bochnia. Less than half an hour away from Krakow, the building boom of early twenty-first century had turned it into a bedroom suburb of the country's historical capital. Parking at the *rynek*, the town square, we walked towards *ulica Biala*, the street on which my father had been raised, stopping in front of the large wooden house which still stood at number 10. Twenty years earlier I had seen the house from the outside, and my older daughter had even stepped inside on her trip to Poland seven years before, but I had never entered it until now. Our driver knocked at the door, explaining to the middle-aged woman who opened it that my father had lived there over ninety years ago and we were just interested in looking at the house and garden. She ushered us in, reassured that we were not about to try and claim the building and its contents as family property.

The house itself had been divided in two with one half having become a pharmacy while the other part remained a residential dwelling. Walking through the small kitchen, I could see a hall and two bedrooms and was trying to visualize what the large house had looked like in its heydey before it was divided. Josh and I reached the back door and descended the rickety wooden steps, only then discovering that the true surprise was the garden, a wonderland of trees, plants and grasses in different shades of green glinting with drops of morning rain. This was the garden in which my father had learned to walk and run over a hundred years earlier. Here was the towering apple tree which he used to climb, imagining how he would escape out the window of his bedroom and hide in its leafy branches if the local priests from the basilica of St. Nicholas would come to take him away.

Leaving the house we walked in a light rain to the local historical museum and from there to the Bochnia archives where the archivist pulled out Polish town records from over a century and a half before. Leafing through the volumes listing town residents, on page 798 of the register I discovered my past. An entry listing the purchase of a house on Biala street by Mendel and Mecha Tidor, born in 1845 and 1850 respectively. The plans of the house including building permits for additions which were contemplated up to the 1930s. The entries listing the births of their three children, Ides, Chaya and Leib. The marriage of their son Leib, born in 1874 to Esther Laufer from Chrzanow born in 1876. The birth of my father Chaskel in 1903 and his sister Ides in 1911. My father's marriage to Beile Grawer in 1930.

Although the spellings had changed throughout the generations, the family name listed alternately as Tydor and Tidor, there they were. My father, aunt, grandparents, great-grandparents, and great aunts. My father's first wife, brothers-in-law and in-laws. Daddy, Tante Ides, Baba Esther, Zeide Yehuda Leib, Baba Mecha, Zeide Menachem Mendel, Tante Chatcha and Tante Yehidis'l. There were Uncle Yosef Greiver and his brother Salo and his sister Beile, his parents Hirsch and Ruchel

Laja. A family reunion brought together by three generations of Polish bureaucrats who had painstakingly taken a nib pen, dipped it into a reservoir of black ink and written our family's names each time in a similarly flourishing script. There was the deed to the house that still stood in which three generations of Tydor's had lived and which a fourth and fifth generation had visited. Here was my great-grandfather's signature on the deed to the house, proof that he could write his name in Polish although I knew that it was my great-grandmother Mecha who had found the house and negotiated a good price. She had been less than sixteen years old at the time.

Although only three of all those Tydors and Greivers listed on the page had a grave that could be visited, at that moment I was torn between the feeling that I was at a family reunion and the sense of visiting a virtual cemetery. Looking at the first massive proof that I had ever seen of my family's past, I could only imagine what Bochnia had been like almost a hundred years earlier when all of them were still alive. Walking through the streets of the town. Playing in the *rynek*. Climbing the apple tree. Sitting on the stoop facing the street and being chided that a young Jewish boy and girl shouldn't sit next to each other in public even if they were first cousins. Walking through the snow-covered streets on the way to *cheder*.

I left the archive building in a daze, barely noticing that the light morning drizzle had turned into a heavy rain. My husband gently held an umbrella over my head as our driver walked with us to our last stop in Bochnia, the newly dedicated memorial to the Jews of the city who had been murdered by the Nazis. Two blocks away from the archive, at the junction of a small intersection, the memorial had been built on a hill that had once been the center of the ghetto. Crossing through the traffic we stood for a long moment at the site, reading the inscriptions in Hebrew and Polish, looking at the stone and metal slabs reminiscent of the ghetto walls. By now the rain was coming down in torrents, as if the heavens were crying for my family, my aunt who had been deported from the ghetto, my brother and sister's mother who had been taken away by the SS, my grandfather who had been shot coming out of a bunker. For all of Bochnia's Jews. For all the Jews of Poland. For all the Jews of Europe.

I turned away from the memorial, taking one more look at the past before turning towards the future as my father had done sixty-two years earlier when he had left Europe for Palestine. "It's time to go home", I said to my husband, the man who had been the guiding force behind this journey to my roots – roots which had now truly made the two of us into a family by reuniting me with the family of my youth. As I sent a last glimpse over my shoulder towards the memorial the rain began to let up, finally stopping as the clouds over Bochnia parted to let a small ray of light be seen between them. *"Betach be'Hashem veAseh Tov"* ("Trust in the Lord and do the right thing", Psalms 37, 3) I thought at that moment.

It was time to go home and begin writing this book.

Further Reading

Introduction

Testimonies and Autobiographies as Documentary Material

Cullom Davis et al. *Oral History from Tape to Type*, Chicago: American Library Association, 1977.

Robert Nathaniel Kraft, "Archival Memory: Representation of the Holocaust in Oral Testimony," *Poetics Today* 27:2 (2006), 311–330.

Laurence Kutler, "Holocaust Diaries and Memoirs," *Holocaust Literature* (1993), 521–532.

Rachel Rosenblum, "'And Till the Ghastly Tale Is Told': Sara Kofman–Primo Levi, Survivors of the 'Shoah' and the Dangers of Testimony," *European Judaism* 33:2 (2000), 81–103.

Immigration, Migration, Deportation and Homelessness

Leon and Rebeca Grinberg, *Psychoanalytic Perspectives on Migration and Exile*, New Haven and London: Yale, 1989.

Jacob Lestschinsky, *Jewish Migration for the Past Hundred Years*, New York: Yiddish Scientific Institute YIVO, 1944.

Mark Wischnitzer, *To Dwell in Safety: The Story of Jewish Migration since 1800*, Philadelphia: JPS, 1948.

http://mjmd.haifa.ac.il/ (23 June 2009)

Political and Social History of the Twentieth Century

Eric Hobsbawm, *The Age of Extremes: The Short Twentieth Century 1914–1991*, London: Michael Joseph, Ltd., 1994.

Chapter 1   Bochnia, 1903–1914

The Jews of Poland

Gershon David Hundert, *Jews in Early Modern Poland*, London: Litmann, 1997.

Joachim Schoenfeld, *Jewish Life in Galicia Under the Austo-Hungarian Empire and in the Reborn Poland 1891–1939* (foreword by Michal Marrus), Hoboken, New Jersey: Ktav, 1985.

The Shtetl

Alina Cala, "The Shtetl: Cultural Evolution in Small Jewish Towns," *Polin* 17 (2004), 133–141.

Samuel David Kassow, "The Shtetl in Interwar Poland," in Steven T. Katz (ed.), *The Shtetl: New Evaluations*, New York: NYU Press, 2007, 121–139

Annamaria Orla-Bukowska, "Shtetl Communities, another Image," *Polin* 8 (1994), 89–113.

Antony Polonsky, "The Shtetl: Myth and Reality," Polin 17 (2004), 3–23.
http://www.logtv.com/films/shtetl/hoffman.html (23 June 2009).

The Hassidic Movement

Martin Buber, *Tales of the Hasidim*. New York: Schocken with Farrar Straus and Young, Inc., 1948.

Zeev Gries, "Hasidism, the Present State of Research and Some Desirable Priorities," *Numen: International Review for the History of Religions* 34:1 (1987), 97–108; 34: 2 (1987), 179–213.

Yaacov Hasdai, "The Origins of the Conflict between Hasidim and Mitnagdim," in Bezalel Safran (ed.), *Hasidism: Continuity or Innovation?* Cambridge, Mass. and London: Harvard University Press, 1988, 27–45.

Moshe J. Rosman, *Founder of Hasidism: A quest for the historical Baal Shem Tov*, Berkeley: University of California Press, 1996.

Stephen Sharot, "Hasidism in Modern Society," in: Gershon David Hundert (ed.), *Essential Papers on Hasidism: Origins to Present*, New York and London: NYU Press, 1991, 511–531.

Elie Wiesel, *Souls on Fire: Portraits and Legends of Hasidic Masters*, New York: Vintage, 1972.

Jewish Orthodoxy and Ultra-Orthodoxy

Menachem Friedman, "The Lost 'Kiddush' Cup: Changes in Ashkenazic Haredi Culture – a Tradition in Crisis," in: Jack Wertheimer (ed.), *The Uses of Tradition: Jewish Continuity in the Modern Era*, New York: Jewish Theological Seminary, 1992, 175–186.

Michael K. Silber, "The Emergency of Ultra-Orthodoxy: The invention of a tradition," in Jack Wertheimer, ed., *The Uses of Tradition: Jewish Continuity in the Modern Era*, New York: Jewish Theological Seminary, 1992, 23–84.

Jewish Women in 19th Century Eastern Europe

Iris Parush, "The Politics of Literacy: Women and Foreign Languages in Jewish Society of 19th Century Eastern Europe," *Modern Judaism* 15: 2 (1995), 183–206.

Iris Parush, *Women Reading: The Advantage of peripheralism in Jewish society in Eastern Europe during the nineteenth century* (Heb.), Tel Aviv: Ofakim: Am-Oved, 2001.

The Cheder System

Diane Roskies, "Alphabet instruction in the East European heder: some comparative and historical notes," *YIVO Annual of Jewish Social Science* 17 (1978), 21–53.

Shaul Stampfer, "Is the Question the Answer? East European Jews, Heder Education, and Possible Antecedents of Contemporary Israeli and Jewish life," *Studia Judaica* 8 (1999), 239–254.

The Bochnia Salt Mine

http://www.go-tarnow.com/english/worth_seeing/bochnia_salt_mine.html (22 June 2009).

Rabbi Yechezkel Shraga of Sieniava

http://www.shtetlinks.jewishgen.org/stropkov/RabbisStropkov5.htm (22 June 2009).

http://uploads.geni.com/people/Rabbi-Yechezkel-Shraga-Halberstam-Shineva-/4430870834180128283 (23 June 2009).

Chapter 2 Munich, 1914–1920

Nikolsburg

http://www.shtetlinks.jewishgen.org/nikolsburg/homeniko.htm (22 June 2009).

Jews in Germany During and After the First World War

Stirling Fishman, "The Assasination of Kurt Eisner: a study of identity in the German Jewish Dialogue," in: Klaus L. Berghahn (ed.), *The German Jewish Dialogue Reconsidered: A symposium in honor of George L. Mosse*, New York: Lang, 1996, 141–154.

George L. Mosse, *The Jews and the German War Experience 1914–1918*, New York: The Leo Baeck Institute, 1977.

Sarah Schneirer and the Bais Yaakov Movement

Pearl Benisch, *Carry Me in Your Heart: the Life and Legacy of Sarah Schneirer, founder and visionary of the Bais Yaakov Movement*, Jerusalem: Feldheim, 2003.

Judith Gruenfeld-Rosenbaum, "Sara Schenierer," in: Leo Jung (ed.), *Jewish Leaders (1750–1940)*, Jerusalem: Boys Town, 1964, 407–432.

Deborah R. Weissman, "Bais Yaakov as an Innovation in Jewish Women's Education: a contribution to the study of education and social change," *Studies in Jewish Education* 7 (1995), 278–299.

Orthodox Jews in Germany

Mordechai Breuer, *Modernity Within Tradition: The Social History of Orthodox Jewry in Imperial Germany*, New York: Columbia UP, 1992.

Adam S. Ferziger, *Exclusion and Hierarchy: Orthodoxy, nonobservance and the emergence of modern Jewish identity*, University of Pennsylvania Press, 2005.

Leo (Yehuda) Levi, "Rabbi Samson Rafael Hirsch, myth and fact," *Tradition* 31:3 (1997), 9–22.

German and Austrian Jewish Soldiers in the First World War

http://www.dw-world.de/dw/article/0,,2960033,00.html (23 June 2009).
http://www.muzeum.tarnow.pl/judaica/jewish.html(23 June 2009).

Commemoration During and After the First World War

George L. Mosse, *Fallen Soldiers: Reshaping the Memory of the World Wars*, New York: Oxford UP, 1990.

Jay Winter, *Sites of Memory, Sites of Mourning: The great war in European Cultural History*, Cambridge: Cambridge UP, 1995.

The Israelitische Realschule in Fürth

Mordechai Eliav, *Juedische Erziehung in Deutschland im Zeitalter der Aufklaerung und der Emanzipation*, Muenster: Waxman, 2001.

http://www.bayerisches-nationalmuseum.de/presse/schulmuseum/index.htm (22 June 2009).

FURTHER READING

Henry Kissinger

Jeremy Suri, *Henry Kissinger and the American Century*, Belknap Press of Harvard University Press, 2007.

Chapter 3   Frankfurt–Lodz–Bochnia–Frankfurt, 1921–1939

Weimar Germany

Alex de Jonge, *The Weimer Chronicle: prelude to Hitler*, New York: Paddington, 1978.

German Jewish Orthodoxy and the Hirsch-Breuer Community

Yehuda Ben-Avner, *Vom orthodoxen Judentum in Deutschland zwischen zwei Weltkriegen*, Hildesheim, Georg Olms Verlag, 1987.

Asher Dominik Biemann, "Isaac Breuer: Zionist against his will?" *Modern Judaism* 20: 2 (2000), 129–146.

Joseph Breuer, "Rav Dr. Salomon Breuer, his life and times," in: *The Living Hirschian Legacy: Essays on "Torah im Derekh Eretz" and the contemporary Hirschian Kehilla*, New York and Jerusalem: Published for K'hal Adath Jeshurun, New York by P. Feldheim, 1988, 25–44.

David Harry Ellenson, "German Jewish Orthodoxy, tradition in the context of culture," in: Jack Wertheimer (ed.), *The Uses of Tradition: Jewish Continuity in the Modern Era*, New York: JTS, 1992, 5–22.

Gershon Greenberg, "Sovereignty as Catastrophy: Jakob Rosenheim's 'hurban weltan-schaaung'," *Holocaust and Genocide Studies* 8:2 (1994), 202–224.

David Landesman, David Kranzler, *Rav Breuer: His Life and Legacy*, Jerusalem: Feldheim, 1998.

Marc B. Shapiro, "Torah and Derekh Eretz in the Shadow of Hitler," *Torah u-Madda Journal* 14 (2006–2007), 84–96.

Yaakov Zur, *Rabbi Dr. Jacob Hoffman, the Man and his Era*, Ramat Gan: Machon Gavoha Letorah Bar Ilan University, 1999.

http://www.tzemachdovid.org/gedolim/ravbreuer.html (22 June 2009).

Jewish Life in Nazi Germany, Kristallnacht and its Aftermath

Martin Gilbert, *Kristallnacht: Prelude to Destruction*, New York: HarperCollins, 2006.

Marion Kaplan, *Between Dignity and Despair: Jewish Life in Nazi Germany*, New York and Oxford: Oxford UP, 1998

Jerzy Tomaszewski, "Letters from Zbaszyn 1939–1940," *Yad Vashem Studies* 19 (1988), 289–315.

http://www1.yadvashem.org/exhibitions/kristallnacht/photos.html (22 June 2009).

Jewish Emigrants from Germany

Yoav Gelber, *New Homeland: The Immigration of Central European Jewry and their Absorption 1933–1948* (Heb.), Jerusalem: Yad Yitzhak Ben-Zvi, 1990.

Doron Neiderland, "Areas of Departure from Nazi Germany and the Social Structure of the Emigrants," in: Werner E. Mosse et al. (eds.), *Second Chance: Two Centuries of German Speaking Jews in the United Kingdom*, Tuebingen: Mohr, 1991, 57–68.

Doron Niederland, "Leaving Germany, emigration patterns of Jews and non-Jews during the Weimar Period," *Tel Aviver Jahrbuch fuer Deutsche Geschichte* 27 (1998), 169–194.

Kindertransports and Children's Rescue

Judith Tydor Baumel, "Great Britain and the Jewish Refugee Children 1933–1943," *European Judaism* 15 (Winter 1981), 19–25.

Mark Jonathan Harris and Deborah Oppenheimer, *Into the Arms of Strangers: Stories of the kindertransport*, New York: Bloomsbury, 2000.

Ernst Papanek and Edward Linn, *Out of the Fire*, New York: Morrow, 1975.

http://www.onethousandchildren.org/ (22 June 2009).

Polish Jewry between the Wars

Lucjan Dobroszydki and Barbara Kirschenblatt-Gimblett, *Image Before My Eyes: A photographic history of Jewish life in Poland 1864–1939*, New York: Schocken, 1977.

Celia S. Heller, *On the Edge of Destruction: the Jews of Poland Between the Two World Wars*, New York: Columbia UP, 1977.

Chapter 4   Buchenwald–Auschwitz–Buchenwald, 1939–1945

Auschwitz, Buna-Monowitz, and Buchenwald

Emil Carlebach et al., *Buchenwald, ein Konzentrationslager: Berichte, Bilder, Dokumenten,* Bonn: Pahl-Rugenstein, 2000.

Yisrael Gutman and Michael Berenbaum (eds.), *Anatomy of the Auschwitz Death Camp*, Bloomington: Indiana UP, 1994.

David A. Hackett (ed.), *The Buchenwald Report*, Boulder: Westview, 1995.

Harry Stein, *Juden in Buchenwald 1937–1942*, Buchenwald: Gedenkstaette Buchenwald, 1992.

Bernd C. Wagner, *IG Auschwitz: Zwangsarbeit und Bernischtung von Haeftlingen des Lagers Monowitz 1941–1945*, Munschen, K.G. Sauer, 2000.

http://www.auschwitz.org.pl/ (22 June 2009).

http://www.buchenwald.de/index_en.html (22 June 2009).

The "Death Marches"

Yehuda Bauer, "The Death Marches, January–May 1945," *Modern Judaism* 3:1 (1983), 1–21.

Daniel Blatman, "The Death Marches January–May 1945: Who was responsible for what?" *Yad Vashem Studies* 28 (2000), 237–271.

Survivor Memoirs of Auschwitz and Buchenwald

Pearl Benisch, *To Vanquish the Dragon*, Jerusalem and New York: Feldheim, 1991.

Reuven Kassel (ed.), *From Day to Day his Salvation: The Story of the Life of Boruch (Bernard) Merzel* (Heb.), Jerusalem: R. Kassel, 2002.

Primo Levi, *The Black Hole of Auschwitz*, Cambridge, UK, Malden, MA: Polity Press, 2005.

Primo Levi, *If this is a Man, and The Truce*, London: Abacus, 1987.

Ernest W. Michel, *And Promises to Keep*, New York: Barricade Books, 1993.

Jack Werber with William B. Helmreich, *Saving Children: Diary of a Buchenwald Survivor and Rescuer*, New Brunswick: Transaction, 1996.

Elie Wiesel, *Night*, London: Penguin, 1960.

Primo Levi

http://www.giotto.org/piccolomini/levi.html (22 June 2009).

Elie Wiesel

http://www.eliewieselfoundation.org/ (22 June 2009).

Bochnia Ghetto

http://www.angelfire.com/my/heritage/ghetto_bochnia/ (22 June 2009).

Chapter 5   Geringshof, 1945

The Displaced Persons

David Bankier, *The Jews Are Coming Back: The Return of the Jews to their Countries of Origin After WWII*, Yad Vashem and Berghahn Books, 2005.

Yehuda Bauer, *Brichah: Flight and Rescue*, New York: Random House, 1970.

Judith Tydor Baumel, "DP's Mothers and Pioneers: Women in the She'erit Hapletah," *Jewish History* 11:2 (Fall 1997), 99–110.

Judith Tydor Baumel, "The Politics of Religious Rehabilitation in the DP Camps," *The Simon Wiesenthal Center Annual* 6 (1990), 57–79.

Michael Brenner, "Displaced Persons," in: Walter Laqueur and Judith Tydor Baumel, *The Holocaust Encyclopedia*, New Haven and London: Yale UP, 2001, 152.

Leonard Dinnerstein, *America and the Survivors of the Holocaust*, New York: Columbia UP, 1982.

Haim Genizi, *Adviser and Builder: Adviser to the American Army on the She'erit Hapletah 1945–1949* (Heb.), Tel Aviv: Moreshet and Sifriyat Poalim, 1987.

Yisrael Gutman and Avital Saf (eds.), *She'erit Hapletah, 1944–1948: Rehabilitation and Political Struggle*, Jerusalem: Yad Vashem, 1990.

Irit Keinan, *The Hunger Hasn't Eased: Holocaust Survivors and Palestine Emissaries: Germany 1945–1948* (Heb.), Tel Aviv: Am Oved, 1996.

Hagit Lavsky, *New Beginnings: Holocaust Survivors in Bergen Belsen and the British Zone in Germany 1945–1950*, Detroit: Wayne State UP, 2002.

Ze'ev W. Mankowitz, *Life between Memory and Hope: The Survivors of the Holocaust in Occupied Germany*, Cambridge: Cambridge UP, 2002.

Koppel S. Pinson, "Jewish Life in Liberated Germany: A Study of the Jewish DP's," *Jewish Social Studies* 9 (April 1947), 101–126.

Leo Schwartz, *The Redeemers: A Saga of the Years 1945–1952*, New York: Farrar, Strauss and Young, 1953.

Francesca M. Wilson, *Aftermath: France, Austria, Yugoslavia, 1945–1946*, West Drayton, Middlesex: Penguin, 1947.

http://www.dpcamps.org/dpcampseurope.html (23 June 2009).

The Young Survivors of Buchenwald

Judith Hemmendinger, *The Children of Buchenwald: Child Survivors of the Holocaust and their Post-war Lives*, Jerusalem and New York: Geffen, 2002.

http://www.scrapbookpages.com/Buchenwald/Liberation1.html (23 June 2009).

Post-war Kibbutzim in Germany

Judith Tydor Baumel, *Kibbutz Buchenwald: Survivors and Pioneers*, New Brunswick, New Jersey: Rutgers UP, 1997.

Judith Tydor Baumel, "Kibbutz Buchenwald and Kibbutz Hafetz Hayyim – Two Experiments in the Rehabilitation of the Jewish Survivors in Germany," *Holocaust and Genocide Studies* 9:2 (1995), 231–249.

Rabbi Dr. Leo Jung

Leo Jung, *The Path of a Pioneer*, London and New York: Soncino, 1980.
Marc Lee Raphael, "Rabbi Leo Jung and the Americanization of Orthodox Judaism: a
biographical essay," in Jacob J. Schacter (ed.), *Reverence, Righteousness and Rahamanut:
Essays in Honor of Rabbi Leo Jung*, New York: Jason Aronson, 1992, 21–91.
http://www.nytimes.com/1987/12/21/obituaries/rabbi-leo-jung-spiritual-leader-of-
new-york-jewish-center-dies.html (23 June 2009).

Rabbi Herschel Schacter

Alex Grobman, *Rekindling the Flame: The American Jewish Chaplains and the Survivors of
European Jewry 1944–1948*, Detroit: Wayne State University Press, 1993.
http://www.pbs.org/auschwitz/learning/guides/reading6.2.pdf (23 June 2009).

Chapter 6 Jerusalem–Tel Aviv, 1945–1951

Holocaust Survivors in Palestine and the State of Israel

Judith Tydor Baumel, "Bridging Myth and Reality: The Absorption of She'erit Hapletah,
1945–1948," *Middle Eastern Studies* 33 (1997), 362–382.
Dvorah Hakohen, *Immigrants in Turmoil: Mass Immigration to Israel and its Repercussions in
the 1950s and After*, Syracuse: Syracuse UP, 2003.
Aviva Halamish, *The Exodus Affair: Holocaust Survivors and the Struggle for Palestine*,
Syracuse and London: Syracuse UP, 1998.
Hanna Yablonka, *Survivors of the Holocaust: Israel after the War*, New York: NYU Press,
1999.

Young Jewish Refugees from Nazism

Judith Tydor Baumel, *Unfulfilled Promise: The Rescue and Resettlement of Jewish Refugee
Children from Germany in the United States 1934–1945*, Juneau: Denali, 1990.
Kathryn Close, *Transplanted Children*, New York: Victor Gollancz, 1953.
Philip K. Jason and Iris Posner, *Don't Wave Goodbye: The Children's Flight from Nazi
Persecution to American Freedom*, Westport, CT and London: Praeger, 2004.
Walter Laqueur, *Generation Exodus: The Fate of Young Jewish Refugees from Nazi Germany*,
Hanover and London: Brandeis UP, 2001.
http://www.onethousandchildren.org/ (23 June 2009).

The Satmar Rebbe, Rabbi Joel Teitelbaum

Yechezkiel Yosef Weisshaus, *The Rebbe, a glimpse into the daily life of the Satmar Rebbe,
Rabbeinu Yoel Teitelbaum*, Brooklyn: Machon Lev Avos, 2008.
Zvi Jonathan Kaplan, "Rabbi Joel Teitelbaum, Zionism, and Hungarian ultra-ortho-
doxy," *Modern Judaism* 24:2 (2004), 165–178.
http://www.jewishvirtuallibrary.org/jsource/biography/teitelbaum.html (23 June
2009).

The Israeli War of Independence

Benny Morris, *1948: A History of the first Arab-Israeli War*, New Haven, CT: Yale
University Press, 2008.
Moshe Naor, "Israel's 1948 War of Independence as a Total War," *Journal of Contemporary
History* 43:2 (2008), 241–257.
http://www.zionism-israel.com/his/Israel_war_independence_1948_timeline.htm (23
June 2009).

German Jews in Israel

Neima Barzel, "The Attitude of Jew of German Origin in Israel to Germany and Germans after the Holocaust 1945–1952," *The Leo Baeck Institute Yearbook* 39 (1994), 271–301.

Yoav Gelber, *New Homeland: The Immigration of Central European Jewry and their Absorption 1933–1948* (Heb.), Jerusalem: Yad Yitzhak Ben-Zvi, 1990.

Chapter 7   New York, 1951–1957

Holocaust Survivors in America

Joseph Berger, *Displaced Persons: Growing up in America after the Holocaust*, New York: Scribner, 2001.

Beth B. Cohen, *Case Closed: Holocaust Survivors in Postwar America*, New Brunswick, NJ: Rutgers UP, published in association with the United States Holocaust Memorial Museum, 2007.

William B. Helmreich, *Against All Odds: Holocaust Survivors and the Successful Lives they Made in America*, New York: Simon and Schuster, 1992.

The 1956 Sinai Campaign

Mordechai Bar-On, *The Gates of Gaza: Israel's Road to Suez and Back 1955–1957*, London, Macmillan, 1994.

Motti Golani, *Israel in Search of a War: The Sinai Campaign 1955–1956*, Brighton and Portland: Sussex Academic Press, 1998.

Benny Morris, *Israel's Border Wars 1949–1956: Arab Infiltration, Israeli Retaliation and the Countdown to the Suez War*, Oxford: Clarendon Press, 1993.

David Tal, "Israel's Road to the 1956 War," *International Journal of Middle East Studies* 28:1 (1996), 59–81.

http://www.jewishvirtuallibrary.org/jsource/Society_&_Culture/56iaf.html (23 June 2009).

American Jewry and Modern Orthodoxy in the United States

Arnold Eisen, "American Judaism: Changing Patterns in Denominational Self-Definition," *Studies in Contemporary Jewry* 8 (1992), 21–49.

Haim Soloveitchik, "Rupture and Reconstruction: The Transformation of Modern Orthodoxy," *Tradition* 28:4 (1994), 64–130.

Chapter 8   Rapid City, South Dakota and Deer Lodge Montana, 1958–1959

Rabbi Robert (Reuven) Hammer

Reuven Hammer, "Commemorations and the Holocaust," Donald G. Schilling (ed.), *Lessons and Legacies II: Teaching the Holocaust in a Changing World*, Evanston: Northwestern UP, 1998, 175–191.

http://www.newlondon.org.uk/rabbis/?biography=2 (23 June 2009).

Buffalo Bill Cody

Dayton Duncan, *Miles From Nowhere: Tales from America's Contemporary Frontier*, University of Nebraska Press, 2000.

Roger A. Hall, *Performing the American Frontier, 1870–1906*, Cambridge UP, 2001.

http://www.buffalobill.org/history.htm (23 June 2009).

217

Deer Lodge, Montana

http://www.bigskyfishing.com/Montana-Info/city-galleries/deer-lodge-mt.shtm (23 June 2009).

Rapid City, South Dakota

http://www.visitrapidcity.com/ (22 June 2009).

Jews of the Northwest

Julie L. Coleman, *Golden Opportunities: A Biographical History of Montana's Jewish Communities*, Billings, Montana: Julia Coleman in cooperation with SkyHouse Publishers, 1994.

Guide to the Jewish Rockies: Colorado, Montana, Wyoming, Denver: Rocky Mountain Jewish Historical Society, 1979.

Chapter 9 New York, 1959–1974

German Reparations and the I.G. Farben Trial

Neima Barzel, "Dignity, Hatred and Memory: Reparations from Germany: The Debates in the 1950s," *Yad Vashem Studies* 24 (1994), 247–280.

Joseph Borkin, *The Crime and Punishment of I.G. Farben*, New York: Pocket Books, 1979.

Benjamin Ferencz, *Less Than Slaves, Jewish forced labor and the quest for compensation*, Cambridge: Harvard UP, 1979.

Nana Sagi, *German Reparations: A History of the Negotiations*, Jerusalem: Magnes, 1980.

http://reformed-theology.org/html/books/wall_street/chapter_02.htm (22 June 2009).

Presenting the Scroll to Eisenhower

Ernest W. Michel, "My Long Journey to Eisenhower", *Readers Digest*, December 1960, 135–139.

http://findarticles.com/p/articles/mi_6970/is_1_34/ai_n31586189/ (23 June 2009).

Rabbi Abraham Besdin

Abraham Besdin, *Reflections of the Rav*, Jerusalem, Department for Torah Education, 1979.

The Six-Day War and the Yom Kippur War

Chaim Herzog, *The War of Atonement: The Inside Story of the Yom Kippur War*, London: Greenhill Books, 1975.

Leonard Fein, "Failing God; American Jews and the Six-Day War," *The Impact of the Six-Day War* (1988), 269–280.

Abraham Rabinovitch, *The Yom Kippur War: The Epic Encounter that Transformed the Middle East*, New York: Schocken, 2005.

http://www.jewishvirtuallibrary.org/jsource/History/1967toc.html (22 june 2009).

http://www.jewishvirtuallibrary.org/jsource/History/73_War.html (22 June 2009).

Alexander Harris

Alexander Harris, *Breaking Borders: one man's journey to erase the lines that divide*, IUniverse, 2008.

Chapter 10: Ramat Gan–Givatayim, 1974–1993

American-Jewish immigration and the Immigrant Experience in Israel

Karin Amit, "The role of Social Networks in the Immigration Decision Making Process: The Case of North American Immigration to Israel," *Immigrants and Minorities* 25:3 (2007), 290–313.

Guy H. Haskell, "The Development of Israeli Anthropological Approaches to Immigration and Ethnicity 1948–1980," *Jewish Folklore and Ethnology Review* 11:1,2 (1989), 19–26.

Liel Leibovitz, *Aliya: Three generations of American immigration to Israel*, New York: St. Martin's Press, 2006.

The 1980 Yad Vashem Conference

Yisrael Gutman, Avital Saf (eds.), *The Nazi Concentration Camps: Structure and aims, the image of the prisoner, the Jews in the camps. Proceedings of the Fourth Yad Vashem International Historical Conference, Jerusalem, January 1980,* Jerusalem: Yad Vashem, 1984.

The Lebanese War of 1982

Zeev Schiff and Eliezer Ya'ari, *Israel's Lebanon War*, New York: Simon and Schuster, 1984.

http://www.jewishvirtuallibrary.org/jsource/History/Lebanon_War.html (22 June 2009).

Epilogue   Bochnia, 2007

The Jewish Cemetery in Bochnia

Iwona Zawidzka, *Miejsce swiete dla wszystkich zyjacych: czyli Rzecz o cmentarzu zydowskim w Bochni*, Bochnia: Muzeum im St. Fischera, 1992.

http://www.angelfire.com/my/heritage/ghetto_bochnia/testimonies/reichberg.htm (22 June 2009).

http://www.kirkuty.xip.pl/bochniaang.htm (22 June 2009).

Memorial to Bochnia Jewry

http://www.shtetlinks.jewishgen.org/krakow/bochnia/Boch_memorial.htm (22 June 2009).

Holocaust Memory, Commemoration, and its Impact on Religious Jewry

Judith Tydor Baumel, "In Perfect Faith: Jewish Religious Commemoration of the Holocaust," *Studies in Religion/Sciences Religieuses* 30:1 (2001), 5–23.

Eliezer Berkowitz, *Faith After the Holocaust*, New York: Ktav, 1973.

Dan Michman, "The Impact of the Holocaust on Religious Jewry," Yisrael Gutman (ed.), *Major Changes Within the Jewish People in the Wake of the Holocaust*, Yad Vashem, Jerusalem 1996, 613–656.

Iwona Irwin-Zarecka, *Frames of Remembrance: The Dynamics of Collective Memory*, New Brunswick: Rutgers UP, 1994.

Barry Schwartz, "The social context of commemoration: A study in collective Memory," *Social Forces* 61:2 (1982), 374–402.

Bibliography

Archival Collections

Private archives of Yechezkel Tydor, Ramat Gan, Israel
YIVO Archives, Center for Jewish History, New York
DP Collection RG 294.
German Jewish Children's Aid RG 249.
Oevre de Secours aus Enfants RG 248.
(Jewish refugee children in the United States, the She'erit Hapleta, and post-war kibbutzim in liberated Germany).

American Friends Service Committee, Philadelphia
Refugee children – files I, II, III.
AFSC general file.
(Rescue of Jewish refugee children from Germany found in France in 1941 to the United States).

Central Archives for the History of the Jewish People (Jerusalem)
Collection of the Israelitische Realschule Fürth. (School records)

Jewish Joint Distribution Committee (New York City)
Refugee children, June 1940–June 1941.
Refugee children, July 1941–December 1942.
(Rescue of Jewish refugee children from Germany found in France in 1941 to the United States).

Leo Baeck Institute, Center for Jewish History, New York
Paul Amann files, AR-7157 VIII A–C.
(Dossiers of German–Jewish refugee children from France coming to America in 1941).

New York Public Library. Manuscript Division, New York, NY
Ernst Papanek Collection.
(Rescue of German-Jewish refugee children from OSE homes in France to the United States in 1941).

Yad Vashem Archives, Jerusalem
Documentation Reichsvertretung: Children's Emigration 1934–1941, 2829/ R.V. (Kindertransports)

Kibbutz Afikim Archives
Kibbutz newspaper, *Afikim*, 1945–1948.

Demographic changes in the course of 1945. Kibbutz Afikim, File K/10.
(Kibbutz Buchenwald in Kibbutz Afikim).

Kibbutz Netzer Sereni Archive
Kibbutz Buchenwald Diary, parts 1, 2.
(Founding of Kibbutz Buchenwald and its existence throughout 1945).

Interviews, Correspondence, Films and Symposia

Author's interviews
Pearl Mandelkern Benisch (Kibbutz Buchenwald), Bnei Brak, 3 October 1988.
Yehudit Berkowitz (Itka Charash), Haifa, 22 July 1987.
Chava Landau Drenger (Kibbutz Buchenwald), Bnei Brak, 12 July 1988.
Yaffa Greiver, Tel Aviv, 2 November 2008.
Eliyahu Gruenbaum (Kibbutz Buchenwald), Tel Aviv, 16 December 1984.
Rivkah Englard Hoffman (Kibbutz Buchenwald), Bnei Brak, 25 October 1984.
Rabbi Dr. Leo Jung 23 August, 1982; (telephone), 9 July 1985.
Luba Englard Lindenbaum (Kibbutz Buchenwald), Bnei Brak, 15 February 1987.
Sara Schlachet Lustiger (Kibbutz Buchenwald), Ramat Gan, 19 February 1989.
Camilla Maas, New York, 1 April 1981.
Hilda Matzdorf (co-worker of Lotte Marcuse, refugee child placement services), Jerusalem, 20 December 1981.
Boruch (Bernard) Merzel, Yad Eliyahu, 22 August 1980.
Sarah Blaugrund Pfeffer (Kibbutz Buchenwald), Petach Tikva, 3 November 1988.
Arthur Poznansky (Kibbutz Buchenwald), Yad Eliyahu, 29 November 1984.
Rabbi Herschel Schacter, New York, 24 July 1985.
Rochel Schanzer Teller (Kibbutz Buchenwald), Tel Aviv, 11 January 1987.
Manfred Tidor, New York, 3 April 1981.
Jacob and Henia Traube (Kibbutz Buchenwald), Bnei Brak, 5 February 1987.
Shirley Tydor, Ramat Gan, 7 December 2008, 4 January 2009.
Yechezkel Tydor, Jerusalem 30 March 1983, Ramat Gan 4 June 1983, Givatayim, September–December 1992.
Norbert Wollheim, New York, 18 April 1981.

Author's correspondence
Tamara Green, daughter of Chaplain Rabbi Robert Marcus, 23 June 2008.
Rabbi Reuven Hammer, 10 December 2008.
Alex Harris, 24 January 2009.
Rabbi Jacob J. Schacter, son of Chaplain Rabbi Herschel Schacter, 30 April 2009.
Filmed interview with Yechezkel Tydor on the history of Kibbutz Buchenwald. From a film series developed by the Open Univeristy of Israel for the course "The Holocaust", Open University 1983–1992.
Symposium held at Netzer Sereni on 8 May 1985 to mark the fortieth anniversary of the liberation of the Buchenwald Camp and Kibbutz Buchenwald's founding. Participants: Avraham Ahuvia, Eliyahu Gruenbaum, Yechezkel Tydor.

Online Resources
http://mjmd.haifa.ac.il/ (23 June 2009).

http://www.logtv.com/films/shtetl/hoffman.html (23 June 2009).

http://www.go-tarnow.com/english/worth_seeing/bochnia_salt_mine.html (22 June 2009).

http://www.shtetlinks.jewishgen.org/stropkov/RabbisStropkov5.htm (22 June 2009).

http://uploads.geni.com/people/Rabbi-Yechezkel-Shraga-Halberstam-Shineva-/4430870834180128283 (23 June 2009).

http://www.shtetlinks.jewishgen.org/nikolsburg/homeniko.htm (22 June 2009).

http://www.dw-world.de/dw/article/0,,2960033,00.html (23 June 2009).

http://www.muzeum.tarnow.pl/judaica/jewish.html (23 June 2009).

http://www.bayerisches-nationalmuseum.de/presse/schulmuseum/index.htm (22 June 2009).

http://www.tzemachdovid.org/gedolim/ravbreuer.html (22 June 2009).

http://www1.yadvashem.org/exhibitions/kristallnacht/photos.html (22 June 2009).

http://www.onethousandchildren.org/ (22 June 2009).

http://www.auschwitz.org.pl/ (22 June 2009).

http://www.buchenwald.de/index_en.html (22 June 2009).

http://www.giotto.org/piccolomini/levi.html (22 June 2009).

http://www.eliewieselfoundation.org/ (22 June 2009).

http://www.angelfire.com/my/heritage/ghetto_bochnia/ (22 June 2009).

http://www.dpcamps.org/dpcampseurope.html (23 June 2009).

http://www.scrapbookpages.com/Buchenwald/Liberation1.html (23 June 2009).

http://www.nytimes.com/1987/12/21/obituaries/rabbi-leo-jung-spiritual-leader-of-new-york-jewish-center-dies.html (23 June 2009).

http://www.pbs.org/auschwitz/learning/guides/reading6.2.pdf (23 June 2009).

http://www.jewishvirtuallibrary.org/jsource/biography/teitelbaum.html (23 June 2009).

http://www.zionism-israel.com/his/Israel_war_independence_1948_timeline.htm (23 June 2009).

http://www.jewishvirtuallibrary.org/jsource/Society_&_Culture/56iaf.html (23 June 2009).

http://www.newlondon.org.uk/rabbis/?biography=2 (23 June 2009).

http://www.buffalobill.org/history.htm (23 June 2009).

http://www.bigskyfishing.com/Montana-Info/city-galleries/deer-lodge-mt.shtm (23 June 2009).

http://www.visitrapidcity.com/ (22 June 2009).

http://reformed-theology.org/html/books/wall_street/chapter_02.htm (22 June 2009).

http://findarticles.com/p/articles/mi_6970/is_1_34/ai_n31586189/ (23 June 2009).

http://www.jewishvirtuallibrary.org/jsource/History/1967toc.html (22 june 2009).

http://www.jewishvirtuallibrary.org/jsource/History/73_War.html (22 June 2009).

http://www.jewishvirtuallibrary.org/jsource/History/Lebanon_War.html (22 June 2009).

http://www.angelfire.com/my/heritage/ghetto_bochnia/testimonies/reichberg.htm (22 June 2009).

http://www.kirkuty.xip.pl/bochniaang.htm (22 June 2009).

http://www.shtetlinks.jewishgen.org/krakow/bochnia/Boch_memorial.htm (22 June 2009).

BIBLIOGRAPHY

Books and Articles

Amit, Karin, "The role of Social Networks in the Immigration Decision Making Process: The Case of North American Immigration to Israel," *Immigrants and Minorities* 25:3 (2007), 290–313.

Bankier, David, *The Jews Are Coming Back: The Return of the Jews to their Countries of Origin After WWII*, Yad Vashem and Berghahn Books, 2005.

Bar-On, Mordechai. *The Gates of Gaza: Israel's Road to Suez and Back 1955–1957*, London: Macmillan, 1994.

Bauer, Yehuda, *Brichah: Flight and Rescue*, New York: Random House, 1970.

Bauer, Yehuda, "The Death Marches, January–May 1945," *Modern Judaism* 3:1 (1983), 1–21.

Barzel, Neima, "The Attitude of Jew of German Origin in Israel to Germany and Germans after the Holocaust 1945–1952," *The Leo Baeck Institute Yearbook* 39 (1994), 271–301.

Barzel, Neima, "Dignity, Hatred and Memory: Reparations from Germany: The Debates in the 1950s," *Yad Vashem Studies* 24 (1994), 247–280.

Baumel, Judith Tydor, "Bridging Myth and Reality: The Absorption of She'erit Hapletah, 1945–1948," *Middle Eastern Studies* 33 (1997), 362–382.

Baumel, Judith Tydor, "DP's Mothers and Pioneers: Women in the She'erit Hapletah," *Jewish History*, 11:2 (Fall 1997), 99–110.

Baumel, Judith Tydor, "Great Britain and the Jewish Refugee Children 1933–1943," *European Judaism* 15 (Winter 1981), 19–25.

Baumel, Judith Tydor, *Kibbutz Buchenwald: Survivors and Pioneers*, New Brunswick, New Jersey: Rutgers UP, 1997.

Baumel, Judith Tydor, "Kibbutz Buchenwald and Kibbutz Hafetz Hayyim – Two Experiments in the Rehabilitation of the Jewish Survivors in Germany," *Holocaust and Genocide Studies* 9:2 (1995), 231–249.

Baumel, Judith Tydor, "The Politics of Religious Rehabilitation in the DP Camps," *The Simon Wiesenthal Center Annual* 6 (1990), 57–79.

Baumel, Judith Tydor, *Unfulfilled Promise: The Rescue and Resettlement of Jewish Refugee Children from Germany in the United States 1934–1945*, Juneau: Denali, 1990.

Baumel, Judith Tydor, "In Perfect Faith: Jewish Religious Commemoration of the Holocaust," *Studies in Religion/Sciences Religieuses* 30:1 (2001), 5–23.

Ben-Avner, Yehuda, *Vom orthodoxen Judentum in Deutschland zwischen zwei Weltkriegen*, Hildesheim, Georg Olms Verlag, 1987.

Benisch, Pearl, *Carry Me in Your Heart: The Life and Legacy of Sarah Schneirer, founder and visionary of the Bais Yaakov Movement*, Jerusalem: Feldheim, 2003.

Benisch, Pearl, *To Vanquish the Dragon*, Jerusalem and New York, Feldheim, 1991.

Berger, Joseph, *Displaced Persons: Growing up in America after the Holocaust*, New York; Scribner, 2001.

Berkowitz, Eliezer, *Faith After the Holocaust*, New York: Ktav, 1973.

Besdin, Abraham, *Reflections of the Rav*, Jerusalem, Department for Torah Education, 1979.

Biemann, Asher Dominik, "Isaac Breuer: Zionist against his will?" *Modern Judaism* 20: 2 (2000), 129–146.

Blatman, Daniel, "The Death Marches January–May 1945: Who was responsible for what?" *Yad Vashem Studies* 28 (2000), 237–271.

Borkin, Joseph, *The Crime and Punishment of I. G. Farben*, New York: Pocket Books, 1979.

Brenner, Michael, "Displaced Persons," in: Walter Laqueur and Judith Tydor Baumel, *The Holocaust Encyclopedia*, New Haven and London: Yale University Press, 2001, 152.

Breuer, Joseph, "Rav Dr. Salomon Breuer, his life and times," in: *The Living Hirschian Legacy: essays on "Torah im Derekh Eretz" and the contemporary Hirschian Kehilla*, New York and Jerusalem: Published for K'hal Adath Jeshurun, New York by P. Feldheim, 1988, 25–44.

Breuer, Mordechai, *Modernity Within Tradition: The Social History of Orthodox Jewry in Imperial Germany*, New York: Columbia UP, 1992.

Buber, Martin, *Tales of the Hasidim*. New York: Schocken with Farrar Straus and Young, Inc., 1948.

Cala, Alina, "The Shtetl: Cultural Evolution in Small Jewish Towns," *Polin* 17 (2004), 133–141.

Carlebach, Emil et al., *Buchenwald, ein Konzentrationslager: Berichte, Bilder, Dokumenten*, Bonn: Pahl-Rugenstein, 2000.

Close, Kathryn, *Transplanted Children*, New York: Victor Gollancz, 1953.

Cohen, Beth B., *Case Closed: Holocaust Survivors in Postwar America*, New Brunswick, NJ: Rutgers University Press, published in association with the United States Holocaust Memorial Museum, 2007.

Coleman, Julie L., *Golden Opportunities: A Biographical History of Montana's Jewish Communities*, Billings, Montana: Julia Coleman in cooperation with SkyHouse Publishers, 1994.

Davis, Cullom et al., *Oral History from Tape to Type*, Chicago: American Library Association, 1977.

Dinnerstein, Leonard, *America and the Survivors of the Holocaust*, New York: Columbia UP, 1982.

Dobroszydki, Lucjan and Kirschenblatt-Gimblett, Barbara, *Image Before My Eyes: A Photographic history of Jewish life in Poland 1864–1939*, New York: Schocken, 1977.

Duncan, Dayton, *Miles From Nowhere: Tales from America's Contemporary Frontier*, University of Nebraska Press, 2000.

Eisen, Arnold, "American Judaism: Changing Patterns in Denominational Self-Definition," *Studies in Contemporary Jewry* 8 (1992), 21–49.

Eliav, Mordechai, *Juedische Erzeihung in Deutschland im Zeitalter der Aufklaerung und der Emanzipation*, Muenster: Waxman, 2001.

Ellenson, David Harry, "German Jewish Orthodoxy, tradition in the context of culture," in: Jack Wertheimer (ed.), *The Uses of Tradition: Jewish Continuity in the Modern Era*, New York: JTS, 1992, 5–22.

Fein, Leonard, "Failing God; American Jews and the Six-Day War," *The Impact of the Six-Day War* (1988), 269–280.

Ferencz, Benjamin, *Less Than Slaves, Jewish forced labor and the quest for compensation*, Cambridge: Harvard UP, 1979.

Ferziger, Adam S., *Exclusion and Hierarchy: Orthodoxy, Nonobservance and the emergence of modern Jewish identity*, University of Pennsylvania Press, 2005.

Fishman, Stirling, "The Assasination of Kurt Eisner: a study of identity in the German Jewish Dialogue," in: Klaus L. Berghahn (ed.), *The German Jewish Dialogue Reconsidered; A symposium in honor of George L. Mosse*, New York: Lang, 1996, 141–154.

Friedman, Menachem, "The Lost 'Kiddush' Cup: Changes in Ashkenazic Haredi Culture – a Tradition in Crisis," in: Jack Wertheimer (ed.), *The Uses of Tradition: Jewish*

Continuity in the Modern Era, New York: Jewish Theological Seminary, 1992, 175–186.

Gelber, Yoav, *New Homeland: The Immigration of Central European Jewry and their Absorption 1933–1948* (Heb.), Jerusalem: Yad Yitzhak Ben-Zvi, 1990.

Genizi, Haim, *Adviser and Builder: Adviser to the American Army on the She'erit Hapletah 1945–1949* (Heb.), Tel Aviv: Moreshet and Sifriyat Poalim, 1987.

Gilbert, Martin, *Kristallnacht: Prelude to Destruction*, New York: HarperCollins, 2006.

Golani, Motti, *Israel in Search of a War: The Sinai Campaign 1955–1956*, Brighton and Portland: Sussex Academic Press, 1998.

Greenberg, Gershon, "Sovereignty as Catastrophy: Jakob Rosenheim's 'hurban weltanschaaung'," *Holocaust and Genocide Studies* 8:2 (1994), 202–224.

Gries, Zeev, "Hasidism, The Present State of Research and Some Desirable Priorities," *Numen: International Review for the History of Religions* 34:1 (1987), 97–108; 34:2 (1987) 179–213.

Grinberg, Leon and Rebeca, *Psychoanalytic Perspectives on Migration and Exile*, New Haven and London: Yale, 1989.

Grobman, Alex, *Rekindling the Flame: The American Jewish Chaplains and the Survivors of European Jewry 1944–1948*, Detroit: Wayne State University Press, 1993.

Gruenfeld-Rosenbaum, Judith, "Sara Schenierer," in: Leo Jung (ed.), *Jewish Leaders (1750–1940)*, Jerusalem: Boys Town, 1964, 407–432.

Guide to the Jewish Rockies: Colorado, Montana, Wyoming, Denver: Rocky Mountain Jewish Historical Society, 1979.

Gutman, Yisrael and Berenbaum, Michael, (eds.), *Anatomy of the Auschwitz Death Camp*, Bloomington: Indiana UP, 1994.

Gutman, Yisrael, Saf, Avital (eds.), *The Nazi Concentration Camps: structure and aims, the image of the prisoner, the Jews in the camps. Proceedings of the Fourth Yad Vashem International Historical Conference, Jerusalem, January 1980*, Jerusalem: Yad Vashem, 1984.

Gutman, Yisrael and Saf, Avital (eds.), *She'erit Hapletah, 1944–1948: Rehabilitation and Political Struggle*, Jerusalem: Yad Vashem, 1990.

Hackett, David A. (ed.), *The Buchenwald Report*, Boulder: Westview, 1995.

Hakohen, Dvorah, *Immigrants in Turmoil: Mass Immigration to Israel and its Repercussions in the 1950s and after*, Syracuse: Syracuse UP, 2003.

Halamish, Aviva, *The Exodus Affair: Holocaust Survivors and the Struggle for Palestine*, Syracuse and London: Syracuse UP, 1998.

Hall, Roger A, *Performing the American Frontier, 1870–1906*, Cambridge UP, 2001.

Hammer, Reuven, "Commemorations and the Holocaust", Donald G. Schilling (ed.) *Lessons and Legacies II: Teaching the Holocaust in a Changing World*, Evanston: Northwestern UP, 1998, 175–191.

Harris, Alexander, *Breaking Borders: one man's journey to erase the lines that divide*, IUniverse, 2008.

Harris, Mark Jonathan and Oppenheimer, Deborah, *Into the Arms of Stranger: Stories of the kindertransport*, New York: Bloomsbury, 2000.

Hasdai, Yaacov, "The Origins of the Conflict between Hasidim and Mitnagdim," in Bezalel Safran (ed.), *Hasidism: Continuity or Innovation?* Cambridge, MA and London: Harvard University Press, 1988, 27–45.

Haskell, Guy H., "The Development of Israeli Anthropological Approaches to Immigration and Ethnicity 1948–1980," *Jewish Folklore and Ethnology Review* 11:1,2 (1989), 19–26.

Hemmendinger, Judith, *The Children of Buchenwald: Child Survivors of the Holocaust and their post-war Lives*, Jerusalem and New York: Geffen, 2002.

Heller, Celia S., *On the Edge of Destruction: the Jews of Poland Between the Two World Wars*, New York: Columbia UP, 1977.

Helmreich, William B., *Against All Odds: Holocaust Survivors and the Successful Lives they Made in America*, New York: Simon and Schuster, 1992.

Herzog, Chaim, *The War of Atonement: The Inside Story of the Yom Kippur War*, London: Greenhill Books, 1975.

Hobsbawn, Eric, *The Age of Extremes: The Short Twentieth Century 1914–1991*, London: Michael Joseph, Ltd., 1994.

Hundert, Gershon David, *Jews in Early Modern Poland*, London: Litmann, 1997.

Irwin-Zarecka, Iwona, *Frames of Remembrance: The Dynamics of Collective* Memory, New Brunswick: Rutgers UP, 1994.

Jason, Philip K. and Posner, Iris, *Don't Wave Goodbye: The Children's Flight from Nazi Persecution to American Freedom*, Westport, CT and London: Praeger, 2004.

Jonge, Alex de, *The Weimer Chronicle: Prelude to Hitler*, New York: Paddington, 1978.

Jung, Leo, *The Path of a Pioneer*, London and New York : Soncino, 1980.

Kaplan, Marion, *Between Dignity and Despair: Jewish Life in Nazi Germany*, New York and Oxford: Oxford UP, 1998.

Kaplan, Zvi Jonathan, "Rabbi Joel Teitelbaum, Zionism, and Hungarian ultra-ortho-doxy," *Modern Judaism* 24:2 (2004), 165–178.

Kassel, Reuven (ed.), *From Day to Day his Salvation: The Story of the Life of Boruch (Bernard) Merzel* (Heb.), Jerusalem: R. Kassel, 2002.

Kassow, Samuel David, "The Shtetl in Interwar Poland," in Steven T. Katz (ed.), *The Shtetl: New Evaluations*, New York; NYU Press, 2007, 121–139.

Keinan, Irit, *The Hunger Hasn't Eased: Holocaust Survivors and Palestine Emissaries: Germany 1945–1948* (Heb.), Tel Aviv: Am Oved, 1996.

Kraft, Robert Nathaniel, "Archival Memory: Representation of the Holocaust in Oral Testimony," *Poetics Today* 27:2 (2006), 311–330.

Kutler, Laurence, "Holocaust Diaries and Memoirs," *Holocaust Literature* (1993), 521–532.

Landesman, David, Kranzler, David, *Rav Breuer: His Life and Legacy*, Jerusalem: Feldheim, 1998.

Laqueur, Walter, *Generation Exodus: The Fate of Young Jewish Refugees from Nazi Germany*, Hanover and London: Brandeis UP, 2001.

Lavsky, Hagit, *New Beginnings: Holocaust Survivors in Bergen Belsen and the British Zone in Germany 1945–1950*, Detroit: Wayne State University Press, 2002.

Leibovitz, Liel, *Aliya: Three generations of American immigration to Israel*, New York: St. Martin's Press, 2006.

Lestschinsky, Jacob, *Jewish Migration for the Past Hundred Years*, New York: Yiddish Scientific Institute YIVO, 1944.

Levi, Leo (Yehuda), "Rabbi Samson Rafael Hirsch, myth and fact," *Tradition* 31:3 (1997), 9–22.

Levi, Primo, *The Black Hole of Auschwitz*, Cambridge, UK, Malden, MA: Polity Press, 2005.

Levi, Primo, *If this is a Man, and The Truce*, London: Abacus, 1987.

Mankowitz, Ze'ev W., *Life between Memory and Hope: The Survivors of the Holocaust in Occupied Germany*, Cambridge: Cambridge UP, 2002.

226

Michel, Ernest W., *And Promises to Keep*, New York: Barricade Books, 1993.

Michel, Ernest, "My Long Journey to Eisenhower", *Readers Digest*, December 1960, 135–139.

Michman, Dan, "The Impact of the Holocaust on Religious Jewry," Yisrael Gutman, ed., *Major Changes Within the Jewish People in the Wake of the Holocaust*, Yad Vashem, Jerusalem, 1996, 613–656.

Morris, Benny, *Israel's Border Wars 1949–1956: Arab Infiltration, Israeli Retaliation and the Countdown to the Suez War*, Oxford: Clarendon Press, 1993.

Morris, Benny, *1948: A History of the fFrst Arab–Israeli War*, New Haven, CT: Yale UP, 2008.

Mosse, George L., *Fallen Soldiers: Reshaping the Memory of the World Wars*, New York: Oxford UP, 1990.

Mosse, George L., *The Jews and the German War Experience 1914–1918*, New York: The Leo Baeck Institute, 1977.

Naor, Moshe, "Israel's 1948 War of Independence as a Total War," *Journal of Contemporary History* 43:2 (2008), 241–257.

Neiderland, Doron, "Areas of Departure from Nazi Germany and the Social Structure of the Emigrants," in: Werner E. Mosse et al., *Second Chance: Two centuries of German speaking Jews in the United Kingdom*, Tuebingen: Mohr, 1991, 57–68.

Niederland, Doron, "Leaving Germany: Emigration patterns of Jews and non-Jews during the Weimar Period," *Tel Aviver Jahrbuch fuer Deutsche Geschichte* 27 (1998), 169–194.

Orla-Bukowska, Annamaria, "Shtetl Communities, another Image," *Polin* 8 (1994), 89–113.

Papanek, Ernst and Linn, Edward, *Out of the Fire*, New York: Morrow, 1975.

Parush, Iris, "The Politics of Literacy: Women and Foreign Languages in Jewish Society of 19th Century Eastern Europe," *Modern Judaism* 15: 2 (1995), 183–206.

Parush, Iris, *Women Reading: The Advantage of peripheralism in Jewish society in Eastern Europe during the nineteenth century* (Heb.), Tel Aviv: Ofakim: Am-Oved, 2001.

Pinson, Koppel S., "Jewish Life in Liberated Germany: A Study of the Jewish DP's," *Jewish Social Studies* 9 (April 1947), 101–126.

Polonsky, Antony, "The Shtetl: Myth and Reality," Polin 17 (2004), 3–23.

Rabinovitch, Abraham, *The Yom Kippur War: The Epic Encounter that Transformed the Middle East*, New York: Schocken, 2005.

Raphael, Marc Lee, "Rabbi Leo Jung and the Americanization of Orthodox Judaism: a biographical essay", in Jacob J. Schacter (ed.), *Reverence, Righteousness and Rahamanut: Essays in Honor of Rabbi Leo Jung*, New York: Jason Aronson, 1992, 21–91.

Rosenblum, Rachel, "'And Till the Ghastly Tale Is Told': Sara Kofman – Primo Levi, Survivors of the 'Shoah' and the Dangers of Testimony," *European Judaism* 33:2 (2000), 81–103.

Roskies, Diane, "Alphabet instruction in the East European heder: some comparative and historical notes," *YIVO Annual of Jewish Social Science* 17 (1978), 21–53.

Rosman, Moshe J., *Founder of Hasidism: A quest for the historical Baal Shem Tov*, Berkeley: University of California Press, 1996.

Sagi, Nana, *German Reparations: A History of the Negotiations*, Jerusalem: Magnes, 1980.

Schiff, Zeev and Ya'ari, Eliezer, *Israel's Lebanon War*, New York: Simon and Schuster, 1984.

Schoenfeld, Joachim, *Jewish Life in Galicia Under the Austo-Hungarian Empire and in the Reborn Poland 1891–1939* (foreword by Michal Marrus), Hoboken, New Jersey: Ktav, 1985.

Schwartz, Barry, "The social context of commemoration: A study in collective Memory," *Social Forces* 61:2 (1982), 374–402.

Schwartz, Leo, *The Redeemers: A Saga of the Years 1945–1952*, New York: Farrar, Strauss and Young, 1953.

Shapiro, Marc B., "Torah and Derekh Eretz in the Shadow of Hitler," *Torah u-Madda Journal* 14 (2006–2007), 84–96.

Sharot, Stephen, "Hasidism in Modern Society," in: Gershon David Hundert (ed.), *Essential Papers on Hasidism: Origins to Present*, New York and London: NYU Press, 1991, 511–531.

Silber, Michael K., "The Emergency of Ultra-Orthodoxy: The invention of a tradition", in Jack Wertheimer (ed,), *The Uses of Tradition: Jewish Continuity in the Modern Era*, New York: Jewish Theological Seminary, 1992, 23–84.

Soloveitchik, Haim, "Rupture and Reconstruction: The Transformation of Modern Orthodoxy," *Tradition* 28:4 (1994), 64–130.

Stampfer, Shaul, "Is the Question the Answer? East European Jews, heder education, and possible antecedents of contemporary Israeli and Jewish life," *Studia Judaica* 8 (1999), 239–254.

Stein, Harry, *Juden in Buchenwald 1937–1942*, Buchenwald: Gedenkstaette Buchenwald, 1992.

Suri, Jeremy, *Henry Kissinger and the American Century*, Belknap Press of Harvard University Press, 2007.

Tal, David, "Israel's Road to the 1956 War," *International Journal of Middle East Studies* 28:1 (1996), 59–81.

Tomaszewski, Jerzy, "Letters from Zbaszyn 1939–1940," *Yad Vashem Studies* 19 (1988), 289–315.

Wagner, Bernd C., *IG Auschwitz: Zwangsarbeit und Bernischtung von Haeftlingen des Lagers Monowitz 1941–1945*, Munich: K.G. Sauer, 2000.

Weisshaus, Yechezkiel Yosef, *The Rebbe, a glimpse into the daily life of the Satmar Rebbe, Rabbeinu Yoel Teitelbaum*, Brooklyn: Machon Lev Avos, 2008.

Weissman, Deborah R., "Bais Yaakov as an Innovation in Jewish Women's Education: a contribution to the study of education and social change," *Studies in Jewish Education* 7 (1995), 278–299.

Werber, Jack with Helmreich, William B., *Saving Children: Diary of a Buchenwald Survivor and Rescuer*, New Brunswick: Transaction, 1996.

Wiesel, Elie, *Night*, London: Penguin, 1960.

Wiesel, Elie, *Souls On Fire: Portraits and Legends of Hasidic Masters*, New York: Vintage, 1972.

Wilson, Francesca M., *Aftermath: France, Austria, Yugoslavia, 1945–1946*, West Drayton, Middlesex: Penguin, 1947.

Winter, Jay, *Sites of Memory, Sites of Mourning: The great war in European Cultural History*, Cambridge: Cambridge UP, 1995.

Wischnitzer, Mark, *To Dwell in Safety: the Story of Jewish Migration Since 1800*, Philadelphia 1948.

Yablonka, Hanna, *Survivors of the Holocaust: Israel after the War*, New York: NYU Press, 1999.

Zawidzka, Iwona, *Miejesce swiete dla wszystkich zyjacych: czyli Rzecz o cmentarzu zydowskim w Bochni*, Bochnia: Muzeum im St. Fischera, 1992.

Zur, Yaakov, *Rabbi Dr. Jacob Hoffman, the Man and his Era*, Ramat Gan: Machon Gavoha Letorah Bar Ilan University, 1999.

Index